HOW TO DO DELIVERANCE MANUAL

By Gene Moody

Deliverance Ministries
Gene B. Moody
14930 Jefferson Highway
Baton Rouge, LA 70817-5217
www.genemoody.com

Telephone: (225) 755-8870
Fax: (225) 755-6120

HOW TO DO DELIVERANCE MANUAL

TABLE OF CONTENTS – JUST THE SECTIONS

HOW TO DO DELIVERANCE MANUAL

TABLE OF CONTENTS - DETAILED

SECTION 1 – PREFACE, SUMMARY & SPIRITUAL WARFARE DIRECTIONS

PREFACE

This lesson applies to a group of any size; there is no limit on the number of people that can be ministered to. **Anyone that can hear your voice, can be delivered.** It is setup primarily for mass deliverance of a group. However, it is also applicable to personal deliverance. You could look at personal deliverance as mass deliverance for a person such as a man, woman or child, or a few persons such as a couple or family. Select the parts of the lesson that are applicable to the people that are being ministered to. For more information on how to do deliverance for a few persons, see the **Deliverance Manual**, Chapter 2.

GENERAL

There are many good deliverance prayers that have been written and printed in books and in loose-leaf form. Some of these prayers are general and some have been written for specific subjects.

The ideal prayer is the one prayed by the individual, being ministered to at that time, to cover the specific area of that person's life (personal deliverance). **The next best prayer** is the form prayer which the person or group repeats after the deliverance leader or reads from the printed prayer.

The following prayers have been used many times by us and others. They have produced good results. One side benefit is that the people can see what is wrong and evil in their lives by what is contained in the prayers. These prayers can be used for individuals, small groups or large groups equally well.

SUMMARY

The first thing we do is to get the people to pray about their **specific problems and sins** (personal deliverance). The Blood of Jesus will cleanse the people, and take away legal rights and grounds that the demons have to remain. Then demons can be cast out. **You must personally repent of your sins!**

Pray out loud for the most power in the spiritual world. If you are working in personal deliverance, get the individual to pray about their specific problems and sins. If you are working in mass deliverance, lead the group in praying the form prayers. Lead the congregation or individual through these scriptures, prayers and commands as fits the situation and as led by The Holy Spirit.

SPIRITUAL WARFARE DIRECTIONS

1. Teach one lesson or several lessons.
2. Customize the deliverance around what was taught especially if only one or several lessons were taught.
3. **Deliverance Warfare Prayers** - These can be used in various ways as indicated by the subtitles: **Short Prayer**, **Medium Prayer** and **Long Prayer.**
4. **Moody's Prayers** - These are good combination prayers.

5. **Deliverance Prayers With Lists** - These can be used in various ways as indicated by the subtitles: **Biblical Curses**, **Soul Ties**, **Occult and False Religions**, **Ungodly Spirits**, **Godly Spirits**, and **Cursed Objects and Demon Infestation.**
6. **Tactics To Win The War Against Satan** - These can be used to drive out demons.
7. **Tormenting Demons** - These are used to torment the demons with their impending doom by using statements based on scripture and using scriptural quotations.
8. **Lists of Demons for Mass Deliverance** - These are lists to be used for mass deliverance in various ways as indicated by the subtitles: **Basic Deliverance**, **Fifty-Three Common Demon Groupings**, **Abused Children**, **Grief and Bitterness**, **Bastards**, **Charismatic Witchcraft**, **Drunkenness and Gluttony**, **Perfecting Love**, **Ingratitude**, **Self**, and **How Not to Do Deliverance**.
9. Customize the deliverance to the situation that is presented. There are many factors to be considered such as time allowed, sequence of events and spiritual climate.
10. **Sequence of Events**

  1. **Teach** - Teach one or more lessons.

  2. **Pray** - Have the people stand up and repeat after you the following prayers that you have selected:

    1. **Deliverance Warfare Prayers**
    2. **Deliverance Warfare Prayers With Lists**
    3. **Tactics To Win The War Against Satan**
    4. **Tormenting Demons**

  6. **Cast Out** - Cast out the demons in mass deliverance from selected lists of demons. It is good to start with **Basic Deliverance** of the families of **Rejection**, **Bitterness** and **Rebellion**, and then go on to other families. A good list to use always is **Fifty-Three Common Demon Families**.

  7. **Deliverance Manual** - There are many lists of demons in the manual. The lists can be selected by topic being taught to the people.

  8. **Audios and Videos** - An excellent tape is **Mass Deliverance** by Win Worley. There are audio and video tapes that have mass deliverance on them after teaching about various topics.

SECTION 2 - BASIC DELIVERANCE - #1
(Rejection, Bitterness, Rebellion and Unforgiveness)

CONTENTS

1. **Prayer**
2. **List of Demons**
    1. **Basic Deliverance**
    2. **Rejection**
3. **Bitterness**
4. **Rebellion**
5. **Schizophrenia**

2. **Fifty-Three Common Demon Groupings**
    1. **Prayer**

REJECTION
LIST OF SCRIPTURE

Matt. 5:3 (Rejected are "poor in spirit") Do you feel poorly?
Matt. 5:43-44 (Love your enemies) Would solve a lot of your problems!
Rom. 12:3 (Not to think of himself more highly) Would not get rejected!
I Cor. 10:12-13 (Take heed lest he fall) Pride - Ego - Vanity
II Cor. 5:14-15 (Not live unto themselves) Be generous and think of others!
Eph. 6:4 (Fathers do not provoke children) Not the mothers! Phil. 4:8 (Think on these things)
James 1:5-8 (Double-minded man) Will not receive anything from God!
I Peter 4:12 (Fiery trial) We go through many trials!

GENERAL

Rejection includes **fear of rejection and self-rejection** in this common demon family. **I am going to spend more time on rejection because it is generally the door opener to demon oppression.**

Except for the sins of the ancestors, rejection is generally where the demons first attack someone and because of the parents, this can be in the womb. Rejection is one of the biggest problems of the human race!

Rejection is defined as reject, refuse, repudiate, decline, deny, rebuff, repel, renounce, discard, throw away, exclude, eliminate and jettison.

Have you had these feelings before? Rejection is very common among Christians. **Love is the opposite of Rejection. The Love of God and God loving through us is a very powerful force which we don't fully understand.**

CHARACTERISTICS OF REJECTION
(The Power Of Love Overcoming Rejection)

Hunger for power. Causes you to seek power in job, family or ministry in order to be accepted and look good to others and Jesus. Has religious ambition. **Over achiever, perfectionist.** Strives for recognition through accomplishments. **Wants to be in control.** You do not want to be vulnerable to being rejected. **Has a roller coaster ride in Christian walk.** One day up and one day down. **Self justification.** Feels like you are being rejected if someone criticizes you or you make a mistake. **Cannot see the truth of God's Word.** There is a cloud over your mind that says God does not love me anyway which causes you not to receive the revelations of truth.

Causes you to commit adultery or fornicate. You are looking for love from anyone or anything because you are starving for the true love of Jesus. **Cannot accept the love of Jesus or anyone else fully.** You can just let others get so personal in fear of being hurt again, including Jesus. **Can't seem to forgive yourself or others from past hurts, mistakes or sin.** Causes you to have a spirit of unbelief and doubt towards the truth; it also lets the spirit of hatred and bitterness come in with it. **You can not see rejection working in you.** Your mind is seared over to the truth. **Causes you to speak negative things about yourself.** Because you can not see or receive the full love of Jesus and you do not love yourself. **Causes anger, strife and murder to come in.** You do not have peace because of fear of being rejected so you act out in anger and even rage at times because you are subconsciously mad at God. **Causes you to receive a Jezebel spirit or a spirit of control.** The spirit of rejection will bring in a spirit of control to work with it because it is afraid if it is not in control of everything it will not prevail or it will be rejected.

EARLINE'S COMMENTS

Rejection Opens Door To A Multitude Of Curses

Looking up rejection in the Bible, I have found that God has not rejected a single person who has not persisted in rejecting God. See I Sam. 8:7; 10:19; 15:23, 26; 16:1; II Kings 17:15, 29; Isa. 53:2; Jer. 6:19; 7:29-30; etc. These scriptures reassure us that if we heed God's call to us, He will not reject us.

We have not found a single person who has escaped the problem of rejection. Even if we are not rejected, rejection works very well when demons can convince us that we are rejected. Rejection is one the best ideas the Devil ever had and it works so well he uses it against all people. Even Jesus did not escape rejection. Isa. 53:3, **He was despised and rejected and forsaken by man, ... He was despised, and we did not appreciate His worth or have any esteem for Him.** Jesus was totally rejected of men. The Devil did not stop using rejection on Jesus even when He was on the cross. Jesus' response was, **Father, forgive them for they don't know what they do.**

The Devil used rejection on Eve when he told her she would be like God. Was not that question in response to what Eve was probably thinking? If she had not been thinking this, she would not have taken the bait.

What does rejection do to you? It makes you open to all kinds of seduction because you do not feel complete nor settled. It may be a respectable seduction like food, work, play, prestige, money or non-respectable like street drugs, abnormal sexual activities, murder, abortion, witchcraft, etc. The person is always trying to find something to fix that spot so they will fell all right.

Rejection is behind over working, lying, greed, denying a problem exists or our ability to control it, deception, etc. The work of the Holy Spirit within us is to bring us into proper self-control, peace and joy (Gal. 5:22-26).

Rejection Leading To Sexual Perversions

Sexual perversions represent an extreme attempt to overcome rejection. Sexual experiences, real or imaginary, can never satisfy the need for genuine love. They are the Devil's substitutes for real love and leave a person ridden with frustration and guilt. **Sex is not love!**

The person who has a deep sense of rejection feels insecure and inferior. Since the person has been rejected or fears rejection he is driven to pamper self ... to push self. He is thereby trying to overcome feelings of rejection. One who feels rejected wants to feel important.

The Roots Of Rejection (Excerpts)

As for my people, children are their oppressors, and women rule over them. 0 my people, they which lead thee cause thee to err, and destroy the way of thy paths" (Isaiah 3:12). Children rule the parents and wife rules the husband; this is a matriarchal society!

The curse of destruction of the family priesthood (which is centered in the father and usually is the result of inherited family curses) paves the way for the spirit of Rejection in a child. **Father is the priest and head of the home!**

Frustrated by his lack of leadership and her inability to respect him as a man, the woman (who herself may have inherited curses of dominance) begins to take over and direct the home by the Jezebel spirit. **Men go after wine, women and song - such as adult toys, outdoors, sports, etc. to escape the wife!**

The child is caught up in the conflict between the parents and becomes its chief victim. **Children are the main victims of divorce!**

The spirits in the mother will coerce the male child, forbidding him to assert his masculinity or to engage in activities which would develop him as a man. **This pattern develops homosexual men!**

The progression of destruction in the life of a female child is much the same as that of the boy, except that she will consciously or unconsciously absorb and manifest the same attitudes and spirits which drive her mother. **Watch how your children have your same bad habits!**

There is a definite pattern to the entrance of Rejection, which in turn opens the door for Rebellion:

1. Curse of **destruction of the family priesthood** (centered in father).
2. Curses and spirits of **withdrawal** of the father and **dominance** by the mother.
3. Spirit of improper discipline (usually works through the mother **(either overpermissive or too harsh)** may associate with the curse of rebellion against discipline on the child's part.
4. Spirit of **lying** to escape punishment.
5. Curse and spirits of **guilt**.
6. Curse and spirits of **distrust** (resulting from guilt).
7. Curse and spirits involving **lack of communication** between parents and child.
8. Curse and spirits of **rejection** ("My parents don't love me" or "I can't even talk to them etc.").

Rejection, Witchcraft Control And Ugliness (Excerpts)

The hellish "ping pong" game played with hapless victims by the spirits of Rejection and Rebellion has been spelled out by the Hammonds. Everyone should read **Pigs in the Parlor** by Frank Hammond, with particular attention to the chapter on Schizophrenia. **The demons of**

Rejection and Rebellion whipsaw the people back and forth between these opposite emotions!

Rejection is such a common malady that it is found everywhere to some degree or another.

Discovery of an out-of-wedlock pregnancy usually results in anger, upset and dismay in the parents of their child.

The curse of **Rejection from the Womb** has opened the door for many tormenting spirits in scores of people with whom we have dealt. **Did you know that you can be rejected by your parents while you are in the womb?**

Over and over people have reported life-long trouble by seemingly groundless but crippling rejection and various kinds of fears.

In some individuals, such spirits only produce discomfort and uneasiness.

A knowledge of the binding and casting out of evil spirits, and loosing the spirits of God (to counter and cancel the evil ones) is essential (Matt. 18:18; Mark 16:17-18).

There is a demonic entity called **Witchcraft Control** and he is able to bind other spirits in a person, particularly those involving habits such as smoking, drinking and sexual lapses. In order for the victim to be freed completely, witchcraft curses must be broken from his family (back to ten generations on both sides) or from any other quarter. Legal holds and legal grounds must be taken from the enemy in the name of Jesus.

We have observed that people with heavy rejection spirits (usually including Rejection from the Womb) sometimes are rather homely and plain. A demon called **Ugliness** is found in many persons.

Perhaps you have noticed that people very often look ten to twenty years younger in their casket than when alive. Many times in deliverance, we see people change before us. They look younger, softer and more relaxed. **Women, would you like to be more beautiful? Then, get your demons cast out!**

Schizophrenia (Excerpts)

Schizophrenia is a very common problem. Some authorities in the field of mental illness estimate there may be as many schizophrenics as one out of eight persons in the United States. Schizophrenics account for half the population in psychiatric hospitals. Of course there are varying degrees of schizophrenia. Some cases are acute while others are quite mild. Many schizophrenics have never been treated professionally. Schizophrenia has remained a very baffling problem to mental health professionals. The cause and cure has remained shrouded in uncertainty.

The disturbance and disintegration of personality known as schizophrenia or dementia praecox is frequently encountered by the deliverance minister. I would estimate that as many as one fourth of those who come to us for deliverance are found to have the schizophrenic pattern. The Lord has graciously given to Frank and Ida Mae Hammond a special revelation on the problem which enables us to deal with such cases more effectively.

The core of the schizophrenic is Rejection and Rebellion.

Schizophrenia always begins with Rejection! It commonly begins in childhood or infancy and sometimes while the child is yet in his mother's womb. There are many causes for rejection. Perhaps the child was not wanted. It may have been the wrong sex desired by one or both parents. The conditions in the home may have been unsettled. There are many "doors" that lead to rejection. **Did you want your children and were they the right sex? How about your parents?**

For example, suppose the schizophrenic nature is in the mother. The demons will pick out one or more of her children to feed down through. The schizophrenic mother feels rejection. She is the one who is primarily responsible for feeding love into the family. The rejection within herself creates problems in her relationships with the child. **The child is opened for rejection by the mother's instability.**

Now, one can have a rejection spirit and not be schizophrenic. In other words, it is in the matter of forming a personality. You can have a rejection spirit and still manage to form your own personality and be secure in yourself.

Rejection is the control demon in one of the personalities set up within the schizophrenic. Rejection depicts a **withdrawn** type personality. (It is a feeling within - it is **agony within** - it is a **starvation of love** - it is **insecurity** - it is **inferiority** - it is **fantasy** - it is **unreality** - it is on the inside - "I don't share in this."). **Do you feel loved? Can you love others? Do you try to avoid contact with other people?**

Sexual perversions represent an extreme attempt to overcome rejection. Sexual experiences, real or imaginary, can never satisfy the need for genuine love. They are the Devil's substitutes for real love and leave a person ridden with frustration and guilt. **Sex is not love; did you know that? How many one-night stands have you had in seeking love?**

The person who has a deep sense of rejection feels insecure and inferior. **Do you feel inferior?**

Since the person has been rejected or fears rejection, he is driven to pamper self...to push self. He is thereby trying to overcome feelings of rejection. **One who feels rejected wants to feel important!**

References

The Power Of Love Overcoming Rejection by James and Janell Lyle, It' Easy With Jesus Printing, Jacksonville, IL
Battling The Hosts Of Hell and **Demolishing The Host Of Hell** by Win Worley, Hegewisch Baptist Church, Lansing, IL
Pigs In The Parlor by Frank and Ida Mae Hammond, Impact Books, Kirkwood, MO
Roget's Thesaurus

BITTERNESS
List Of Scripture

Deut. 29:18-20 (Root of Gall & Wormwood) Break this curse.
I Sam. 1:10 (Bitterness of Soul)
I Sam. 15:32 (Bitterness of Death)
II Sam. 2:26 (Bitterness in the latter end)
Ps. 10:7 **(Cursing, Deceit, Oppression, Mischief, Iniquity)**
Pr. 14:10 (Bitterness to Heart)
Pr. 17:25 (Bitterness of Mother)
Ezek. 27:31 (Bitter Wailing)
Zec. 12:10 (Bitterness for only son) **(Loss of Byron, our only son)**
Acts 8:22-24 (Gall of Bitterness, Bond of Iniquity)
Rom. 3:13-14 (Cursing and Bitterness)
Eph. 4:31-32 (Bitterness, Wrath, Anger, Clamor)
Col. 3:8-9 (Anger, Wrath, Malice, Slander, Lies)
Heb. 12:14-16 (Root of Bitterness) Break this curse.

General

Bitterness includes **Resentment, Hatred, Unforgiveness, Violence, Temper, Anger, Retaliation and Murder** in a common demon family.

Generally, after a person becomes rejected, they become bitter and unforgiving. The opposite of bitterness is forgiveness.

Bitterness is defined as bitterly curse, rebellious, sharp, acrid, grief, embitter, poisonous, violently, provoke, vex, grieve, sorrow, bitter herb, calamity, bile, venom, angry, chafed, most bitterly, rebel and provoke.

Have you had these feelings before? Unforgiveness, which is a form of bitterness, is very common among Christians.

Gall is defined as **poison** or **bile**. Bound is defined as **control** and **uniting**. Root is defined as **root** and **thought**. Wormwood is defined as **cursed**.

Dealing With Bitterness (Excerpts)

Bitterness is a hurt that will not heal, a wound in the spirit (Prov. 18:14). It comes into a life because of a failure to appropriate God's grace (Heb. 12:15); by refusing to forgive others (Matt. 6:14-15; 7:1-2; 18:21-35); or refusing to thank God for all things (Eph. 5:20; Phil. 4:6). **Forgiveness is the most important thing that God has taught us about deliverance!**

However, each time we remember the things which happened, we are suddenly flooded with hurt and/or anger again. This indicates unhealed bitterness. This is called a spirit of memory recall.

Vengeance is mine, I will repay, saith the Lord (Heb. 10:30). It is too heavy for us to carry and besides it belongs to God. Earline had a problem with getting even until God delivered her.

Forgive eagerly (Matt. 18:12), remembering that unforgiveness is torture (Matt. 18:34-35).

We must remember that God loves us (Rom. 8:32-34), and not look at what others say, what we think or even at the situation itself.

We must go to the God of comfort (II Cor. 1:3) for His Holy Spirit is our Comforter (John 14:16) and He earnestly desires to comfort us (Psalm 103:13).

When we go to God, we will find peace that passes understanding which will keep (guard, garrison) our hearts and minds (emotions and thoughts) (Phil. 4:4-9). God's peace guards our mind!

Focus on God and give Him thanks (Eph. 5:20; Rom. 8:28) rejoicing because your name is written in the Lamb's Book of Life (Luke 10:20; Phil. 4:4) and ask for grace, comfort and peace (Matt.7:7-11). **Say, Lord Jesus give me grace, comfort and peace. Amen.**

Focusing on God and letting Him be our judge is absolutely necessary.

Proverbs 29:25 contrasts the **fear of man** with trust in God. Perfect love for God casts out fear because we trust in Him! **Say, Lord Jesus forgive me for fear of man. Amen.**

To receive comfort and heal the bitterness in your spirit, you must die to works of righteousness (trying to earn God's love and favor) by drowning in the ocean of God's love and grace, rejoicing that He has chosen you.

References

Conquering The Hosts Of Hell by Win Worley, Hegewisch Baptist Church, Lansing, IL

REBELLION

List Of Scripture

I Sam. 15:23 (for **rebellion** is as the sin of witchcraft, **stubbornness** is as iniquity and idolatry) Are you practicing witchcraft or idolatry?
Heb. 2:2 (**disobedience** received a just reward) You will be punished.
Heb. 13:17 (**submit** yourselves) (**Anti-submissiveness**) Pastors should not try to control their flock; the flock should submit to the pastor.
2 Peter 2:10 (Presumptuous are they, **self-willed**)

General

Rebellion includes **Self-Will, Stubbornness, Disobedience and Anti-Submissiveness** in this common demon family.

Synonyms for Rebellion are Treason, Self-Will, Obduracy, Stubbornness, **Disobedience**, Denunciation, and Anti - submissiveness. **Antonyms** for Rebellion are Willfulness, **Obedience** and Submissiveness.

Generally, after a person has become bitter, they rebel.

Disobedience means to disobey, transgress, violate, disregard, defy, infringe, shirk, resist, mutiny, rebel and revolt.

Have you had these feelings before? Rebellion is very common among Christians. **Obedience is the opposite of Rebellion**.

The word **Rebellion** occurs infrequently in the Bible. Therefore, we must use other words as **rebellious** and **to rebel**. The next best word to describe Rebellion is **Disobedience** or the opposite of **Obedience**.

Study Of Rebellion

How To Study

The best way to study rebellion is as **disobedience to God** and from the opposite view of **the need to be obedient to God**. There are many instances of disobedience to God and the corresponding punishment in the Bible for the sin.

Disobedience to God Scripture

Lev. 26:14-46 (A curse to those that break the commandments) There is a curse for each disobedience.
Numbers 14:11-24 (People murmur - God threatens them) **Are you murmuring?**
Numbers 32:8-13 (Moses reproves the Reubenites and Gadites - rebels.)
Deut. 18:19 (God will require it of you the people if you rebel.)
Deut. 28:15-68 (The curse for disobedience)

Helpful Scripture and Bible Stories of Rebellion

Genesis Ch. 3 The Fall of Man
II Samuel Ch. 13 Absalom Avenges Tamar
II Samuel Ch. 15 Absalom's Conspiracy
I Kings Ch. 16-22 Ahab/Jezebel Rebellion
Isa. 3:12 **Children Oppress, Women Rule (Ahab/Jezebel Complex) A picture of our society: women will not follow and men will not lead!**
Isa. Ch. 14 Satan's Fall
Eze. Ch. 28 Satan's Rebellion
Malachi 4:5-6 Smite the Earth with a Curse
II Thes. 2:9-12 Strong Delusion, Believing Lies
James 3:13-18 Earthly, Unspiritual, Devilish Wisdom

Nelson's Expository Dictionary Of The Old Testament

The words **to rebel, rebellion and rebellious** are defined by the following phrases: Be contentious, make angry, contend with, dispute with, stubborn headed, opposition to someone motivated by pride, stubborn and rebellious, speech and actions are against the Lord, rebellious attitude against God, disobey, act of defying the command of God, rebellious and defiled, listens to no voice, accepts no correction, make bitter, provoke, reject, not recognize, rebellion and stiff neck, double rebellion and rebellious house.

Rebellion can also be defined as revolt, overthrow, mutiny, breakup, destruction, spasm, convulsion, resistance, interference, friction, withstand, repulse and disobedient.

Rebellious can also be defined as revolutionary, defiance, aggressiveness, dare and scorn.

Eve Rebels (The Original Rebellion Of Man)

We can trace our curses back to Adam and Eve. Adam also rebelled against God. This is the Jezebel / Ahab Complex. There are **many ingredients** in Eve's rebellion:
1. She was **seduced** by conversation and greed for power and knowledge.
2. The **price of seduction** was experiencing a knowledge of good and evil.
3. The **action of rebellion** resulted in shame, attempting to correct the mistake or cover it up, fear, withdrawing from God's presence, loss of esteemed position, pain in childbirth, hard work and toil, and birth of rebellious children.

Absalom Rebels

Absalom's sister, Tamar, was **raped** by his half-brother, Amnon (II Sam. 13).

Hate entered Absalom's heart because of his sister being raped. He plotted and planned for two years to murder Amnon.

Absalom again falls prey to resentment and burns Joab's field because he would not go to David for him. By trying to force David to see him, he is acting out rebellion.

He came to repentance but didn't really repent; it was surface repentance only.

After he had his audience with David, he quickly got busy with his **plans for rebellion**.

Absalom got favor with the people by acting as if he loved them and claiming great concern for their welfare. After he had **seduced them**, he declared himself King.

Some demons that probably were in Absalom were **hate, anger, resentment, deceit, trickery, witchcraft, betrayal, pride, pompousness, false love, backstabbing, lying, arrogance, unrighteous judgement and self-serving.**

Jezebel Rebels

She killed God's prophets which is **rebellion against God**. She exhibited hate, retaliation and threatenings.

She turns from role of woman and wife to trying to upstage the King, her husband. She belittled him, connived behind his back, and plotted murder and control of people. **Some women/men today use seemingly pure religious motives to control others such as soulish prophecy - telling others what to do!**

Another motive behind her rebellion was that she wanted **worship and admiration**. Jezebel is **true sorcery**. Rebellious Jezebelic males/females will ask questions aimed at causing the other person to doubt his worth, ability, decisions, etc. She ended up being thrown out a window, run over by chariots and eaten by dogs. **Did she go to Hell; what do you think?**

Ahab Rebels

Worshiping Idols Is Worst Rebellion Against God

This is called spiritual adultery. The **major rebellion was against God** in Baal worship. He went after idols. Abortion is worship of the god of sex, Satan, and is similar to Baal worship!

Ahab exhibited characteristics of **complete confusion, disobedience, resentfulness, sullenness, greed, accomplice to Jezebel, believed lying spirit, refused to believe God, and begat rebellious children.**

Perfect Family

Eph. 5:22 & 25; 6:1 & 4: Families repeat after me:
1. **Husbands love your wives.**
2. **Wives submit to your husbands.**
3. **Children obey your parents.**
4. **Fathers do not provoke your children.**

Classic Examples Of Rebellion

1. Nation of Israel - rebelled many times. Study the rise and fall of Israel!
2. Satan and Fallen Angels - original rebellion.
3. Queen Jezebel - rebellious woman.
4. King Ahab - rebellious man

Ahab-Jezebel Rebellious Influence In World Today

1. Divorce - one parent families. Men don't want responsibility - just sex!
2. Felinism - pictures bungling father and clever mother. Watch TV brain washing.
3. Sex - no restrictions. There is no free sex; only curses of God in the future.
4. Young people - confused, rebellious.
5. Drugs - Sex - Music.
6. Society with emotional problems.
7. Effeminate, emotional, weak spiritual and weak physical men.
8. Women's false strength - put to test usually fails.
9. Children - fear, insecurity, frustration, difficulty learning, potential corruption, discord, growth in occult and cults, selfishness, doubt, inability to achieve, hypochondriacs and church splits.

You And People Around You

Such qualities as these **have unnatural power to seduce you,** even overwhelm you. It is not charisma but seduction, and it creates bondage. You may have a friend whom you at times have a great desire to be free of, and the next moment feel guilt or condemnation for desiring your freedom. Consider why you are attracted to your friend.

Look out for mothers/dads who try to dominate married children's lives, and men/women who **cannot delegate authority** but try to mind every detail.

Women/men shouldn't try to force mate into a religious experience but win him/her by quiet and joyful submission to the Christian life **fulfilling your role as God established it**.

Summary

A study of the Bible shows clearly that God hates rebellion and that He will punish the people for their sins.

The people are blessed when they obey the Bible and they are **cursed when they disobey the Bible commandments.** There is a curse for every violation of Bible!

Rebellion is against God. For example, when a wife rebels against her husband, she is not just rebelling against him but against God who put the husband in authority over the wife. Finally, **rebellion can be very costly** while **obedience can be very rewarding**. The Bible applies equally to an individual, family, church, community, nation, etc.

References

Nelson's Expository Dictionary of the Old Testament

UNFORGIVENESS

List Of Scripture

Psa. 85:2 (Forgiven iniquity and covered sin - God)
Psa. 86:5 (Ready to forgive and plenteous in mercy - God)
Psa. 103:3 & 12 (Forgiveth all & removed as far as east from west - God)
Isa. 1:18 (Sins shall be as white as snow - God)
Isa. 43:25 (Blotteth out and will not remember - God)
Matt. 5:44 (Forgive your enemies.)
Matt. 6:14-15 (Forgive men or not be forgiven by God - man)
Matt. 18:21-35 (Law of Forgiveness - man)
Mark 11:25-26 (Forgive men or not be forgiven by God - man)
Luke 17:3-4 (Rebuke man and forgive seven times a day - man)
Eph. 4:32 (King, tenderhearted, forgiving as God does - man)
Col. 2:13 (Forgiven you all trespasses - God)
Col. 3:12-13 (Mercies, kindness, humbleness, meekness, long-suffering, forbearing and forgiving one another - man)
Heb. 8:12 (Merciful to unrighteous and remember not sins - God)
Heb. 10:17 (Remember not sins and iniquities - God)
I John 1:9 (Confessing, forgiveness, cleansing from unrighteousness)

General

Generally a person's demons cannot be cast out if he has unforgiveness in his heart. The opposite of unforgiveness is forgiveness.

Matt. 18:21-35 (**Law of Forgiveness** - Key Chapter); God sends demons to torment these with unforgiveness. Forgive your fellowman 70 x 7 = 490 times.

Kingdom of Heaven (is likened to): God (is The King), the Rich Man (is You); and the Poor Man (is anyone you have not forgiven).

1. Talent = 750 oz. of silver; Pence = 1/8 oz. of silver.
2. 10,000 talents x 750 = 7,500,000 oz. = $52,800,000 ($600,000).

3. 100 Pence x 1/8 = 2 1/2 oz. = $44.00 ($1.00).
4. Forgave 600,000 times as much.
5. Tormentors are Satan and his demons.
6. Prison is being in jail with Satan as warden and his demons as guards.

This is the crucifixion of the flesh until you come to your senses, forgive your fellowman and then ask God to forgive you! **The consequence of unforgiveness is the most important lesson that God has taught us about deliverance!**

Cancer and arthritis can come in through the sin of unforgiveness. If you know a Christian with these diseases, see if they have unforgiveness. They cannot be healed if the demons have a right to be there.

Pattern for being delivered and healed: forgive others, ask God for forgiveness, and forgive self. Cast out unforgiveness and bitterness. Cast out cancer and arthritis. **Anoint with oil and pray for healing: first deliverance then healing.**

Analysis Of Matthew 5:44

But I say unto you, Love your enemies, bless them that curse you, do good to them that hate you, and pray for them which despitefully use you, and persecute you. Forgive your enemies; there are no excuses! Whites forgive blacks; blacks forgive whites.
1. **Love your enemies.** We do not have to love Satan! Love in a social or moral sense: beloved. Enemy is an adversary: foe.
2. **Bless them that curse you.** Speak well of: thank or invoke a benediction upon. Curse is to execrate: to doom.
3. **Do good to them that hate you.** Do good honestly: full well. Hate is to detest: especially to persecute.
4. **Pray for them that despitefully use you and persecute you.** Pray earnestly for: supplicate. Despitefully is to insult: slander and falsely accuse. Persecute is to pursue: to suffer.

Forgiveness (Excerpts)

Forgiveness is hard to give because it hurts to extend it to undeserving and hard-hearted ones. To release a wrong-doer instead of exacting a just penalty requires that we reach out in love, rejecting the temptation to hold bitterness and resentment. This is contrary to our natural inclinations, thus the old adage, **To err is human, to forgive divine.**

Forgiveness is not forgetting the wrong done; some hurts are so deep that this would be impossible. We can forget the anger and hurt we felt, but the act is branded in our minds. Forgiveness takes place when the victim accepts the loss and/or injury done him and deliberately cancels the debt owed him by the offending person. **This is an act of your will and God will honor it.**

Anger must be dealt with openly and honestly, not denied or ignored. Either it must be vented in retaliation or the injured party must accept his own anger, bear the burden of it, and confess it in prayer to release himself and to set the other party free. **Revenge always hurts the revenger far more than the one at whom it is leveled!**

In other words , our pattern must be the grievous and substitutionary death of Christ. He willingly received the hurt and evil of the entire human race in His own body on the tree (I Peter 2:21-24) to pay the debt for our guilt. He now offers what He has wrought as a free gift to undeserving and guilty persons so they can be free (Rom. 6:23; John 10:28-30).

As nothing else will, forgiveness takes us into the mysteries of grace where God forgives unconditionally on the basis of the substitutionary payment by another (Mark 11:25-26).

One of the fruits of the Holy Spirit's work in a life is the quality of meekness. It is a quality which is nurtured and abetted by practicing forgiveness.

This highly prized quality will cause us to be able to accept God's dealings with us as good, without disputing or resisting them. Meekness will also cause us to be able to **bear one another's burden's** cheerfully and for Jesus' sake, enabling us to enter into the mystery of Christ's sufferings.

Because unforgiveness, and the resentment and bitterness it generates is so deadly, it is not optional, but necessary that it be dealt with. Cancer and arthritis spirits definitely root into this fertile ground. To be bitter and unforgiving costs far more than it is worth.

Husbands forgive your wives. Wives forgive your husbands. Children forgive your parents. **In Jesus' Name, I forgive my wife or husband and my parents. Amen.**

References

Conquering The Hosts Of Hell, Forgiveness

5. PRAYERS AND LISTS OF DEMONS FOR MASS DELIVERANCE

1. **Basic Deliverance**
    1. **Prayer**
    2. **List of Demons**
        1. **Basic Deliverance**
        2. **Rejection**
    3. **Bitterness**
    4. **Rebellion**
    5. **Schizophrenia**
2. **Fifty-Three Common Demon Groupings**
    1. **Prayer**

SECTION 3 - BASIC DELIVERANCE SUMMARY - #2
(Rejection, Bitterness, Rebellion and Unforgiveness)
ATTACK - ATTACK - ATTACK

CONTENTS

GENERAL

Preface

This is the most important lesson that I can teach you. Be sure and understand the very important principle of forgiveness / unforgiveness which is the basis of deliverance.

The Three R's of deliverance are **Rejection, Root of Bitterness and Rebellion.** This is the most important grouping - like reading, riting and rithmetic.

These three families, **The Three R's**, of demons are the root causes of most of our problems as Christians. We must work to cleanse our lives of rejection, bitterness and rebellion so that we are not controlled in any way by these emotions and reactions.

Unforgiveness is very detrimental to our lives. We must forgive everyone who has done anything to us - actual or imagined. Hate, vengeance, envy and strife have no part in our lives.

The order of becoming demonized is as follows: familiar spirits from the sins of the ancestors, spirit of conception in lust, spirits of rejection in the womb, traumatic birth, unprotected child before the age of accountability and sins after becoming accountable to GOD. The order of basic deliverance demonization is as follows: Rejection, Bitterness including Unforgiveness, Rebellion and other demon families such as Sexual Sins. People began to get demonized from the sins of the ancestors, then basic demonization and finally advanced demonization.

I have ministered to thousands of Christians in deliverance: lay persons, five-fold ministers and deliverance ministers across the BODY OF CHRIST. Christians are demonized, not demon possessed. You simply have demons within your soul and body but not spirit.

Whatever your age, I would say that you have spent that time plus nine months getting demonized. It is going to take time to get free of demons. The rate of freedom is a function of how you work at it. Deliverance is a way of life, not a grand event. You can get saved, BAPTIZED IN THE HOLY SPIRIT and divinely healed instantaneously. But you will be working out your deliverance throughout your life time.

I try to take everyone through the basic deliverance. Many times the Christians will begin to get delivered from the family of Rejection. Rejection generally starts with the parents rejecting the child. **It is very important how the parents treat the child!**

Testimony About How God Taught Us Deliverance

After Byron, our only son died, our marriage was breaking up and Marie, our daughter, was in rejection and rebellion because she felt that we did not love her. We were trying to recover from Byron's death. We fasted, prayed and sought the LORD for about two years for GOD to help us in our terrible situation.

One night, Earline told me that she threw her Bible across the family room into the corner and told GOD that she was going to quit Christianity if He didn't do something for our family. **The LORD then appeared to Earline in a series of visions. A window shade came down and He told Earline to get me to pray deliverance.** She argued with GOD; she didn't want me to pray or anyone else. Many people had prayed for us with no results. **The window shade came down the second time and GOD repeated the command.** Earline argued with GOD again. **The window shade came down a third time; GOD laughed at Earline and told her, "Didn't I tell you to get Gene to pray deliverance?"** She came back to the bedroom where I was in bed, but not asleep, and told me what GOD had said.

I made my arguments too about not knowing about deliverance and why not get our pastor to do it. Finally, I gave in not knowing what to do, I prayed in English and then in Tongues, The Heavenly Language. Then THE HOLY SPIRIT began to call out names of demons through my voice which then came out of us. Marie was in the next bedroom but she also received deliverance. The next day she was a smiling teenager. Deliverance saved our marriage and family, and began our ministry around 35 years ago.

While I was praying in THE HOLY SPIRIT with my eyes closed, Earline said that she clasped her hands together into a fist to hit me in the side of the head. When the demon of Rebellion came out, she realized that deliverance was real and didn't hit me. THANK GOD!

THE HOLY SPIRIT personally taught us basic deliverance, the demonic families of Rejection, Bitterness and Rebellion. Almighty God taught us this lesson in the middle of the night in our bed about thirty years ago.

We did not learn from reading a book or listening to someone teach us. We did not receive any books or teaching by man until about six months after our supernatural deliverance by GOD. Then we heard Frank and Ida Mae Hammond teach about deliverance and discuss the book, **Pigs In The Parlor**. The churches we went to did not teach deliverance which was about a third of JESUS CHRIST's ministry here on earth. JESUS CHRIST came to preach the Gospel, heal the sick and cast out demons which is what Christians should do.

(First) REJECTION (Opposite is Love)
Scripture

Rejection includes fear of rejection and self-rejection.

Except for the sins of the ancestors, rejection is generally where the demons first attack someone. Because of the parents, this can be in the womb.

Matt. 5:3 (rejected feel poorly in their spirit) If you are rejected, your spirit feels poorly.
Matt. 5:43-44 (love your enemies) You wouldn't have some of your problems if you loved your enemies.
II Cor. 5:14-15 (should not live unto themselves) Selfishness is a family of demons.
Eph. 6:4 (fathers provoke not your children to wrath) Notice it did not say mothers.

Rejection is defined as reject, refuse, repudiate, decline, deny, rebuff, repel, renounce, discard, throw away, exclude, eliminate and jettison.

Have you had these feelings before? **Rejection is common among Christians.**

Man's Rejection
(Family Deliverance Manual)

Rejection of God and the truth, over-protection, wrong sex, broken home, guilt complex, treacherous comparison, envy, conditional love, worthlessness, Jezebel influence, depression, internal temper tantrum, controlled by emotions, thinks with feeling, introspection, guilt, lack of responsibility, worries, doubts, fear, unbelief, anxiety, fear of failure prevents attempting, braggart, criticism, obstinacy, loner, perfectionism, compliance, defiance, shyness, **self-deprecating, discipline, condemnation and hatred**.

Man's Symptoms Of Rejection
(Family Deliverance Manual)

Body is tense, high blood pressure, grinding teeth, goes to the refrigerator for relaxation, feels that one does not fit in, not a part, looks for happiness in things, wounded spirit, drive to lead, to have own way rather than serve, clash easily with other people close to you, easily offended, moralist, needs to receive credit, considers self bold and unafraid, intolerant of neurotic people, impatient of slow movers, trouble submitting, argumentative, quick tempered, angry person, suspicious, over-achiever and timidity.

Man's Inter-Personal Effects Of Rejection
(Family Deliverance Manual)

Wishing you were never born, feelings of inferiority, inability to express feelings, depression, emotional insulation, subjectively, perfectionism, lack of self-discipline, irresponsibility, handicaps, conditional love, self-condemnation, inability to express feelings.

Earline's Testimony About Rejection

Rejection is the basic cause of abuse. All types of rejection work to destroy the mental and emotional health of an individual.

I had often wondered about certain problems I had: (1) an inordinate desire to please, (2) inability to say no to things I didn't want to do, (3) always setting goals, working hard to accomplish them and then stopping short of success, (4) always feeling I had to do things better than anyone else, and (5) trying to make everything around me and about me look better than I thought it was. (<u>Do you have some of the problems that Earline had</u>?)

I cut off part of my finger in an accident loading a horse into a trailer. **It was the first time I had need of a hospital in many years.** (<u>Our family lived in divine health for about a dozen years after we learned about divine healing</u>.) I was put to sleep and my finger was sewn into my palm. The next day I was supposed to be quiet and take it easy.

For five years, I had been trying to help my mom get resettled after my dad's death. At times she would tell me what she wanted me to do and I would start to do it. **Right in the middle of my doing it, she would suddenly, without telling me, change her mind and have one of my brothers doing an entirely different thing.**

Two years ago I took her to Maine to see my brother. Back in Chattanooga she accused me of wanting and trying to kill her. This really puzzled me because I thought we got along very well.

After the operation, I was being still on the sofa praying. I asked God **Why can't I help mom? Why does she think I want to kill her?**

I had a vision. (Have you had visions?) I was standing in the room I had as a child. I was high near the ceiling. I was witnessing a terrible thing. A woman was beating, not whipping, a child. I went down to see who this was and to stop it; I saw it was my mom. I went beside the bed, bent down and looked; the child was me. (Earline was a physically and mentally abused child. Have you been physically and mentally abused?)

Thinking I was hallucinating because of the drugs from the operation the day before, I quickly decided to get up and get busy. One-handed work was hard to find, so I swept the carport.

My brother called me or I called him. Since I sounded a little funny, he asked what was wrong. I told him next time they could sew me up awake. Then I related this story to him. He was silent, then he asked me if I remembered that day.

He said he had told my dad that if my mom didn't stop beating me for no reason, he would kill her. The only words said in the scene were by my dad; he said to my mom that he would kill her if he ever heard of this happening again. I was not a small child. I was ten or twelve years old when the beatings stopped.

For some reason, I simply cannot remember this today. He thought her fear that I wanted to kill her came from the guilt for what she did to me.

About eight to nine years before this incident, Gene and I had fasted and prayed for me for two years. When I got the Baptism of the Holy Spirit, there was only initial joy. Immediately, I began to have more fears than before, my emotions were out of control and I couldn't think clearly. God does not give us a spirit of fear but a spirit of power, love, calm, well-balanced mind, discipline and self control.

Neither of us knew about deliverance from demons, so God had to teach us. After a long time of praying one night, Gene began to call out **Rejection, Rebellion, Bitterness, etc.** I was very different after this.

I had to learn how to stay free by studying the Bible. No one in our town believed a Christian could have a demon, so we had to rely on God and His Word.

I was doing very well until the scene passed before my eyes and I learned of my early life. Immediately, I began to have times of panic for no apparent reason. I was hostile. I noticed a panic when those who had authority over me were present. I would become fearful if a policeman came near me, and when the pastor or principal came into my school room. I felt I had to challenge Gene's decisions.

We prayed and felt that I needed more deliverance. Gene was led to call out the same things as before. **We realized at this point that we were working on my subconscious mind.** (When you have very traumatic events that the conscious mind can not handle, they are submerged in your subconscious min.)

(Second) BITTERNESS (Opposite is Forgiveness)

Scripture

Bitterness includes resentment, hatred, unforgiveness, violence, temper, anger, retaliation and murder.

Generally, after a person becomes rejected, they become bitter.

Acts 8:22-24 (in gall of bitterness and in bond of iniquity) Are you?
Rom. 3:13-14 (mouth is full of cursing and bitterness) Are these in your mouth?
Eph. 4:31-32 (bitterness---forgiving one another) Can you forgive?
Heb. 12:14-16 (peace---root of bitterness defiles) Are you defiled?

Bitterness is defined as bitterly curse, rebellious, sharp, acrid, grief, embitter, poisonous, violently, provoke, vex, grieve, sorrow, bitter herb, calamity, bile, venom, angry, chafed, most bitterly, rebel and provoke.

Have you had these feelings before? Bitterness is common among Christians.

Roots
(Family Deliverance Manual)

Anger, jealousy, irritating behavior, habits, irritability, loathing, mad, madness, malice, murder, offending, idle, pouting, provoking to wrath, pugnacious, quarrelsome, rage, destructive, enraged, rebellion, repugnance, repulsive, resentment, retaliation, revenge, rough, sassy, sassiness, savage, seething, self-abuse, accusation, blame, condemnation, guilt, criticism, destruction, infliction, punishment, torture, sharp tongue, spite, strife, strong will, struggle, suicide wish, suicide, tempter tantrum, tortured, troubled, torn relations, adolescent, vehement, vicious, violence, warring, wild child, unforgiveness, ugliness, unbridled tongue, uncontrollable child, unforgiveness, unruly child and uncooperative adult.

Earline's Testimony About The Curse Of The Bastard

(Do you know what a bastard is? It is a child conceived out of wedlock. The sin has been committed and it doesn't matter if you get married later.) Great grandfather marries great grandmother in church. All seems well; they have three children. Great grandfather dies. Great grandmother discovers she can not get his railroad pension because she is his fifth wife. My grandfather becomes very bitter and a little paranoid. My mom is paranoid and schizophrenic (like father - like daughter). She abused me physically.

(Check yourself and see if you have any of these problems.) Here are some of the problems created for me by this bastard curse. Never feeling at home in any church for long. Never feeling good about myself. Being ashamed for people to look at me even though I didn't know what I wanted to hide, overriding fear, striving excessively to succeed and stopping short of realizing the goal, fear of failure, fear of authority, resisting authority, fighting verbally and physically, demonic pressure to sexual activities, and not much joy in natural or spiritual life.

(Raise your hand if you were born out of wedlock (marriage). Raise your hand if you conceived a child out of wedlock. Raise your hand if your child conceived a child out of wedlock. You can notice the continuation of the curse of the bastard. We have worked with four or five generations of bastards.)

(Third) REBELLION (Opposite is Obedience)

Rebellion includes self-will, stubbornness, disobedience and anti-submissiveness.

Generally after a person has become bitter, they rebel.

Scripture

1 Sam. 15:23 (for rebellion is as the sin of witchcraft, and stubbornness is as iniquity and idolatry. A Christian in rebellion is practicing witchcraft.)
Heb. 2:2 (disobedience received a just reward. You will receive a reward that you don't want.)
Heb. 13:17 (obey and submit yourselves. This is a two edged sword: pastor and congregation.)
2 Pet. 2:10 (presumptuous are they, self-willed. Are you presumptuous?)

Disobedience means to disobey, transgress, violate, disregard, defy, infringe, shirk, resist, mutiny, rebel and revolt.

Have you had these feelings before? Rebellion is common among Christians.

Earline's Testimony About Ancestral Background

(The following testimony will help you understand how the soul (mind, will and emotions) works. It will also show you how Satan attacks the physical body with demons by curses.)

I have an Indian - English - German - French background. There are nationality curses on each of these people. The sins of the nations will fall on those of that nationality. Some Indians worshipped demons; some English and Europeans were Druids - they worshipped Satan.

In innocence, my father participated in some occult practices: **wart removal and water witching**. From my father came curses of Masons and Indians. Physical problems came as a result of curses on Indian worship: inactive thyroid, female disorders and heart disease.

My father removed the warts from my brother by mountain medicine (charming which is a type of witchcraft). This occult practice was something in the order of tying strings, going out under the drip of the eave and burying the strings. The occult practice removed the warts but he got spinal meningitis. (Apparently, a demon of spinal meningitis was swapped for a demon of warts.)

Satan doesn't give anything away for free; there is a greater price to pay. Spinal meningitis killed him. He went to Heaven and saw two siblings which had died early in life; God sent him back to earth. I had to nurse him back to health.

My mother was a paranoid schizophrenic with an Indian - English background. Her emotional illness caused me to need a lot of deliverance from emotional problems.

Spiritual Bondage

Generally a person's demons can not be cast out if he has unforgiveness in his heart! Do you want to keep your demons - then keep your unforgiveness!

Law Of Forgiveness: Key Chapter - Matt. 18:21-35

1. Forgive your fellowman 70 x 7 = 490 times.
2. Actually, you should forgive your fellowman an unlimited number of times. How would you like it if GOD only forgave you 490 times?
3.God sends demons to torment these with unforgiveness. Tormentors are Satan and his demons. Prison is being in jail with Satan as Warden and his demons as guards.

Kingdom Of Heaven Is Likened To

This is a parable. God (**is The King**), the Rich Man (**is You**); and the Poor Man (**is anyone you have not forgiven**).

The Value Of Money

Talent = 750 oz. of silver; Pence = 1/8 oz. of silver.
10,000 talents x 750 = 7,500,000 oz. = $52,800,000.
100 Pence x 1/8 = 12-1/2 oz. = $44.00.

The Value Of Your Salvation

Your salvation is worth $52,800,000.
Your unforgiveness is worth $44.00.
This is a ratio of 600,000 to 1.
God forgave you 600,000 times as much as you are willing to forgive others.

This is the crucifixion of the flesh until you come to your senses and forgive your fellowman and then ask God to forgive you!

Earline's Testimony About Heart Condition

Earline's Comments

Earline had Cherokee Indian ancestors on both sides of the family. I had a heart condition which was unusual. It never occurred with regularity or under any specific condition.

God gave me a vision of an Indian Shaman or Witch Doctor at an elevated funeral pyre which was burning dead bodies. He was chanting and waving, and saying on the descendents and descendents. The Shaman or Witch Doctor is not of GOD and was using demonic power. This was supposed to be a blessing, but in actuality was a curse, because many Indians worship demons. This was a curse that came down on my family causing heart problems.

Gene's Comments

This is a sign of demonic symptoms of disease brought about by a curse. It doesn't follow the medical guidelines. All they can say is that it is inherited.

Earline's Comments

While taking a tread mill test, I experienced tremendous pain in the chest, arms and neck. I was examined by a **heart specialist** in Minneapolis who told me that my heart was good but he had written **death by heart attack** on many people's certificates like myself.

Gene's Comments
These were people who didn't really have anything wrong with their hearts physically but had a spiritual root to the disease. The prayer of faith will not heal a disease that has a spiritual root that must be dealt with as sin to be confessed. Then the curse can be broken and the person prayed for to be healed.

God is beginning to show the Christian world spiritual roots of various diseases. Pastor Henry Wright of Molena, Georgia and Art Mathias in Anchorage, Alaska are pioneers in this area. I took the one week course in Thomaston, Georgia and have met Art Mathias in Alaska. I recommend that every Christian purchase the book, **A More Excellent Way** by Henry Wright.

Earline's Comments

A year or so after my dad's death, I found my heart acting up again. Sometimes one to five years would elapse between seizures. I began to ask God to show me why my brothers, dad, dad's brothers and his dad had heart problems.

God showed me Exodus 20 and Ezekiel 18. He told me to repent for my ancestors and myself for the sin of idol worship in Leviticus 26:40-41. The curse of idol worship follows the blood line down to the descendants. I did these things and have been free from these attacks for over twenty years. I was only the second generation from previous generations of Indians that sinned before God.

Gene's Comments

You have to forgive your ancestors and ask for forgiveness for yourself. Earline took her older brother, Clyde, through breaking the curse and he is still alive after a heart attack.

Exodus 20 lists the Ten Commandments which are still applicable today. The scriptures about worshipping other gods are verses 3, 4 and 5. This outlines the curse for idol worship which lasts three or four generations according to God's purposes. (Does anybody know why God curses some sins for three generations and some sins for four generations?)

Ezekiel 18 shows the equity of God's dealings with us. The sin of idol worship is defined as eating upon the mountains (in the groves), lifting up the eyes to the idols (worship), and not walking in God's statutes and judgments (disobedience).

This was a **revelation of the sins of the ancestors** that God gave Earline through prayer about why her family was plagued by heart attack and death by heart attack. This was primarily the men that were attacked but even Earline, a woman, was attacked. The revelation was the effect of the sins of the ancestors in her family coming through the Indians to cause heart problems and early death. The sin was disobeying the Ten Commandments of having no other gods before you, which is idol worship, that the Indians committed. Up to that time, we had never heard about the sins of the ancestors.

Earline had Cherokee Indian ancestry coming through her father and mother. We were raised in and around Chattanooga, Tennessee which was not far from Cherokee, North Carolina which had a demonic draw upon Earline. We were drawn to make a pilgrimage to the Smokey Mountains every year although we did not make it every year. In the fall, Earline would long to go to the mountains. After Earline was delivered from Indian spirits, she did not have that draw to go to the Smokey Mountains.

When you are a person of mixed races, you inherit the curses coming down through the different races, languages, customs, religions and nationalities. If you have Indian ancestry and are Caucasian, you receive the curses from the Indians and the Caucasians. How many of you have Indian ancestry? It is amazing how many do!

The curse would come from those ancestors that had sinned. This means that you can be cursed for ten generations (2046 ancestors) from both sides of your family.

Which of your ancestors didn't sin or that you know didn't sin? It is a good assumption that you have the curse of incest and the curse of the bastard on you. It could come from any of 2046 ancestors back to the tenth generation that sinned assuming it has not been properly broken. You will see the sin repeating itself generation after generation such as bastard after bastard.

We worked with one Indian woman who was a Christian. She had a hard time getting free of Indian curses and demons brought upon her by her ancestral lineage and sexual abuse. She was cursed by being an Indian and by incest which is very hard on a woman being abused by her blood relatives.

Consequence Of Unforgiveness

The consequence of unforgiveness is the most important lesson that God has taught us about deliverance. The opposite is the importance of forgiveness.

Cancer, arthritis and certain other diseases can come in through the sin of unforgiveness. If you know a Christian with cancer and arthritis, see if they have unforgiveness. They cannot be healed if the demons have a right to be there.

Pattern For Being Delivered And Healed

Forgive ancestors, descendents and others, ask God for forgiveness, and forgive self. Cast out unforgiveness and bitterness. Cast out cancer and arthritis. Anoint with oil and pray for healing. **Try this pattern on all diseases: first deliverance then healing.** This is what GOD taught me about thirty years ago. First take people through deliverance and then pray for healing.

REFERENCE

Family Deliverance Manual by Pat Holliday, 9252 San Jose Blvd., Apt. 2804, Jacksonville, FL

SECTION 4 - OVERVIEW OF DELIVERANCE

SEQUENCE OF DEMONIZATION

Six Basic Steps To Becoming Demonized

1. Sins of the Ancestors (three - four - ten generation curses)
2. Conception in Sin (fornication - adultery - lust - bastard - incest - other)
3. Rejection in Womb (unwanted - threat of abortion - death curse)
4. Birth (anesthesia - cutting of flesh - surgery - trauma - other)
5. Before the Age of Accountability (sin against innocent child)
6. After the Age of Accountability (sin by accountable adult)

SPIRITUAL HISTORY

How To Determine Demonization

A spiritual history lists the spiritual events that have taken place in a person's life that cause problems in the spirit, soul and body. These include traumatic events, sins, problems and anything that would open the door for a demon to come into the person's soul or body. Each event has to be dealt with spiritually.

Look at the **Six Basic Steps To Becoming Demonized** and the sequence of events. What sins did the ancestors do that would have cursed the descendents to the third, fourth or tenth generation? What spirits were active when you were conceived? Were you rejected or did they try to kill you when you were in the womb? Was your mother operated on to deliver you? Were you molested before GOD held you accountable for sin? What sins did you commit after GOD held you accountable?

Sit down and write the spiritual history. Once the spiritual history has been developed, you have identified the problems. Look at the **Six Basic Steps To Becoming Delivered**, get right with GOD and break demonic ties for each event. Now you are ready to cast out demons and pray for healing. Then discipline your life, change your way of thinking and acting, go and sin no more.

SEQUENCE OF DELIVERANCE

Six Basic Steps To Becoming Delivered

1. Identify Problems (do a Spiritual History - short or long)
2. Get Right With God (forgive - repent - renounce as appropriate)
3. Break Demonic Ties (curses - soul ties - demonic holds - demonic ties)
4. Cast Out Demons (In THE NAME OF JESUS CHRIST OF NAZARETH)
5. Pray for Healing (soul (mind - will - emotions) - body (organs - systems)
6. Discipline Life (change way of thinking and acting - go and sin no more)

COMMENTS

1. A person can spent a lifetime, including instant of conception and time in womb, in accumulating demons.
2. Deliverance is a way of life, a process, not a grand event. It is a lifetime walk on the way to Heaven.
3. It is easy to cast out demons but hard to discipline the soul and body. GOD will not do it for you and no one else can either.

CURSES

The following is an outline and origin of primary curses on people:

NATIONALITIES
ANCESTORS (10 generations of bloodline)
OURSELVES (after the age of accountability)
OTHERS OUTSIDE OF BLOODLINE

SPIRITUAL AUTHORITY
SECULAR AUTHORITY
CARNAL AUTHORITY (generally from sexual sins)

CONCEPTION
WOMB
BIRTH
BEFORE THE AGE OF ACCOUNTABILITY
AFTER THE AGE OF ACCOUNTABILITY

MENTAL
PHYSICAL (including operations)
SPIRITUAL
FINANCIAL

HOLY BIBLE (disobeying GOD)
HOUSE (cursed home)
POSSESSIONS (cursed objects)

THINKING
SPEAKING
ACTING

MALE
FEMALE

FALSE RELIGIONS
APOSTATE CHURCH
DEMONIC PRACTICES

General: Biblical, nationalities, bloodline, ancestral, ourselves, descendents, mates, others, male, female, innocent blood, sexual, out of divine order, objects, house, word, slavery, religious, idolatry, New Age, Occult, Witchcraft and Satanism.

SECTION 5 - HOW TO MINISTER BASIC DELIVERANCE

REASON FOR LEARNING

The main reason we are teaching you how to do basic deliverance is that every Christian should be able to cast out demons at least in their own family. Later on God may lead you to do deliverance in your home or church. **God told us to train an army for His use; you are part of that army!** The bottom line of deliverance is the casting out of demons.

Deliverance will assist in establishing family order and God's order. Every Christian should cast out demons (**Mark 16:17**). There are not many "Deliverance Ministers" to help people. Christians have many demons; proper deliverance takes a lot of time. Deliverance is a way of life and not a grand event.

Parents are the best persons to minister to their children; husband to wife and wife to husband. Parents need to protect their children and set the family free from demons.

Deliverance gives an understanding of God's and Satan's kingdoms that you will not get any other way. Deliverance allows you to see into the spiritual world by the manifestations of demons.

GENERAL

Basic Deliverance consists of setting a person free from three common demon families: rejection, bitterness and rebellion (also common to schizophrenia).

Typically a person becomes rejected, then becomes bitter, and finally rebels (then come other problems).

The most important key in setting a person free from these families is to get the person to forgive anyone that has hurt him!

First, unforgiveness should be dealt with before the families of rejection, bitterness and rebellion are cast out.

After basic deliverance, then other demon families can be attacked. For example, cancer and arthritis can come into a person thru the open door of unforgiveness. After basic deliverance, cast out the spirits of cancer and arthritis.

A person may have become demonized while in the womb by **sins of the ancestors** for causes other than rejection, bitterness and rebellion. If so, another approach is required.

Again, the most important key in setting a person free from the sins of the ancestors is to get the person to **forgive his ancestors**, and ask God to forgive them and bless them (parents are also ancestors).

After forgiveness for any hurt or sin, then any demonic ties should be broken. For example, curses of the ancestors passed down thru the generations, or soul ties caused by sexual sin or witchcraft control are demonic ties.

After **breaking curses and soul ties**, we ask God to restore the fragmented soul -mind, will and emotions. We ask God to send out angels to restore anything that the demons have stolen.

After **restoration of the fragmented soul**, we ask God to stir up the demons in the subconscious mind so that they can be identified and cast out.

The person can then be led in a general prayer of **salvation / deliverance** to God. There are many good prayers.

The leader should then pray and take authority over the demonic spirit world.

After the grounds for deliverance are established (taking away the demons' legal rights before God which allow the demons to stay), then start casting out demons.

Use all the **weapons of the warfare in the Bible** against the demons. These include reading scripture to the demons, exercising the Gifts of the Holy Spirit, causing the demons to reveal information against themselves, seeking discernment from God thru the Holy Spirit, praying to God in other tongues, asking Jesus for help, and any other methods that are helpful in gathering data, taking away legal rights and casting out. **By all means, do what God tells you to do even if you do not understand it. Caution - make sure it is God and not Satan telling you what to do.**

Unforgiveness - get the person to forgive others by an act of his will which God will honor. It may be very difficult for the person but God accepts their willingness to forgive. **Unforgiveness** - Cancer or Arthritis may come into the person later on.

Before any deliverance starts, a person should be given an opportunity to discuss his problems and background so that you can get to know the person and properly minister to him.

After deliverance is ended, a person should be counseled about how to walk out his deliverance and discipline his life.

It is good if teaching on basic deliverance or sins of ancestors precedes the deliverance.

After counseling, anoint with oil and pray for any healing needed. Pray for scars in the body where the demons left. **The practice of Inner Healing is not a substitute for Deliverance!**

COMMON DEMON FAMILIES OF BASIC DELIVERANCE
(From Pigs In The Parlor)

Do you have the following problems?

Rejection
Fear of Rejection
Self-Rejection
Unforgiveness
Violence

Bitterness
Resentment
Hatred
Disobedience
Antisubmissiveness

Rebellion
Self-will
Stubbornness

Temper	Anger Retaliation Murder

STEPS TO MINISTER DELIVERANCE

A. Steps For Basic Deliverance For Personal Ministry To An Individual

1. Find out about the person's problems and background.
2. Some discussion about how they got into trouble will be helpful.
3. Get the person to forgive others and lead him in a specific prayer about his problems.
4. **Start casting out the families of Rejection, then Bitterness and finally Rebellion.**
5. Counsel the person how to walk out his deliverance and how to discipline his life.
6. Anoint with oil and pray for healing.
7. The above steps could be used after a church service at the altar, or in the prayer room, home or over the phone.

B. Steps For Sins Of Ancestors For Personal Ministry To An Individual

1. Find out about the person's problems and background.
2. Some discussion about how they got into trouble may be helpful.
3. Get the person to forgive others and lead him in a specific prayer about his problems.
4. **Lead the person thru a prayer to break curses and soul ties, restore the fragmented soul, stir up the demons in the sub-conscious mind, and finally salvation/deliverance.**
5. **Here again, it is good to start with basic deliverance of Rejection, Bitterness and Rebellion. Then go into other areas that have been identified and legal grounds established for casting out.**
6. Counsel the person how to walk out his deliverance and how to discipline his life.
7. Anoint with oil and pray for healing.
8. The above steps could be used after a church service at the altar or in the prayer room, in the home or over the phone.

C. Steps For Basic Deliverance And/Or Sins Of Ancestors For A Group Or A Church (We will do that today after the teaching.)

1. Teach on Basic Deliverance, Sins of Ancestors, or any other deliverance topic.
2. Lead the congregation in a mass prayer about that topic, and include curses, soul ties, fragmented soul, subconscious mind, unforgiveness and salvation.
3. The pastor/evangelist will then pray and take authority over the demonic spiritual world and ask God to send his forces and take charge of the deliverance.
4. Start the mass deliverance with basic deliverance and then go to any other topic. Workers shall help individuals having trouble getting free.
5. After mass deliverance, work with individuals.
6. Counsel the person how to walk out his deliverance and how to discipline his life.
7. Anoint with oil and pray for healing.
8. The above steps could be used after a church service at the altar or in the prayer room, in the home or over the phone.
9. The above steps could be used in a prayer group, church, home or any meeting about deliverance.

D. Steps For Basic Deliverance/Sins Of Ancestors For The Home Counseling /

Ministry Meeting

1. Provide specific counseling to the individuals as God leads.
2. Find out about the person's problems and background.
3. Some discussion about how they got into trouble may be helpful.
4. Take a refreshment/bathroom break of about 15 minutes.
5. Get the person to forgive others and lead him in a specific prayer about his problems.
6. Lead the congregation in a mass prayer about that topic, and include curses, soul ties, fragmented soul, subconscious mind, unforgiveness and salvation.
7. The pastor/evangelist will then pray and take authority over the demonic spiritual world and ask God to send his forces and take charge of the deliverance.
8. Start the mass deliverance with basic deliverance and then go to any other topic. Workers shall help individuals having trouble getting free.
9. After mass deliverance, work with individuals.

E. Variations

The above procedures can be varied to fit the situation or at the leadership of the Holy Spirit.

F. Subjects Omitted

This lesson deals with Basic Deliverance primarily. There are many subjects omitted. Please see the **Deliverance Manual** Table of Contents for other subjects and a listing of demons. It is four books in one: **Basic Deliverance, Advanced Deliverance, Mass Deliverance,** and **How To Do Deliverance**.

HOW TO LEARN ABOUT DELIVERANCE

1. Get Experience - start casting out demons and get involved.
2. Study Bible - use a concordance and study Gospels mainly.
3. Fast and pray - seek the Lord about your problems.
4. Study deliverance books - learn as much as you can.
5. Study books on the mind, will and emotions.
6. Go to deliverance meetings - participate in teaching and ministry: mass, small groups and individuals.
7. Study Satan from a Christian viewpoint - to see how he is trying to destroy you, your family and your church.
8. Emphasize practical methods - put the Bible to work.
9. Clean out your house - get rid of demonic objects.
10. Be persistent - keep after the demons in an area of your life until you are successful.
11. Learn to research a subject - use encyclopedias, dictionaries, medical and psychiatric books.
12. Learn the three phases of deliverance: How to Determine the Need for Deliverance, How go Get Delivered, and How to Stay Delivered.
13. Deliverance is a constant learning process. Satan has spent thousands of years weaving a very complicated system to trap people.

PRACTICAL DELIVERANCE BOOKS

Basic - Pigs In The Parlor - Frank and Ida Mae Hammond, Impac Books, 137 W. Jefferson, Kirkwood, MO 63122.

Advanced - Battling The Hosts Of Hell; Conquering The Hosts Of Hell; Demolishing The Hosts Of Hell; Annihilating The Hosts Of Hell, Volume I; Annihilating The Hosts Of Hell, Volume II; Eradicating The Hosts Of Hell; and Smashing The Hosts Of Hell, eleven books and fifty booklets by Win Worley, Hegewisch Baptist Church, Highland, Indiana 46322

Mind - War On The Saints - Unabridged Edition, Jessie Penn-Lewis & Evans Roberts, Thomas E. Lowe, LTD., New York, New York.

DELIVERANCE PRAYERS

There are many **good deliverance prayers** that have been written and printed in books and in loose-leaf form. Some of these prayers are general and some have been written for specific purposes.

The **ideal prayer** is the one prayed by the individual to cover the specific area of the person's life that is being ministered to at that time. The next best prayer is the form prayer which the person repeats after the deliverance leader.

The following prayers have been used many times by us and **have produced good results**. One side benefit is that the people can see what is wrong and evil in their lives by what is contained in the prayers.

These prayers can be used for individuals, small groups or large groups equally well.

Short Prayer - Lord Jesus Christ, I believe you died on the cross for my sins and rose again from the dead. You redeemed me by your blood and I belong to you, and I want to live for you. I confess all my sins--known and unknown--I'm sorry for them all. I renounce them all. I forgive all others as I want you to forgive me. Forgive me now and cleanse me with your blood. I thank you for the blood of Jesus Christ which cleanses me now from all sin. And I come to you now as my deliverer. You know my special needs--the thing that binds, that torments, that defiles; that evil spirit, that unclean spirit--I claim the promise of your word, "Whosoever that calleth on the name of the Lord shall be delivered." I call upon you now. In the name of the Lord Jesus Christ, deliver me and set me free. Satan, I renounce you and all your works. I loose myself from you, in the name of Jesus, and I command you to leave me right now in Jesus' name. Amen!

The **Short Prayer** is my favorite prayer because it is short and effective. The first part is **salvation** and the last part is **deliverance**. You can pause after the sentence underlined about **"forgiveness"** and let the people forgive others as the Holy Spirit leads them. This prayer was written by Derek Prince. We will use it later on.

Moody's Prayers - The first thing we do is get the people to **pray about their specific problems and sins**, so that the blood of Jesus can cleanse the people and take away legal rights that the demons have to remain, and God can begin to act.

Then we get the people to repeat the **Short Prayer** out loud with sincerity after me.

Finally, we lead the people in a combination prayer out loud that covers **Sins of Ancestors, Curses, Soul Ties, Fragmented Soul, and Subconscious Mind** as follows:

Lord Jesus Christ, I forgive my ancestors and descendants, and I ask you to forgive and bless them. Forgive me for my many sins and I forgive myself for sins against my body. I break all curses, hexes, vexes and demonic ties that bind. I break all soul ties caused by witchcraft or sexual sins. Lord Jesus, restore my fragmented soul: mind, will and emotions; send your angels out to recover anything that was stolen from me. Lord Jesus, stir up the demons in my subconscious mind so that they can be identified and cast out. All these things we ask in the blessed name of our Lord Jesus Christ: Our Lord, Master and Savior. We now take authority over Satan and all the forces of evil according to the whole Word of God and command that you obey it. In the Name of Jesus Christ, we ask these things. Amen.

After the people have prayed and been led in prayer, then **I take spiritual authority over the meeting as follows**:

Satan, we come against all powers, principalities, evil forces in this world and spiritual wickedness in high places. We come against all demons inside or outside of anyone present, over this city, state, nation and world, in Hell or out of Hell. The Bible says, 'Behold, I give unto you power to tread on serpents and scorpions, and over all the power of the enemy: and nothing shall by any means hurt you.' We intend to exercise that power to set ourselves free. Satan, we come against you by the power and blood of Jesus Christ, by the Word of God, by the name of Jesus, by the authority of the believer, in the unity of our spirits. Satan, we tell you that we sit in heavenly places with our Christ Jesus. We are over you, your fallen angels, your demons and all forces of evil. We command you to line up in rank and file and order, and come out quickly. We bind every power that you have and loose ourselves from you in the name of Jesus.

Lord Jesus, we ask that you would send the gifts of the Holy Spirit as needed to minister to the needs of the people and to accomplish what you want done here tonight. We are careful to give you all the glory, honor, praise and credit for everything that is said or done. We ask all these things in the blessed name of Jesus Christ, our Lord and Master and Savior. And we take authority over Satan according to the whole Word of God. For it's in Jesus name we pray. Amen!" Now start casting out demons!

SECTION 6 - SCHOOL OF DELIVERANCE

CONTENTS

TEACHING TIME

The teaching time for each subject will vary depending on the schedule set by the leader and what is to be accomplished in the program. The format could include a school, seminar, conference or service. It could be one session or a number of sessions. It could last hours, days or weeks.

After the teaching, time could be allowed for questions and answers, or testimonies about individual deliverances.

Personal ministry to individuals could be a part of the schedule. Personal ministry would be scheduled allowing some interval for each appointment such as thirty minutes, one hour, one and a half hour or two hours depending on how many individuals want deliverance or what the situation requires.

MINISTRY AFTER TEACHING

After the teaching, ministry could include mass deliverance for the group and/or individual deliverance for those standing in line. Give each person about five minutes for prayer and/or individual deliverance.

LESSONS

The Manuals are written as lessons. The **Deliverance Manual** contains about a hundred lessons. Other Manuals are written in the same format.

The general format is scripture, lesson, prayer and list of demons. Go through the scripture using The Holy Bible King James Version, teach the lesson, take the group through a standing prayer and cast out the demons. The prayer and mass deliverance could be omitted if only teaching is desired.

TEACHING MANUALS

The **Deliverance Manual** and the eight topic deliverance manuals can be used for teaching. The **Deliverance Manual** contains four Manuals: **Basic Deliverance Manual, Advanced Deliverance Manual, Mass Deliverance Manual and How To Do Deliverance Manual**. These nine books provide twelve topic manuals to choose from.

FAMILY TESTIMONIES

The minister can choose testimonies to present along with the lessons. They can be personal family testimonies or testimonies about other people by omitting their names and testifying in a way that they can not be recognized. The following are testimonies found in the deliverance manuals:

1. BYRON'S DEATH
- **1. FROM DEATH INTO REAL LIFE**
- **2. GENE'S TESTIMONY ABOUT BYRON'S DEATH**
- **3. EARLINE'S TESTIMONY ABOUT BYRON'S DEATH**
- **4. EARLINE'S TESTIMONY ABOUT GRIEF OVER BYRON'S DEATH**

2. EARLINE'S DEATH
- **1. GENE'S TESTIMONY ABOUT EARLINE'S HOMECOMING**
  - **1. Job's Test**
  - **2. Hospital Experience**
  - **3. The Perfect Number Seven**
  - **4. The Future**
- **2. GENE'S MEMORIAL FOR EARLINE**
  - **1. Persecution**
  - **2. Testimony About How GOD Taught Us Deliverance**
  - **3. Declaration**

3. OUR DELIVERANCE TESTIMONY
- **1. General**
- **2. Pigs In The Parlor**
- **3. Faith Tabernacle**
- **4. Can A Christian Have A Demon?**
- **5. All Christians**
- **6. Our Family**
- **7. Our Ministry**

4. GENE'S TESTIMONY
- **1. GENE'S TESTIMONY ABOUT AHAB CHARACTERISTICS**

5. EARLINE'S TESTIMONY
- **1. EARLINE'S MAIN TESTIMONY ABOUT DELIVERANCE**
- **2. EARLINE'S TESTIMONY ABOUT REJECTION**
- **3. EARLINE'S TESTIMONY ABOUT ANCESTRAL BACKGROUND**
- **4. EARLINE'S TESTIMONY ABOUT HEART CONDITION**
  - **1. Earline's Comments**
  - **2. Gene's Comments**
- **5. EARLINE'S TESTIMONY ABOUT THE CURSE OF THE BASTARD**
- **6. EARLINE'S TESTIMONY ABOUT EATING**
  - **1. Gene's Comments**
- **7. EARLINE'S TESTIMONY ABOUT MAINTAINING DELIVERANCE**
- **8. EARLINE'S TESTIMONY ABOUT SCHIZOPHRENIA DELIVERANCE**
- **9. EARLINE'S TESTIMONY ABOUT DELIVERANCE FROM INDIAN CURSES**

6. MARIE'S TESTIMONY
- **1. EARLINE'S TESTIMONY ABOUT MARIE'S SALVATION**
- **2. OUR TESTIMONY ABOUT JESUS SETTING MARIE'S BROKEN SHOULDER**
- **3. MARIE'S TESTIMONY ABOUT EXPERIENCE WITH DEMONIC OBJECTS**

7. PSYCHIC PRAYERS
- **1. OUR TESTIMONY ABOUT PSYCHIC PRAYERS**

1. Gene's Comments

MAIN TEACHING NOTEBOOK
SPIRITUAL WARFARE MANUAL
(Always carry **SPIRITUAL WARFARE PRAYER BOOK** with me.)

Spiritual Warfare (23)
Spiritual Warfare Personal (22)

Spiritual Warfare General Portions (17)
Spiritual Warfare General Scripture (11)
(Portions and Scripture Work Together.)

(Combination Of Topics)

Spiritual Warfare General Scripture (11)
Spiritual Warfare Combination (31)
(Scripture and Combination Work Together.)

(Breakdown of **Spiritual Warfare Combination**)

Spiritual Warfare Scripture (7)
Proclamations (4)
Declarations (4)
Confessions (4)
Other (1)
Prayers (5)
Testimonies (5)

Tactics To Win The War (17)
Judgement Of THE LORD (12)

General Topic Compilation (21)
(Always carry with me.)

The Christian Life - Salvation, Baptism In Water, Deliverance, Baptism In Holy Spirit, And Healing (4)
Why We Need Deliverance (3)
Are You On The Road To Hell? (5)
Cracks In Your Armor (3)
A Christian Can Have A Demon (6/1)

HOW TO DO DELIVERANCE MANUAL

Basic Deliverance (14)
Basic Deliverance Summary (10)

(Always carry with me.)

Individual And Mass Deliverance (13)
Prayers And List Of Demons For Individual and Mass Deliverance (14)
(Work these two together.)

Spiritual Warfare Statements (4)

SEXUAL DELIVERANCE MANUAL

Sexual Sins Summary (21)
Sexual Lust (6)
Prayers And List Of Sexual Demons (12)
(Work these three together.)

WITCHCRAFT DELIVERANCE MANUAL

Witchcraft Related Subjects (22)
Witchcraft Related Summary (14)
Prayers And List Of Witchcraft Demons (10)
(Work these three together.)

Caribbean Witchcraft (10/6)

CURSES DELIVERANCE MANUAL

Overall Curses (7)
House Curses (10/1)

HEALING DELIVERANCE MANUAL

Body Cured And Healed By Deliverance (8/4)
Spiritual Roots Of Disease (4/2)
Deliverance And Healing For Cancer and Arthritis (6/2+6T)

Family Testimonies (Use with lessons - 33T.)

SECTION 7 - SPIRITUAL WARFARE DIRECTIONS

1. Teach one lesson or several lessons.

2. You can customize the deliverance around what was taught especially if only one or several lessons were taught.

3. **Deliverance Warfare Prayers** - these can be used in various ways as indicated by the subtitles: **Short Prayer, Medium Prayer, Long Prayer,** and **Moodys' Prayers.**

4. **Deliverance Related Subjects** - these can be used in various ways as indicated by the subtitles: **Biblical Curses, Soul Ties, Occult and False Religions, Ungodly Spirits, Godly Spirits, and Cursed Objects and Demon Infestation.**

5. **Tactics To Win The War Against Satan** - can be used to drive out demons.

6. **Tormenting Demons** - these are used to torment the demons with their impending doom by using statements based on scripture, and using scriptural quotations.

7. **Lists of Demons for Mass Deliverance** - these are lists to be used for mass deliverance in various ways as indicated by the subtitles: **Basic Deliverance, Fifty-Three Common Demon Groupings, Abused Children, Grief and Bitterness, Bastards, Charismatic Witchcraft, Drunkenness and Gluttony, Perfecting Love, Ingratitude, Self, and How Not to Do Deliverance**.

8. Customize the deliverance to the situation that is presented. There are many factors to be considered such as time allowed, sequence of events and spiritual climate.

9. **Sequence of Events**

   1. **Teach** - one or more lessons.
   2. **Deliverance Warfare Prayers** - have the people stand up and repeat selected prayers after you.
   3. **Deliverance Related Subjects** - have the people stand up and pray selected subjects after you.
   4. **Tactics To Win The War Against Satan** - have the people stand up and repeat the scripture, prayers and commands after you.
   5. **Tormenting Demons** - have the people stand up and repeat the selected scripture and statements.
   6. **Cast Out** - cast out the demons in mass deliverance from selected lists of demons. It is good to start with **Basic Deliverance** of the families of **Rejection, Bitterness and Rebellion**, and then go on to other families. A good list to use always is **Fifty-Three Common Demon Families**.
   7. **Deliverance Manual** - there are many lists of demons in the manual. The lists can be selected by topic being taught to the people.
   8. **Audios and Videos** - An excellent tape is **Mass Deliverance** by Win Worley. There are audio and video tapes that have mass deliverance on them after teaching about various topics.

SECTION 8 - HOW I DO DELIVERANCE

CONTENTS

LESSONS

I felt like GOD told Earline and me to teach Christians around the world how to do deliverance. The ten deliverance manuals are written as how-to-do-it-books and are my main teaching aids. The primary book is the **DELIVERANCE MANUAL** which took Earline and me twenty years to write: a productive year of my life and a productive year of her life. **SPIRITUAL WARFARE MANUAL, HOW TO DO DELIVERANCE MANUAL, SEXUAL DELIVERANCE MANUAL, WITCHCRAFT DELIVERANCE MANUAL, CURSES DELIVERANCE MANUAL, HEALING DELIVERANCE MANUAL, SPIRITUAL WARFARE PRAYER BOOK**, **MINI DELIVERANCE MANUAL, END TIME MANUAL** AND **PRAYER MANUAL** are the notebook deliverance manuals.

The format is scripture, lesson, prayer and list of demons. Take the people through the scripture references, the written lesson, have them stand up and pray the prayer out loud, and cast out the demons in mass deliverance.

The lessons are already worked out. All you have to do is to choose what you want to teach about. You can do this by yourself or with your family, group or church.

MASS DELIVERANCE

Mass deliverance is simply calling out demons from a group of Christians of any size. It can be in any location: home, church, hotel/motel, jail/prison or anywhere Christians are congregating. Take away the legal right of the demons before casting out or the demons may get violent.

First teach, take people through the prayer, then cast out demons. After the service, counsel and pray for individuals. Any Christian can do this with the help of the nine deliverance manuals.

GROUP MINISTRY

There are alternatives to the ministry. You can go through the above procedure with or without mass deliverance. After the teaching, people can line up for individual prayer; I do what I call the five-minute prayer for deliverance and healing.

You can allow the people to ask questions during the lesson or after the lesson. You can allow them to make comments but not preach. GOD may have some special ministry for you to do during or after the teaching. Be led by The Holy Spirit.

TEAM MINISTRY

Set a schedule for the seminar by the hour for personal ministry, eating and group ministry. If there are not too many people, allow an hour per person. If there are more people than time, allow thirty minutes per person. Deliverance can even be done in fifteen minutes in an emergency. You are going to work on what the person asks, not their whole life. You do what you can to help the person in the time you have. Deliverance is a process and way of life, not a grand event.

Find a comfortable room to minister in with a restroom nearby. There needs to be space for a number of people and some privacy for the person.

Start the personal ministry with the leader of the church or group praying for the day. Anoint with oil symbolic of The Holy Spirit. Ask the person what they want ministry for. Keep notes on a pad and give this to the person after the session to maintain their confidentiality. Have the person pray about what they have told you. Lay hands on the head and cast out the demons. Pray for the healing of the body and soul. Ask the person how they are feeling and what happened in deliverance. It is interesting to see what happened inside and outside of the person. External manifestations you can observe; most internally manifestations you can not.

When I have people working with me, they become my assistants, witnesses, prayer partners, learners and helpers. They are being taught to be a part of or to lead deliverance teams. They observe that everything is decent and in godly order. They pray silently or softly out loud, in English or Other Tongues, to backup and support the leader. They help by laying hands on women or men in appropriate places: women on women and men on men. They are to interrupt the leader and tell him or her what THE HOLY SPIRIT is saying to do: pray, cast out a specific demon or family of demons, read Scripture or some other function.

The deliverance team needs a leader who directs and coordinates the deliverance. If it is a large team, it can have assistant leaders. Some demons do not come out easily and may take some time to drive out. If the leader becomes tired, then an assistant leader can take over. Everyone submits to the leader and does what is asked. Everyone is to be in agreement with the leader for spiritual power. They wait on THE LORD for discernment and instructions. Follow the leader in what demons or families are being cast out.

Generally the person does not have to be held if the legal rights have been taken away from the demon. Sometimes an angel holds the person to prevent violence to the person and those ministering. If violence occurs, then the team should call on THE LORD for restraint and spiritually bind the person. If necessary the team members will physically restrain the person.

Avoid strife and envy among team workers. GOD uses one and then another in most deliverance sessions. Often a heavy anointing is on one person in the team while praying for an individual, and then the anointing shifts to another during the same session or one following soon thereafter.

TELEPHONE MINISTRY

You can minister to anyone in the world over the telephone. You can touch the lives of people around the world in a few hours on the telephone and watch The Holy Spirit spread deliverance. I can not travel to every person or have them travel to me. The Holy Spirit can then move in that persons life and spread deliverance in that area. It is gratifying to see what GOD will do. Here again, the key is to take away the legal rights of the demons before casting out. I normally minister by appointment at 7:30 p.m. onward during Monday through Friday.

HOME MINISTRY

You can invite people into your home for deliverance. I minister to men or couples by myself. I minister to a woman with a witness present. I have never asked Christians to sign a legal release in over thirty years of ministry. I believe that GOD protects me when I keep things decent and in order according to The Holy Bible. I have invited people into my home during the week and over the weekends by appointment.

INTERNET

Stan and Elizabeth Madrak have an internet site, **demonbuster.com** where they have our nine deliverance manuals. The site has touched the lives of over seven million people around the world. Our website is **bedelivered.com** which was setup by Elijah Hughes.

TRAVELING MINISTRY

I travel to local, national and international sites to minister. The ministry is primarily deliverance with healing or other topics as requested. I primarily travel around the United States with some trips overseas.

TYPES OF MINISTRY

Over the Internet and telephone; in the mail and home: local, national and international travel, mass and personal deliverance are types of ministry. When I travel, the ministry consists generally of two things: teaching and personal ministry. My main goal is to teach people around the world how to do deliverance. I do personal ministry primarily to set people free but also to teach them how to do personal ministry. I mail packages around the world containing deliverance material. I consider my congregation to be the whole world. Every Christian is a minister, has a ministry and one or more gifts of The Holy Spirit.

FUNCTIONS

My functions include licensed and ordained minister, apostle, teacher, writer, counselor, spiritual father and grandfather, apostle of churches, and pastor of pastors. I believe that GOD told me that I am one of the fathers and pioneers of modern deliverance. I have been told that I have Derek Prince mantle and anointing.

GOALS

My goal is to help Christians fulfill their ministry and especially help those with deliverance and healing. I license and ordain ministers. I counsel with the five-fold ministry and consider it an honor to help ministers do their job. They can come to me without being concerned with competition. I maintain their confidentiality.

TITHES AND OFFERINGS

And as ye go, preach, saying, The Kingdom Of Heaven is at hand. Heal the sick, cleanse the lepers, raise the dead, cast out devils: <u>freely ye have received, freely give</u> (Mark 10:7-8). This is my motto and I love to sing the chorus. I believe that deliverance should be freely given. I do not charge for ministry. GOD told me to take any offering that a person presents so that he could bless that person or organization.

SECTION 9 - HOW TO DO DELIVERANCE
ATTACK - ATTACK - ATTACK

CONTENTS

PREFACE

The purpose of this lesson is to teach everyone how to do deliverance and cast out demons. You start with yourself, then your mate, your family, then others in your home, in home groups, and in churches in that order.

You have the same authority that I have. The authority is the right to use The Name of Jesus Christ to cast out demons. Even small children can cast out demons.

There are various classes of Christians: pastors and leaders, deliverance ministers and workers, those who have cast out a demon, those who have had a demon cast out of them, and those who deliverance is all new to them. The most important person to teach deliverance to is the pastor because he can teach his congregation.

COMPANION LESSONS

Work this lesson with the lessons in the **How To Do Deliverance Manual**.

HOW TO MINISTER DELIVERANCE

Ways To Do Deliverance

Naturally, the proper way to do deliverance is to follow the Bible. Jesus is our example. Probably, no two people do deliverance exactly alike. Everyone has different backgrounds; they are led by The Holy Spirit as they are able to hear God. We have the advantages of our fathers of deliverance who have written, taught, and demonstrated deliverance. Pastor Win Worley, now with The Lord, was the foremost deliverance minister in the world in my estimation. He believed that you should force the demons to manifest. This required a team to hold people that became violent.

I believe that the key to doing deliverance is to take away the demons legal rights before God that are in a person. I believe in doing deliverance the natural way. If the demons manifest, fine and if they don't fine. This way I can do deliverance anywhere by myself.

Reason For Learning

The main reason we are teaching you how to do deliverance is that every Christian should be able to cast out demons at least in their own family. Later on God may lead you to do deliverance in your home or church. Every Christian is a minister, has a ministry, and has gifts given by The Holy Spirit. **God told us to train an army for His use; you are part of that end-time army!**

The bottom line of deliverance is the casting out of demons. Deliverance will assist in establishing family order and God's order. Every Christian should cast out demons **(Mark 16:17)**. There are not many **Deliverance Ministers** to help people. Christians have many demons; proper deliverance takes a lot of time. Deliverance is a way of life and not a grand event.

Parents are the best persons to minister to their children; husband to wife and wife to husband. Parents need to set the family free from demons and protect their children.

Deliverance gives an understanding of God's and Satan's kingdoms that you will not get any other way. Deliverance allows you to see into the spiritual world by the manifestations of demons.

General

The requirements for receiving deliverance is that the person be a Christian. It is the children's' bread. Demons should not be cast out of a person who is not a Christian.

Basic Deliverance consists of setting a person free from three common demon families: **Rejection, Bitterness and Rebellion** (also common to Schizophrenia).

Typically a person becomes rejected, then becomes bitter, and finally rebels (then come other problems).

The most important key in setting a person free from these families is to get the person to forgive anyone that has hurt him!

First, unforgiveness should be dealt with before the families of rejection, bitterness and rebellion are cast out.

After basic deliverance, then other demonic families can be attacked. For example, cancer and arthritis can come into a person thru the open door of unforgiveness. If you know of a Christian that has cancer or arthritis, check to see if they have unforgiveness. After basic deliverance, cast out the spirits of cancer and arthritis.

A person may have become demonized while in the womb by **sins of the ancestors** for causes other than their own rejection, bitterness and rebellion. If so, another approach is required.

Again, the most important key in setting a person free from the sins of the ancestors is to get the person to **forgive his ancestors**, and ask God to forgive them and bless them (parents are the first line of ancestors).

After forgiveness for any hurt or sin, then any demonic ties should be broken. For example, curses of the ancestors passed down thru the generations, or soul ties caused by sexual sin or witchcraft control are demonic ties.

After **breaking curses and soul ties**, we ask God to restore the fragmented soul - mind, will and emotions. We ask God to send out angels to restore anything that the demons have stolen.

After **restoration of the fragmented soul**, we ask God to stir up the demons in the subconscious mind so that they can be identified and cast out.

The person can then be led in a general prayer of **salvation and/or deliverance** to God. There are many good prayers.

The leader should then pray and take authority over the demonic spirit world.

After the grounds for deliverance are established (taking away the demons' legal rights before God which allow the demons to stay), then start casting out demons.

Use all the **weapons of the warfare in the Bible** against the demons. These include reading scripture to the demons, exercising the Gifts of the Holy Spirit, causing the demons to reveal information against themselves, seeking discernment from God thru the Holy Spirit, praying to God in other tongues, asking Jesus for help, and any other methods that are helpful in gathering data, taking away legal rights and casting out.

By all means, do what God tells you to do even if you do not understand it. Caution - make sure it is God and not Satan telling you what to do.

Unforgiveness

Get the person to forgive others by an act of his will which God will honor. It may be very difficult for the person but God accepts their willingness to forgive. **Unforgiveness** - Cancer or Arthritis may come into the person later on.

Before any deliverance starts, a person should be given an opportunity to discuss his problems and background so that you can get to know the person and properly minister to him.

After deliverance is ended, a person should be counseled about how to walk out his deliverance and discipline his life.

It is good if teaching on basic deliverance or sins of ancestors precedes the deliverance.

After counseling, anoint with oil and pray for any healing needed. Pray for damage to the body that the demons left.

The practice of Inner Healing is not a substitute for Deliverance! Some aspects are demonic.

Summary For Deliverance To An Individual

1. The leader can be any lay Christian and does not have to be in the five-fold ministry. This is a very important summary and we have used it successfully many times.
1. **As the leader**, you are to find out what the individual's problems are (use spiritual history and Gifts of The Holy Spirit).
2. Have the person forgive, pray and get right with God (get the sins under The Blood of Jesus Christ: forgive - repent - renounce).
3. Have the person break the curses, soul ties and demonic holds on them and their descendents.
4. **As the leader**, you are to cast out their demons.
5. **As the leader**, you are to anoint with oil and pray for healing of soul and body.
6. **As the leader**, you are to teach them that they must discipline their life by changing their way of thinking and acting. Go and sin no more!

It is easy to cast out demons but hard to discipline your life! You have to do it; God won't and we can't.

STEPS TO MINISTER DELIVERANCE

Initial Steps For An Individual

1. Find out about the person's problems and background.
2. Some discussion about how they got into trouble will be helpful.
3. Get the person to forgive others and lead them in a specific prayer about their problems.
4. Lead the person thru a prayer to break curses and soul ties, restore the fragmented soul, stir up the demons in the sub-conscious mind, and finally salvation / deliverance (Moodys' Prayers).

Steps For Basic Deliverance For Ministry To An Individual

1. Cast out the families of Rejection, then Bitterness and finally Rebellion.

Steps For Sins Of Ancestors For Ministry To An Individual

1. Start with basic deliverance of Rejection, Bitterness and Rebellion. Then go into other areas that have been identified and legal grounds established for casting out demons.

Steps For Basic Deliverance, Sins Of Ancestors Or Other Topic For The Home Meeting

1. Teach on Basic Deliverance, Sins of Ancestors, or any other deliverance topic.
2. Take a refreshment / bathroom break of about 15 minutes.
3. One way is to have a prayer meeting with people sitting in a circle talking about their problems. You can write them down. Get each person to forgive others and lead them in a specific prayer about their problems.
4.Lead the group in a mass prayer about that topic, and include curses, soul ties, fragmented soul, subconscious mind, unforgiveness and salvation (Moodys' Prayers).

5. The leader will then pray and take authority over the demonic spiritual world, and ask God to send his forces and take charge of the deliverance.
6. Start the mass deliverance with basic deliverance and then go to any other topic.

Steps For Basic Deliverance, Sins Of Ancestors Or Other Topic For A Group

1. Teach on Basic Deliverance, Sins of Ancestors, or any other deliverance topic.
2. Lead the congregation in a mass prayer about that topic, and include curses, soul ties, fragmented soul, subconscious mind, unforgiveness and salvation (Moodys' Prayers).
3. The leader will then pray and take authority over the demonic spiritual world, and ask God to send his forces and take charge of the deliverance.
4. Start the mass deliverance with basic deliverance and then go to any other topic.

Final Steps

1. During mass deliverance, workers shall help individuals having trouble getting free.
2. After mass deliverance, work with individuals.
3. Counsel the person about how to walk out their deliverance and how to discipline their life.
4. Anoint with oil and pray for healing.

Variations

1. The above steps could be used over the phone, in the home, in a church service, at the altar, in the prayer room or wherever the opportunity presents itself in public or private.
2. The above procedures can be varied to fit the situation or at the direction of the Holy Spirit.

Subjects Omitted

Please see the **Deliverance Manual** Table of Contents for other subjects and Lists of Demons. It is four books in one: **Basic Deliverance**, **Advanced Deliverance**, **Mass Deliverance,** and **How To Do Deliverance**. The sequel to the **Deliverance Manual** are **Spiritual Warfare Manual**, **How To Do Deliverance Manual**, **Sexual Deliverance Manual**, **Witchcraft Deliverance Manual**, **Curses Deliverance Manual**, and **Healing Deliverance Manual**.

An ideal way to use these manuals is to look up the full context of the Bible verses, read the lesson, pray the prayer out loud, then cast the demons out of yourself. The manuals are how to do it manuals to teach people around the world how to do deliverance.

DON DICKERMAN METHOD

(Serpents In The Sanctuary and Turmoil In The Temple)

Prayer

1. I renounce my sinful activities.
2. I repent for my sins.
3. I break soul ties.
4. I confess that I am born again.
5. I confess that JESUS IS SAVIOR, LORD, DELIVERER and HEALER.
6. I confess that JESUS CHRIST has broken the power of the curse.
7. I confess that I desire to be free.

Commands

1. We put the demons under oath before JEHOVAH GOD.
2. We command you to obey JEHOVAH GOD, JESUS CHRIST, THE HOLY SPIRIT and us.
3. We bind the demon powers according to THE HOLY BIBLE in THE NAME OF JESUS CHRIST.
4. We command the prince, the ruler of the kingdom, to identify himself by name or function.
5. Where are you located?
6. Do you have a right to stay?
7. We command that the right be revealed.
8. We pray, confess and cancel the right.
9. We command you to reveal how many demons are present.
10. We command you to tell us what their functions or assignments are.
11. We cancel the functions or assignments in THE NAME OF JESUS CHRIST.
12. What damage have you done to the body?
13. We command that you restore the damage done and repair any disorder.
14. We command the spirits to become one spirit, with no passing on of duties, and leave the individuals.
15. We command the spirits to go into the abyss and never return in JESUS NAME.
16. We pray anointing and protection for the individuals to help them to walk in continued freedom.

HOW TO LEARN ABOUT DELIVERANCE

1. **Get Experience** - start casting out demons and get involved. Head knowledge of deliverance is insufficient! You can memorize The Bible and go to Hell!
2. **Study Bible** - use a concordance and study Gospels mainly.
3. **Fast and pray** - seek the Lord about your problems.
4. **Study deliverance books** - learn as much as you can.
5. **Study books on the mind, will and emotions.**
6. **Go to deliverance meetings** - participate in teaching and ministry: mass, small groups and individuals.
7. **Study Satan from a Christian viewpoint** - to see how he is trying to destroy you, your family and your church.
8. **Emphasize practical methods** - put the Bible to work.
9. **Clean out your house** - get rid of demonic objects.
10. **Be persistent** - keep after the demons in an area of your life until you are successful.
11. **Learn to research a subject** - use encyclopedias, dictionaries, medical and psychiatric books.
12. **Learn the three phases of deliverance** - How to Determine the Need for Deliverance, How go Get Delivered, and How to Stay Delivered.
13. **Deliverance is a constant learning process.** Satan has spent thousands of years weaving a very complicated system to destroy people.

PRACTICAL DELIVERANCE BOOKS

Basic - Pigs In The Parlor - Frank and Ida Mae Hammond, Impact Books

Advanced - Battling The Hosts Of Hell; Conquering The Hosts Of Hell; Demolishing The Hosts Of Hell; Annihilating The Hosts Of Hell, Volumes I and II; Eradicating The Hosts Of Hell; Smashing The Hosts Of Hell; The Alcoholic Syndrome; Grappling with the Host

of Hell; Freedom from the Hosts of Hell; and **Harassing The Host of Hell**, eleven books (and fifty booklets covering particular topics) by Win Worley, Hegewisch Baptist Church, Highland, Indiana
Mind - War On The Saints - Unabridged Edition, Jessie Penn-Lewis & Evans Roberts, Thomas E. Lowe, LTD.

REFERENCES

Deliverance Manual by Gene and Earline Moody
Serpents In The Sanctuary and **Turmoil In The Temple** by Don Dickerman, Impac Christian Books

SECTION 10 - HOW TO IDENTIFY AND DETECT A DEMON

CONTENTS

WAYS TO DETERMINE THE NEED FOR DELIVERANCE

Discernment And Detection

The presence and nature of evil spirits can be known by two principle methods:

1. **Discernment**: I Cor. 12:10 lists **discerning of spirits** as one of the nine supernatural gifts of THE HOLY SPIRIT.

2. **Detection**: the second method of knowing the presence and nature of evil spirits. Detection is simply observing what spirits are doing to a person (Mark 7:24-30).

Common Symptoms

Some of the most common symptoms of indwelling demons are as follows:

1. Disturbances in the **emotions** which persist or recur.
2. Disturbances in the **mind or thought** life.
3. Outbursts or uncontrolled use of the **tongue**.
4. Recurring unclean thoughts and acts regarding **sex**.
5. **Addictions** to nicotine, alcohol, drugs, medicines, caffeine, food, etc.
6. Many diseases and physical afflictions are due to **spirits of infirmity** (Luke 13:11).

Religious Error

Involvement to any degree in **religious error** can open the door for demons as follows:

1. **False religions**, e.g. Eastern religions, pagan religions, philosophies and mind sciences.
2. **Christian Cults** - all such cults may be classified as **bloodless religions** having a form of godliness, but denying the power thereof (II Tim. 3:5).
3. **Occult and Spiritism** - Any method of seeking supernatural knowledge, wisdom, guidance and power apart from GOD is forbidden (Deut. 18:9-15)!
4. **False Doctrine** - a great increase of doctrinal errors will be promoted by deceiving and seducing spirits in the last days (I Tim. 4:1).

ARE YOU ON THE ROAD TO HELL?

Spiritual Death Sentence Of Occultism

Witchcraft, enchanter, song spell, augur, soothsayer, sorcerer, divination, fortune teller, witch, wizard, clairvoyant, physic, charmer, serpent charmer, consulter with familiar spirits, medium, sorceress, pharmakia, necromancy, seance, observer of times, star gazing, occult decorations and television, and children to pass through the fire.

Modern Terminology

Magical arts, divination, wizardry, jugglers, enchantments, secret arts, sorcery, omens, witchcraft, horoscopes, signs, lucky days, mediums, familiar spirits, abortion, soothsaying, augury, charmer, necromancer, rebellion, stubbornness, idolatry, good luck images, sold to Satan, burned incense, abominable customs, foretelling future events, consult the dead, false prophecy, lying, power of evil spirits, dreamers, magic protective charms, profaned God, slaying Christians, deceptive vails, strengthen hands of the wicked, false visions, astrology, **spiritual harlotry and whoredoms**, household idols, adulterers, false swearers, **oppress the hireling, widow and fatherless**, turn aside the temporary resident, fear not God, discover hidden knowledge, curious arts, resisting God's authority, blinding unbeliever's minds, practices of the flesh, immorality, impurity, indecency, enmity, strife, jealousy, anger, ill temper, selfishness, **divisions and dissensions**, party spirit, factions, heresies, sects with peculiar opinions, envy, drunkenness, carousing, **deluding and seducing spirits**, doctrines that demons teach, deadly charms, **depraved and distorted minds**, reprobate, counterfeit, worship works of own hands, paying homage to demons, magic spells, poisonous charm, cowards, ignoble, contemptible, cravenly lacking in courage, cowardly submission, unbelieving, faithless, **depraved and defiled with abominations**, murderers, lewd, adulterous, dogs, impurity, **loves and deals in falsehood**, untruth, error, deception, cheating.

WARNING SIGNALS - POSSIBLE NEED FOR DELIVERANCE

Characteristics noted below merit a closer look when they are pronounced, persistent or recurrent over a period of time, or progressive - tending to become more, rather than less, extreme. The following thumbnail descriptions of behavior can be a call for help:

1. Confused or disordered thinking: loss of touch with reality - delusions (persistence of erroneous convictions in the face of contrary evidence) - hallucinations; disconnected speech.
2. Obsessions: absorption with a subject or idea to the exclusion of others - compulsions - uncontrollable urges.
3. Inability to cope: with minor problems - with daily routine.
4. Difficulty in making and/or keeping friends: poor social skills - isolation, withdrawal from society - **loner life -style.**
5. A pattern of failure across the board: at school - at work - in sports - in personal relationships.
6. Prolonged or severe depression: suicide threats and/or attempts.
7. Immaturity: infantile behavior (such as bed-wetting) - over dependence on the mother (excessive clinging as a child and continuing dependence in teens and twenties) - failure to keep pace with peer group.
8. A series of physical ailments which do not run a typical course and/or fail to respond to treatment.
9. Neglect of personal hygiene (disheveled and unsanitary surroundings) or exaggerated concern for order and for cleanliness.
10. Difficulty adjusting to new people and places.
11. Undue anxiety and worry: phobias - feelings of being persecuted.
12. Too much or too little sleep.
13. Excessive self-centeredness: indifference to other people's feelings, doings, ideas - lack of sympathy with another's pain or need.
14. Substantial rapid weight - gain or loss.
15. Muted, **flat emotions** (absence of angry / delighted / sorrowing reactions to stimuli) or inappropriate emotions (sharp, inexplicable mood swings - silliness at serious moments, unpredictable tears).
16. Negative self-image and outlook: **inferiority complex** - feelings of worthlessness.
17. Frequent random changes of plans: inability to stick with a job, a school program, a living arrangement - failure to keep appointments, abide by decisions.
18. Extreme aggressiveness (combativeness, hostility - violence, rage) or exaggerated docility (lack of normal competitiveness and self-assertion - refusal to confront, avoidance of argument).
19. Risk-taking.
20. Lack of zest and enthusiasm: listlessness, sadness, **mood habitually down** - limited or missing sense of humor.

HOW TO IDENTIFY GODLY AND UNGODLY SPIRITS

How To Recognize Evil Spirits (Excerpts)

1. **Discerning of spirits**, word of knowledge and word of wisdom: three gifts of The Holy Spirit.
2. Names claimed by demons which describe their work: such as anger - to make angry.
3. Counterfeiting and imitating spirits of God (spirit of divination for word of knowledge).

4. Synonyms for evil spirits (Roget's Thesaurus).
5. Personality of demon (soul - mind, will and emotions). Just like you are except it does not have a physical body.
6. Cause demons to manifest and identify their names and characteristics (spiritual warfare).
7. Detection by common symptoms or problems: emotional, mental, speech, sex, addictions, physical and religious (false religions, Christian cults, occult and spiritism, false doctrine).

The Spirits Of God And Satan (Excerpts)

1. **Beloved, believe not every spirit, but try the spirits whether they are of God** (I John 4:1).
2. We can bind and loose spirits.
3. Therefore, we are safe in assuming that for every ministering spirit of the Lord, there will be one, and often many satanic counter spirits.
4. Loosing spirits from the Lord.

General

1. We **bind** the spirits (demons) of Satan and **loose** the spirits (angels) of God. We cast the demons out of people and God directs the angels to minister to our needs.
2. Godly spirits commonly mentioned are spirit, Spirit of God, Spirit of the Lord, Holy Spirit (human spirit, angels and Holy Spirit).
3. Ungodly spirits commonly mentioned are evil spirits, demons and devils. There is actually only one Devil, Satan; demons are the correct terminology. There are millions of fallen angels and billions of demons.
4. The following are lists of godly and ungodly spirits found in the Bible. You can identify many more after you have been in deliverance awhile. Ungodly spirits generally are found grouped in families. Where you find one demon, you frequently find a family of demons with the same characteristics with one demon as the leader (strong man or ruler demon).

Godly Spirits

Spirit of Wisdom (Ex. 28:3), Poor in spirit (Matt. 5:3), Spirit of God (Gen. 1:2), Spirit of your father (Matt. 10:20), Spirit of the Lord (Jud. 3:10), Strong in spirit (Luke 1:30), Right spirit (Psalm 51:10), Spirit of truth (John 14:17), Holy Spirit (Psalm 51:11), Spirit of life (Rom. 8:2), Broken spirit (Psalm 51:17), Spirit of adoption (Rom. 8:15), Spirit of princes (Psalm 76:12), Fervent in spirit (Rom. 12:11), Faithful spirit (Prov. 11:13), Spirit of meekness (I Cor. 4:21), Humble spirit (Prov. 16:19), Spirit of faith (II Cor. 4:13), Excellent spirit (Prov. 17:27), Spirit of Jesus Christ (Phil. 1:19), Spirit of man (Prov. 20:27), Eternal spirit (Heb. 9:14), Patient in spirit (Ecc. 7:8), Meek and quite spirit (I Pet. 3:4), Spirit of the ruler (Ecc. 10:4), Spirit of glory (I Pet. 4:14), Spirit of judgment (Isa. 4:4), Spirit of prophecy (Rev. 19:10), Spirit of understanding (Is. 11:2), Spirit of Elijah (II Kings 2:15), Spirit of counsel / might (Is. 11:2), Contrite spirit (Psalm 34:18), Spirit of knowledge (Is. 11:2), Good spirit (Psalm 143:10), New spirit (Ezek. 11:19), Spirit of deep sleep (Isa. 29:10), Spirit of holy gods (Dan. 4:8), Spirit of living creature, (Ez. 1:20), Spirit of grace and supplication (Zec. 12:10), Spirit of holiness (Rom. 1:4), Spirit of Christ (Rom. 8:9), Spirit of grace (Heb. 10:29), Quickening spirit (I Cor. 15:45, Free spirit (Psalm 51:12)

Ungodly Spirits (Families)

Spirit of infirmity or weakness (Luke 13:11), Spirit of Antichrist (I John 4:3), Spirit of fear (II Tim. 1:7), Deaf spirit (Mark 9:25), Perverse spirit (Isa. 19:14), Dumb spirit (Mark 9:25), Sorrowful spirit (I Sam. 1:15), Blind spirit (Matt. 9:27), Spirit of slumber (Rom. 11:8), Foul spirit (Mark 9:25; Rev. 18:2), Spirit of whoredoms (Hos. 5:4), Unclean spirit (Matt. 14:43; Mark 1:23, 26; 3:30; 5:2,8, 7:25), Destroying spirit (Deut. 13:15), Evil spirit (Judges 9:23; I Sam. 16:14-16, 23; 18:10; 19:9), Spirit of divination (Acts 16:16), Another spirit (II Cor. 11:4), Spirit of bondage (Rom. 8:15), Hasty of spirit (Prov. 14:29), Spirit of error (I John 4:6), Haughty spirit (Prov. 16:18), Spirit of false doctrines (Ex. 23:1; Matt. 16:12), Perverse spirit (Isa. 19:14), Spirit of jealousy (Num. 5:14), Seducing spirits (I Tim. 4:1), Sad spirit (I Kings 21:5), Jealous spirit (Num. 5:14, 30), Wounded spirit (Prov. 18:14), Lying spirit (I Kings 22:22-23; II Ch. 18:21-22), Proud in spirit (Ecc. 7:8), Spirit of burning (Isa. 4:4), Familiar spirit (Lev. 20:27; I Sam. 28:7-8; I Ch. 10:13; II Ch. 33:6), Spirit of Egypt (Isa. 19:3), Spirit of heaviness (Isa. 61:3), Spirit of unclean devil (Luke 4:33), Spirit of the world (I Cor. 2:12)

Dictionary Of Classical Mythology

"A knowledge of the classics and an acquaintance with the **imaginary characters, places, and incidents of ancient mythology** which have been such an inspiring influence to writers of all ages adds greatly to ones enjoyment of literature, art and conversation. The people outside literary and educational pursuits have sufficient opportunity or leisure to acquire or keep up a knowledge of this popular branch of learning. It is important, therefore, to present in dictionary form the story of **gods, goddesses, heroes, and heroines of the old Grecian and Roman literature**. It will lead to a better understanding of the countless references which are made from time to time in the literature of the day to classic subjects. It is a great wonderland of posy and romance, and forms a realm all its own, **the realm of antiquity's gods and demons and of prehistoric heroes**."

Notice the highlighting and what it says to you. It is talking about gods, goddesses and demons. **There is a demon behind every god and goddess worshiped by man!**

You are seeing products with these names more and more today. Is this innocent or deliberate? The definitions of these names can be found in unabridged dictionaries. We recommend that you purchase one for spiritual research.

Idols Worshipped By Countries

The names of idols are the same as names of demons. There is a demon behind every idol that is worshipped by man. Notice that there are male and female gods and goddesses. Satan has something for everyone. Temple prostitutes included male homosexuals, female lesbians and female prostitutes.

Taber's Cyclopedic Medical Dictionary

The following is Taber's definition of **multiple sclerosis**: "A chronic, slowly progressive disease of the **central nervous** system characterized by development of disseminated demyelinated glial patches called **plaques**. Symptoms and signs are numerous, but in later stages those of **Charcot's triad (nystagmus, scanning speech, and intention tremor)** are common. Occurs in the form of many clinical syndromes, the most common being the **cerebral, brain stem-**

cerebellar, and spinal. A history of remissions and exacerbations is diagnostic. **Etiology is unknown and there is no specific therapy." This means that the doctors don't know what causes the disease and how to cure it.**

Notice the high lighted words. **They tell you the symptoms of the disease and where it is located in the body.** With this information, you can pray more effectively. The symptoms can be called out as names of demons such as plaques, Charcot's triad, nystagmus, scanning speech and intention tremor. **Demons will answer to their medical names, common names, symptoms or names they are given in the spiritual world.**

We worked with a woman in deliverance who had this disease by using the above method. We would get manifestations as we called out the demons by their medical names. She was delivered and healed. **The key is forgiving your ancestors and anyone in spiritual authority over you for their sins and asking for forgiveness for your sins that opened the door to the disease.**

Neurotic And Abnormal Personalities
Psychoneurosis, Psychoneurotic and Psychopsychosis

These lists of demons help you to understand those you are ministering to who have these personalities. A study of psychology and psychiatry can be very helpful in deliverance. The method of treatment can also open the door to demons. **The medical profession identifies the names of demons but they don't know about deliverance.**

Phobias

Phobias are fears. There are 210 phobias recognized by psychiatrists.

Using A Thesaurus In Deliverance (Excerpts)

1. Because demons tend to "cluster" in family groupings, the thesaurus can be an amazingly helpful instrument to identify demons within a specific category.
2. When the spirit is forced to manifest, his name, located in the thesaurus, becomes a tool to uncover his supportive network of demons.
3. This method has been tried in the laboratory of experience and many times has been the key to a breakthrough in cases where the demons have a particularly stronghold on the individual.

False Religions
Source and Branches

The first false religion in the Bible can be traced back to **Nimrod, his wife Semiramus and her child Tammuz**. From this source branched out other false religions. The Catholic religion is for those **who want to be RELIGIOUS**. The Masonic religion is for those **who want BUSINESS SUCCESS**. The Occult religion is for those **who want POWER, SEX AND DRUGS**. This is true of anyone who follows a bloodless religion without the blood of Jesus Christ and has not had a born-again experience with Jesus Christ, our Lord, Master and Savior.

Prayer

I break curses back to the first false religion of Nimrod. I forgive anyone who is Catholic, Masonic or Occult. I break curses coming from these sources. I command those spirits to leave me in the Name of Jesus Christ. Amen.

IDENTIFYING DEMONS

Satan is the Great Imitator; he imitates everything good that God has created with evil spirits. There is a name of a demon for everything that is contrary to the Word of God. This is the simplest way to identify demons.

God gave me a revelation in Montgomery. The names of demons change to fit their assignment by Satan as they leave one body and enter into another body.

LIST OF DEMONS FOR MASS DELIVERANCE

Refer to the **Deliverance Manual**, Mass Deliverance Manual, page 271 for a Table of Contents of the Lists of Demons. Use these lists with the lessons or as needed.

PIGS IN THE PARLOR by Frank Hammond

Basic Deliverance (Rejection - Bitterness - Rebellion)

Fifty Three Common Demon Groupings

PROPER NAMES OF DEMONS by Win Worley

Hegewisch Baptist Church, Highland, IN

DELIVERANCE WARFARE PRAYERS WITH LISTS

Biblical Curses

Lord Jesus Christ, I forgive my ancestors and others that have cursed me. I ask that God forgive me and them. I break curses placed on me and my descendants from uttering a wish of evil against one; to imprecate evil, to call for mischief and injury to fall upon; to execrate, to bring evil upon and to; to blast, vex, harass and torment with great calamities. I break the curses back to ten generations and even to Adam and Eve on both sides of my family, and destroy legal holds and grounds that demons have to work in my life.

I rebuke, break, loose myself and my children from evil curses, charms, vexes, hexes, spells, jinxes, psychic powers, bewitchment, witchcraft and sorcery, that have been put upon me and my family line from persons, occult and psychic sources, and I cancel connected and related spirits and command them to leave me. I thank you, Lord, for setting me free. **But it shall come to pass, if thou wilt not hearken unto the voice of the Lord thy God, to observe to do all His commandments and His statutes which I command thee this day; that all these curses shall come upon thee, and overtake thee.** I break these curses and those that follow in the name of the Lord Jesus Christ.

Mistreating God's Chosen People, Willing Deceivers, Adultery, Harlotry and Prostitution, Disobedience to Bible, Idolatry, Keeping Cursed Objects, Refusing To Fight For God, House of Wicked, Not Giving To Poor, Stealing, Swearing Falsely By God, Failing To Give Glory to God, Robbing God of Tithes, Dishonoring Parents, Hearkening to Wives Rather Than God, Making Graven Images, Cheating People Out of Property, Taking Advantage of Blind, Oppressing Strangers, Widows and Orphans, Bestiality, Incest With Sister or Mother, Murder Secretly and For Hire, Pride, Putting Trust In Man, Doing The Work of God Deceitfully, Rewarding Evil For Good, Abortion and Causing Unborn To Die, Having Bastards, Murdering Indirectly, Striking Parents, Kidnapping, Cursing Parents, Not Preventing Death, Sacrificing to Gods, Witchcraft, Turning Someone Away From God, Following Horoscopes, Rebelling Against Pastors, Losing

Virginity Before Marriage, False Prophets, Rape, Not Disciplining Children, Teaching Rebellion Against God, Cursing Rulers, Refusing To Warn Sinners, Defiling The Sabbath, Sacrificing Humans, Seances and Fortune Telling, Intercourse During Menstruation, Homosexuals and Lesbians, Necromancers, Blaspheming Lord's Name, Being Carnally Minded, Oral and Anal Sex, Children Rebelling, Nonproductivity, Fugitive and Vagabond, Improper Family Structure, Destruction of Family Priesthood, Refusing To Do The Word of God, Family Disorder, Failure and Poverty, Sins Worthy of Death, Touching God's Anointed, Perversion of Gospel, Loving Cursing, Choosing That Which God Delights Not In, Looking To World For Help, Stubbornness and Rebellion, Offending Children Believing Christ, Adding To and Taking Away From Bible, **and Biblical Curses not listed Above.**

Soul Ties

Lord Jesus Christ, I break and renounce evil soul ties with lodges, adulterers, close friends, husbands, wives, engagements, cults and binding agreements between buddies.

Forgive me for developing evil soul ties. I forgive those who would control me. I renounce these evil soul ties, break them and wash them away with the shed blood of the Lord Jesus Christ:

Beasts; Those I Have Had Sex With Outside of Marriage; Divorced Mates; By Incest, Rape, Fornication, Adultery, Homosexuality, Bestiality and Lesbianism; Bloodless Religions and Religious Cults; Blood Brothers and Sisters By Rites; Witchcraft, Occult and Satan Worship; Fortune Tellers and Mediums; Psychiatrists, Social Workers, Psychologists and Mental Institutions. **Finally, I break agreements with those that form evil soul ties.**

Occult And False Religion

Lord Jesus Christ, I confess seeking from Satan the help that should only come from God. I confess occultism and false religions as sin. I repent and renounce these sins and ask you to forgive me. I renounce Satan and his works: I hate his demons; I count them my enemies. I close the door on occult practices, and I command such spirits to leave me.

I renounce, break and loose myself and my children from psychic powers, bondages, and bonds of physical and mental illness, upon me and my family line, as the results of parents and other ancestors.

I renounce, break and loose myself from demonic subjection to my mother, father, grandparents, and other human beings, living and dead, that have dominated me.

I forgive my ancestors and ask that you would forgive me for participating in occult and false religion. I renounce fortune telling, magic practices and spiritism, cults and false teachings, and Satan worship. I break curses and soul ties brought about by psychic heredity, occult contacts and religious cults. I break demonic holds on my family line due to supernatural experiences apart from God including the following forbidden practices:

Enchantments, Wizardry, Necromancy, Witchcraft, Observer of Times, Fortune Telling, Consulting With Familiar Spirits, Occult Practices, Spiritism, Sorcery, Magic Practices, Son or Daughter Passing Through Fire, Divination, Charmers, False Religious Cults **and other Occult and False Religious Practice.**

Ungodly Spirits

Lord Jesus Christ, I forgive my ancestors and ask that you forgive me for the following families of ungodly spirits and command that they come out as their name is called:

Spirit of Infirmity and Weakness, Spirit of Antichrist, Spirit of Fear, Deaf Spirit, Perverse Spirit, Dumb Spirit, Sorrowful Spirit, Blind Spirit, Spirit of Slumber, Foul Spirit, Spirit of Whoredoms, Unclean Spirit, Destroying Spirit, Evil Spirit, Spirit of Divination, Another Spirit, Spirit of Bondage, Hasty of Spirit, Spirit of Error, Haughty Spirit, Spirit of False Doctrines, Perverse Spirit, Spirit of Jealousy, Seducing Spirits, Sad Spirit, Jealous Spirit, Wounded Spirit, Lying Spirit, Proud in Spirit, Spirit of Burning, Familiar Spirit, Spirit of Egypt, Spirit of Heaviness, Spirit of Unclean Devil, Spirit of the World **and other families of Ungodly Spirits.**

Godly Spirits

Lord Jesus Christ, we ask that you direct the angels to minister to our needs. We loose warring angels, ministering angels, the Holy Spirit and the Seven-Fold Spirit of God. We loose legions of angels including the following Godly spirits:

Spirit of Wisdom, Poor in Spirit, Spirit of God, Spirit of Your Father, Spirit of the Lord, Strong in Spirit, Right Spirit, Spirit of Truth, Holy Spirit, Spirit of Life, Broken Spirit, Spirit of Adoption, Spirit of Princes, Fervent in Spirit, Faithful Spirit, Spirit of Meekness, Humble Spirit, Spirit of Faith, Excellent Spirit, Spirit of Jesus Christ, Spirit of Man, Eternal Spirit, Patient in Spirit, Meek and Quite Spirit, Spirit of the Ruler, Spirit of Glory, Spirit of Judgment, Spirit of Prophecy, Spirit of Understanding, Spirit of Elijah, Spirit of Counsel/Might, Contrite Spirit, Spirit of Knowledge, Good Spirit, New Spirit, Spirit of Deep Sleep, Spirit of Holy Gods, Spirit of Living Creature, Spirit of Grace and Supplication, Spirit of Holiness, Spirit of Christ, Spirit of Grace, Quickening Spirit, Free Spirit **and other Godly Spirits.**

Cursed Objects And Demon Infestation

Lord Jesus Christ, I ask that you forgive me for having cursed objects in my home. Show me by The Holy Spirit what to destroy:

1. Books and objects identified with Satan's Kingdom.
2. Sinful activities of former residents that left curses.
3. Knocking and noisy ghosts and apparitions (poltergeist).
4. Owl and frog images.
5. Witch's mask and fetishes used by witch doctors.
6. Objects and literature that pertain to false religions, cults, the occult and spiritism.
7. Graven images of gods (demons).
8. Idols and artifacts dedicated to demons.
9. Ouija boards and other occult paraphernalia.
10. Prayers and worship to demons bring curses on home.
11. Mexican sun gods; idols, incense; Buddhas; hand carved objects from Africa and the Orient; astrology, horoscopes, fortune telling; books and objects associated with witchcraft, good luck charms and cult religions (Christian Science, Jehovah's Witnesses, metaphysics); rock and roll records and tapes and other demonic objects.

12. Jewelry given to a person by someone in witchcraft, hex signs, ancient geometric and mystical motifs, jewelry designed to bring good luck and act as talisman to chase evil.
13. Egyptian ankh, Polynesian tikkis of gods, broken cross (peace symbol), chais, African jujus, Italian horn, protectors from the evil eye, hand with index and little fingers pointing up, crosses, clovers, stars, wishbones, lucky coins, mystic medals, horseshoes, religious fetishes and statues.
14. Products with hidden, secret, occult curses.
15. Puppets, cult objects and representations. Dolls used for witchcraft and magic.

OPERATIONS

When you have an operation, your spiritual armor is not in place due to anesthesia and cutting of the flesh. GOD does not want us to depend on surgery. It is the same as if you were drunk and passed out. Demons can come into the body and soul at that time.

GOD's perfect will for you is to be delivered and healed by the Power Of God rather than to be cut on and passed out by surgery and medicine. His permissive will is for you to go to the medical profession for healing. However, you pay the spiritual consequences for using the world rather than God's methods.

I found this out by experience with my wife, Earline. She had an operation after cutting the tip of her finger off. She lost her joy in THE LORD after sewing her finger into her palm to make a new finger tip. Win Worley and another pastor took her through deliverance in our home. When she was to have the final operation of cutting her finger out of her palm, I stayed outside of the operating room and prayed constantly to prevent this from happening again. I was not able to do this and had to take Earline through deliverance again.

SECTION 11 - HOW TO IDENTIFY SPIRITS

SCRIPTURE
Godly Spirits

Spirit Of Wisdom (Ex. 28:3)
Spirit of GOD (Gen. 1:2)
Spirit of the Lord (Jud. 3:10)
Spirit of truth (John 14:17)
Spirit of life (Rom. 8:2)
Spirit of adoption (Rom. 8:15)
Spirit of princes (Psalm 76:12)
Spirit of faith (II Cor. 4:13)
Spirit of man (Prov. 20:27)
Spirit of the ruler (Ecc. 10:4)
Spirit of judgment (Isa. 4:4)
Spirit of glory (I Pet. 4:14)
Spirit of understanding (Is. 11:2)
Spirit of counsel and might (Is. 11:2)
Spirit of knowledge (Is. 11:2)
Spirit of deep sleep (Isa. 29:10)
Spirit of holy gods (Dan. 4:8)
Spirit of holiness (Rom. 1:4)
Spirit of Christ (Rom. 8:9)
Spirit of grace (Heb. 10:29)
Spirit of Jesus Christ (Phil. 1:19)
Spirit of prophecy (Rev. 19:10)
Spirit of Elijah (II Kings 2:15)
Spirit of living creature (Ez. 1:20)
Spirit of grace and supplication (Zec. 12:10)
Spirit of your father (Matt. 10:20)
Spirit of meekness (I Cor. 4:21)

Contrite spirit (Psalm 34:18)
Strong in spirit (Luke 1:30)
Right spirit (Psalm 51:10)
Holy Spirit (Psalm 51:11)
Broken spirit (Psalm 51:17)
Faithful spirit (Prov. 11:13)
Humble spirit (Prov. 16:19)
Excellent spirit (Prov. 17:27)
Eternal spirit (Heb. 9:14)
Patient in spirit (Ecc. 7:8)
Good spirit (Psalm 143:10)
New spirit (Ezek. 11:19)
Free spirit (Psalm 51:12)
Fervent in spirit (Rom. 12:11)
Meek and quite spirit (I Pet. 3:4)

Quickening spirit (I Cor. 15:45)
Poor in spirit (Matt. 5:3)

Ungodly Spirits

Spirit of Antichrist (I John 4:3)
Spirit of fear (II Tim. 1:7)
Spirit of slumber (Rom. 11:8)
Spirit of divination (Acts 16:16)
Spirit of bondage (Rom. 8:15)
Spirit of error (I John 4:6)
Spirit of jealousy (Num. 5:14)
Spirit of burning (Isa. 4:4)
Spirit of Egypt (Isa. 19:3)
Spirit of heaviness (Isa. 61:3)
Spirit of unclean devil (Luke 4:33)
Spirit of the world (I Cor. 2:12)
Spirit of infirmity or weakness (Luke 13:11)
Spirit of whoredoms (Hos. 5:4)
Spirit of false doctrines (Ex. 23:1; Matt. 16:12)

Deaf spirit (Mark 9:25)
Perverse spirit (Isa. 19:14)
Dumb spirit (Mark 9:25)
Sorrowful spirit (I Sam. 1:15)
Blind spirit (Matt. 9:27)
Hasty of spirit (Prov. 14:29)
Haughty spirit (Prov. 16:18)
Perverse spirit (Isa. 19:14)
Seducing spirits (I Tim. 4:1)
Sad spirit (I Kings 21:5)
Jealous spirit (Num. 5:14, 30)
Wounded spirit (Prov. 18:14)
Proud in spirit (Ecc. 7:8)
Destroying spirit (Deut. 13:15)
Another spirit (II Cor. 11:4)

Lying spirit (I Kings 22:22-23; II Ch. 18:21-22)
Foul spirit (Mark 9:25; Rev. 18:2; Sam. 16:14-16, 23; 18:10; 19:9)
Familiar spirit (Lev. 20:27; I Sam. 28:7-8; I Ch. 10:13; II Ch. 33:6)
Unclean spirit (Matt. 14:43; Mark 1:23, 26; 3:30; 5:2,8; 7:25)
Evil spirit (Judges 9:23; 7:25; I Sam. 16:14-16, 23; 18:10; 19:9))

GENERAL

1. We **bind** the spirits (demons) of Satan and **loose** the spirits (angels) of GOD. We cast the demons out of people and GOD directs the angels to minister to our needs.
2. Godly spirits commonly mentioned are spirit, SPIRIT OF GOD, Spirit of the Lord, Holy Spirit: **human spirit, angels and Holy Spirit.**

3. Ungodly spirits commonly mentioned are evil spirits, demons and devils. There is actually only one Devil, Satan; demons are the correct terminology. There are millions of fallen angels and billions of demons.
4. The following are lists of godly and ungodly spirits found in the Bible. You can identify many more after you have been in deliverance awhile. Ungodly spirits generally are found grouped in families. Where you find one demon, you frequently find a family of demons with the similar characteristics.

SIX STEPS TO DELIVERANCE OF AN INDIVIDUAL

1. Find out what the individual's problems are.
2. Forgive, pray and get yourself right with GOD.
3. Break the curses and soul ties on you and your descendents.
4. Cast out the demons.
5. Pray for healing of soul and body.
6. Discipline your life by changing your ways of thinking and acting.

THE SPIRITS OF GOD AND SATAN

1. **Beloved, believe not every spirit, but try the spirits whether they are of GOD** (I John 4:1).
2. We can bind and loose spirits.
3. Therefore, we are safe in assuming that for every ministering spirit of the Lord, there will be one, and often many satanic counter spirits.
4. Loosing spirits from the Lord.

DICTIONARY OF CLASSICAL MYTHOLOGY

"A knowledge of the classics and an acquaintance with the **imaginary characters, places, and incidents of ancient mythology** which have been such an inspiring influence to writers of all ages adds greatly to ones enjoyment of literature, art and conversation. The people outside literary and educational pursuits have sufficient opportunity or leisure to acquire or keep up a knowledge of this popular branch of learning. It is important, therefore, to present in dictionary form the story of **gods, goddesses, heroes, and heroines of the old Grecian and Roman literature**. It will lead to a better understanding of the countless references which are made from time to time in the literature of the day to classic subjects. It is a great wonderland of posy and romance, and forms a realm all its own, **the realm of antiquity's gods and demons and of prehistoric heroes**."

Notice the words in bold letters and what they say to you. It is talking about gods, goddesses and demons. There is a **demon** behind every god and goddess worshiped by man!

You are seeing products with these names more and more today. Is this innocent or deliberate? The definitions of these names can be found in unabridged dictionaries. We recommend that you purchase one for spiritual research.

IDOLS WORSHIPPED BY COUNTRIES

The names of idols are the same as names of demons. There is a demon behind every idol that is worshipped by man. Notice that there are male and female gods and goddesses. Satan has something for everyone. Temple prostitutes included male homosexuals, female lesbians and female prostitutes.

TABER'S CYCLOPEDIC MEDICAL DICTIONARY

The following is Taber's definition of **multiple sclerosis**: "A chronic, slowly progressive disease of the **central nervous** system characterized by development of disseminated demyelinated glial patches called **plaques**. Symptoms and signs are numerous, but in later stages those of **Charcot's triad (nystagmus, scanning speech, and intention tremor)** are common. Occurs in the form of many clinical syndromes, the most common being the **cerebral, brain stem-cerebellar, and spinal**. A history of remissions and exacerbations is diagnostic. Etiology is unknown and there is no specific therapy."

Notice the words highlighted. **They tell you the symptoms of the disease and where it is located in the body.** With this information, you can pray more effectively. The symptoms can be called out as names of demons such as plaques, Charcot's triad, nystagmus, scanning speech and intention tremor. **Demons will answer to their medical names, symptoms, common names or names they are given in the spiritual world.**

We worked with a woman in deliverance who had this disease by using the above method. We would get manifestations as we called out the demons by their medical names. She was delivered and healed.

NEUROTIC AND ABNORMAL PERSONALITIES

(Psychoneurosis, Psychoneurotic And Psychopsychosis)

These lists of demons help you to understand those you are ministering to who have these personalities. A study of psychology and psychiatry can be very helpful in deliverance. The method of treatment can also open the door to demons.

Phobias

Phobias are fears. There are 210 phobias recognized by psychiatrists.

SOURCE AND BRANCHES OF FALSE RELIGIONS

The first false religion in the Bible can be traced back to **Nimrod, his wife, Semiramus, and her child, Tammuz**. From this source branched out other false religions. The Catholic religion is for those **who want to be religious**. The Masonic religion is for those **who want business success**. The Occult religion is for those **who want power, sex and drugs**. This is true of anyone who follows a bloodless religion without the blood of Jesus Christ and has not had a born-again experience with Jesus Christ: Lord, Master and Savior.

It is easy to cast out demons but hard to discipline your life!

SPECIAL SPIRITS

Location

Soul: Mind - Will - Emotions
Conscious - Subconscious - Unconscious
Body: Physical - Brain - Sexual Organs

Types

Wer Beasts: Vampires - Werewolves - Zombies

Manifestations: Changelings - Incubi/Succubi - Dopple Gangers
Objects: Familiar Objects - Fetish, Talisman and Amulets - Marks - Hagstones - Biofeedback
Curses: Spells - Incantations - Hexes - Vexes

Demons: Son of Satan - Mind Control - Death - Occult - Magic - Witchcraft - Drugs - Child Abuse - Fornication - Demonic Healing - Eastern Religions - Demonic Inheritance - Demonic Games - Rock Music - Voodoo - Familiar and Guiding Spirits - Forces and Powers

DELIVERANCE WARFARE PRAYERS WITH LISTS

Biblical Curses

But it shall come to pass, if thou wilt not hearken unto the voice of the Lord thy GOD, to observe to do all His commandments and His statutes which I command thee this day; that all these curses shall come upon thee, and overtake thee (Deut. 28:15).

I forgive my ancestors and anyone else that has cursed me. I ask that GOD forgive me and them. **I break any curses placed on me or my descendants from uttering a wish of evil against one; to imprecate evil, to call for mischief or injury to fall upon; to execrate, to bring evil upon or to; to blast, vex, harass or torment with great calamities.** I break these curses in Jesus' name. I break the curses back to ten generations or even to Adam and Eve on both sides of my family, and destroy every legal hold and every legal ground that demons have to work in my life. I break curses that follow in the name of the Lord Jesus Christ.

In the Name of Jesus Christ, I now rebuke, break, loose myself and my children from any and all evil curses, charms, vexes, hexes, spells, jinxes, psychic powers, bewitchment, witchcraft and sorcery, that have been put upon me or my family line from any persons or from any occult or psychic sources, and I cancel all connected or related spirits and command them to leave me. I thank you, Lord, for setting me free.

Mistreating GOD's Chosen People, Willing Deceivers, Adultery, Harlotry and Prostitution, Disobedience to Bible, Idolatry, Keeping Cursed Objects, Refusing To Fight For GOD, House of Wicked, Not Giving To Poor, Stealing, Swearing Falsely By GOD, Failing To Give Glory to GOD, Robbing GOD of Tithes, Dishonoring Parents, Hearkening to Wives Rather Than GOD, Making Graven Images, Cheating People Out of Property, Taking Advantage of Blind, Oppressing Strangers, Widows and Orphans, Bestiality, Incest With Sister or Mother, Murder Secretly or For Hire, Pride, Putting Trust In Man, Doing The Work of GOD Deceitfully, Rewarding Evil For Good, Abortion or Causing Unborn To Die, Having Bastards, Murdering Indirectly, Striking Parents, Kidnapping, Cursing Parents, Not Preventing Death, Sacrificing to gods, Witchcraft, Turning Someone Away From GOD, Following Horoscopes, Rebelling Against Pastors, Losing Virginity Before Marriage, False Prophets, Rape, Not Disciplining Children, Teaching Rebellion Against GOD, Cursing Rulers, Refusing To Warn Sinners, Defiling The Sabbath, Sacrificing Humans, Seances and Fortune Telling, Intercourse During Menstruation, Homosexuals and Lesbians, Necromancers, Blaspheming Lord's Name, Being Carnally Minded, Oral and Anal Sex, Children Rebelling, Nonproductivity, Fugitive and Vagabond, Improper Family Structure, Destruction of Family Priesthood, Refusing To Do The Word of GOD, Family Disorder, Failure and Poverty, Any Sin Worthy of Death, Touching GOD's Anointed, Perversion of Gospel, Loving Cursing, Choosing That Which GOD Delights

Not In, Looking To World For Help, Stubbornness and Rebellion, Offending Children Believing Christ, Adding To or Taking Away From Bible, **and all Biblical Curses not listed Above.**

Soul Ties

Father, I break and renounce evil soul ties that I have had or may have had with lodges, adulterers, close friends, husbands, wives, engagements, cults and binding agreements between buddies.

Forgive me for developing soul ties with anyone. I forgive those who would control me. I renounce these evil soul ties, break them and wash them away with the shed blood of the Lord Jesus Christ. I break all evil soul ties with the following:

1. Beasts
2. Anyone I Have Had Sex With Outside of Marriage
3. Divorced Mates
4. By Incest, Rape, Fornication, Adultery, Homosexuality, Bestiality, Lesbianism
5. Bloodless Religions, Religious Cults
6. Blood Brothers and Sisters By Rites
7. Witchcraft, Occult, Satan Worship
8. Fortune Tellers, Mediums
9. Psychiatrists, Social Workers, Psychologists, Mental Institutions
10. **Finally, I break any agreement with anyone that forms an evil soul tie.**

Occult And False Religion

Lord, I now confess seeking from Satan the help that should only come from GOD. I now confess occultism and false religions as sin. Lord, I now repent and renounce these sins and ask you to forgive me. I renounce Satan and his works; I hate his demons and count them my enemies. In the Name of Jesus Christ I now close the door on occult practices, and I command such spirits to leave me in the Name of Jesus Christ.

In the Name of Jesus Christ, I now renounce, break and loose myself and my children from psychic powers or bondages and bonds of physical or mental illness, upon me or my family line, as the results of parents or any other ancestors. I thank you Lord, for setting me free.

In the Name of Jesus Christ, I now renounce, break and loose myself from demonic subjection to my mother, father, grandparents, or any other human beings, living or dead, that have dominated me in any way, and I thank you, Lord, for setting me free.

I forgive my ancestors and ask that You would forgive me for participating in occult and false religion. I renounce all fortune telling, magic practices and spiritism, cults and false teachings and Satan worship. I break every curse and soul tie brought about by psychic heredity, occult contacts and religious cults. I now break any demonic hold on my family line due to supernatural experiences apart from GOD including the following forbidden practices and all that they entail:

Enchantments, Wizardry, Necromancy, Witchcraft, Observer of Times, Fortune Telling, Consulting With Familiar Spirits, Occult Practices, Spiritism, Sorcery, Magic Practices, Son or

Daughter Passing Through Fire, Divination, Charmers, False Religious Cults **and any other Occult or False Religious Practice.**

Ungodly Spirits

Lord Jesus, I forgive my ancestors and ask that you forgive me for the following families of ungodly spirits and command that they come out as their name is called:

Spirit of Infirmity or Weakness, Spirit of Antichrist, Spirit of Fear, Deaf Spirit, Perverse Spirit, Dumb Spirit, Sorrowful Spirit, Blind Spirit, Spirit of Slumber, Foul Spirit, Spirit of Whoredoms, Unclean Spirit, Destroying Spirit, Evil Spirit, Spirit of Divination, Another Spirit, Spirit of Bondage, Hasty of Spirit, Spirit of Error, Haughty Spirit, Spirit of False Doctrines, Perverse Spirit, Spirit of Jealousy, Seducing Spirits, Sad Spirit, Jealous Spirit, Wounded Spirit, Lying Spirit, Proud in Spirit, Spirit of Burning, Familiar Spirit, Spirit of Egypt, Spirit of Heaviness, Spirit of Unclean Devil, Spirit of the World **and all other families of Ungodly Spirits.**

Godly Spirits

Lord Jesus Christ, we ask that you direct the angels to minister to our needs. We loose warring angels, ministering angels, the Holy Spirit and the SEVEN-FOLD SPIRIT OF GOD. We loose legions of angels including the following godly spirits:

Spirit of Wisdom, Poor in Spirit, SPIRIT OF GOD, Spirit of Your Father, Spirit of the Lord, Strong in Spirit, Right Spirit, Spirit of Truth, Holy Spirit, Spirit of Life, Broken Spirit, Spirit of Adoption, Spirit of Princes, Fervent in Spirit, Faithful Spirit, Spirit of Meekness, Humble Spirit, Spirit of Faith, Excellent Spirit, Spirit of Jesus Christ, Spirit of Man, Eternal Spirit, Patient in Spirit, Meek and Quite Spirit, Spirit of the Ruler, Spirit of Glory, Spirit of Judgment, Spirit of Prophecy, Spirit of Understanding, Spirit of Elijah, Spirit of Counsel/Might, Contrite Spirit, Spirit of Knowledge, Good Spirit, New Spirit, Spirit of Deep Sleep, SPIRIT OF HOLY GODS, Spirit of Living Creature, Spirit of Grace and Supplication, Spirit of Holiness, Spirit of Christ, Spirit of Grace, Quickening Spirit, Free Spirit **and all other godly spirits.**

SECTION 12 - FIFTY-THREE COMMON DEMON GROUPINGS

We have used this list many times. We recommend that you use this list in your ministry. You can use it for mass or individual deliverance. Start with **Basic Deliverance of Rejection, Bitterness and Rebellion** in the Unconscious, Subconscious and Conscious Mind.

PRAYER

In The Name of Jesus Christ, I command the spirits to come out of the Unconscious, Subconscious and Conscious Mind. I command the families of Rejection, Bitterness and Rebellion, and other families to come out of me and bring their works with them as your name is called:

Bitterness
Resentment
Hatred
Unforgiveness
Violence
Temper
Anger
Retaliation
Murder
Insecurity
Rebellion
Self-will
Stubbornness
Disobedience
Anti-Submissiveness
Inadequacy
Strife
Contention
Argument
Quarreling
Fighting
Distrust
Control
Possessiveness
Dominance
Witchcraft
Daydreaming
Retaliation
Destruction
Spite
Hatred
Sadism
Hurt
Cruelty
Passivity
Sensitiveness

Accusation
Judging
Criticism
Faultfinding
Lethargy
Rejection
Fear of Rejection
Self-Rejection
Despondency
Discouragement
Inferiority
Self-Pity
Loneliness
Timidity
Shyness
Insomnia
Ineptness

Jealousy
Envy
Suspicion
Disgust
Selfishness
Worry
Withdrawal
Pouting
Dread
Fantasy
Pretension
Unreality
Tension
Escape
Indifference
Stoicism
Excitement
Sleepiness

Passivity
Funk
Indifference
Listlessness

Depression
Despair

Defeatism
Dejection
Hopelessness
Suicide
Death

Morbidity

Heaviness
Gloom
Burden

Anxiety
Fear

Apprehension

Nervousness

Headache
Nervous Habits
Restlessness

Insomnia

Self-Awareness
Fear of Man
Fear of Disapproval
Perfection
Persecution
Unfairness
Fear of Judgment
Fear of Condemnation
Fear of Accusation
Fear of Reproof
Sensitiveness
Anger
Mental Illness
Insanity
Madness
Mania
Retardation
Senility
Schizophrenia
Paranoia
Hallucinations
Frustration
Paranoia
Jealousy
Envy
Suspicion
Distrust
Persecution
Fears
Confrontation
Grief
Confusion
Frustration
Incoherence
Forgetfulness
Sadness
Doubt
Unbelief
Skepticism
Tiredness
Death
Laziness
Indecision
Procrastination
Compromise
Confusion
Forgetfulness

Alcohol
Drugs
Sexual Impurity
Lust
Pride
Vanity
Ego
Frustration
Criticism
Irritability
Intolerance
Harlotry
Rape
Competition
Driving
Argument
Pride
Ego
Christian Science
Impatience
Agitation
Urantia
Intolerance
Resentment
Criticism
Mormonism
False Burden
False Responsibility
False Compassion
and social agencies
using the Bible &
Sorrow
Heartache
Heartbreak
Crying

Cruelty
Ouija Board
Fatigue
Handwriting Analysis
Weariness

ESP
Infirmity
(May include
any disease
or sickness)

Roving

Fantasy Lust
Masturbation
Homosexuality
Lesbianism
Adultery
Fornication
Incest

Exposure
Frigidity

Cults
Jehovah's Witnesses

Rosicrucianism
Theosophy

Subud
Latihan
Unity

Bahaism
Unitarianism
Lodges, societies

God as a basis but
omitting the blood
atonement of Jesus
Christ)

Occult

Palmistry

Automatic Handwriting

Hypnotism
Horoscope
Astrology
Levitation

Indifference
Inheritance
Self Deception
Self-Delusion
Self-Seduction
Pride
White Magic
Mind Binding
Confusion
Fear of Man
Fear of Failure
Occult Spirits
Spiritism Spirits
Blasphemy
Mind Idolatry
Intellectualism
Rationalization
Pride
Ego
Belittling
Fears (All Kinds)
Phobias (All Kinds)
Hysteria
Compulsive
Fear of Authority
Lying
Deceit
Caffeine
Pride
Ego
Vanity
Self-Righteousness
Haughtiness
Importance
Arrogance
Frustration
Affectation
Theatrics
Playacting
Sophistication
Pretension
Self-Hatred
Self-Condemnation

Fortune Telling
Water Witching
(Physical)
(Emotional)
(Mental)
(Curses)

Hyperactivity
Restlessness
Driving
Pressure

Cursing
Ritualism
Course Jesting
Gossip
Criticism
Backbiting
Mockery
Fear of Lost Salvation
Railing
Etc.
Addictive &
Spiritism
Nicotine
Alcohol
Drugs

Medications
Gluttony
Taoism
Gluttony
Nervousness
Compulsive Eating
Resentment
Etc.
Idleness
Self-Pity
Self-Reward
Kleptomania
Self Accusation
Greed
Discontent

Tarot Cards
Pendulum
Witchcraft
Black Magic

Conjuration
Incantation
Fetishes
Etc.

Religious

Formalism
Legalism
Doctrinal Obsession
Fear of God
Fear of Hell

Religiosity

Seance
Spirit Guide
Necromancy

False Religions
Buddhism

Hinduism
Islam
Shintoism
Confucianism

Covetousness
Stealing

Material Lust

SECTION 13 - CHILDREN'S DELIVERANCE

CONTENTS

THE CURSE OF FAMILIES OUT OF DIVINE ORDER

As for my people, children are their oppressors, and women rule over them. O my people, they which lead thee cause thee to err, and destroy the way of thy paths (Isa. 3:12). This is the result of the family not following the Bible and being out of divine order.

CURSES ON CHILDREN

The following are some special curses on children:

1. Children born from incestuous unions (Gen. 19:36-38).
2. **Curse of idol worship extends to 4TH generation of great grandchildren** (Exodus 20:1-5).
3. Children who strike their parents (Exodus 21:15).
4. Those who curse their parents (Exodus 21:17).
5. Iniquity of fathers on children (Exodus 34:6-7).
6. Children wandered for 40 years (Numbers 14:18 & 33).
7. Idol worship (Deut. 5:9-10).
8. Rebellious children (Deut. 21:18-21).
9. **Curse of the bastard extends to tenth generation of descendants** (Deut. 23:2).
10. In son's days evil will come on his house (I Kings 21:19).
11. The iniquity of the father upon the children (Jer. 32:18).

EFFECT ON CHILDREN OF AHAB / JEZEBEL PARENTS

Children are open to violence or death, even early death, because of tensions, confusions, hurts and insults given them by the family structure being out of order (Eze. 38:8-9). Confusion, frustration, disgust, hate, etc. lead to suicide. In trying to find their place, these children frequently give in to spirits which drive them to love of power, money, praise, fame, etc. (I Ki. 21:20).

Children have fear, insecurity, frustration and difficulty learning. It leads to potential corruption, discord, growth in occult and cults, selfishness, doubt, inability to achieve, fake sickness, hypochondriacs and church splits.

Ahab fathers place curses on male children; Jezebel mothers -female children. Male children tend to become homosexuals; the female children - lesbians. Children will have broken marriages and families like their parents. Jezebel mothers cause children to be manipulative. Children are full of rebellion and under pressure to prove their love to their parents. **Finally, children are open to satanic attack and will usually become like their parents!**

BREAKING CURSES

I break curses placed on me or my descendants from uttering a wish of evil against one; to imprecate evil, to call for mischief or injury to fall upon; to execrate, to bring evil upon or to; to blast, vex, harass or torment with great calamities. I break these curses in Jesus' name. I break the curses back to ten generations or even to Adam and Eve on both sides of my family, and destroy legal hold and legal ground that demons have to work in my life. I break curses that follow in the name of the Lord Jesus Christ.

PERFECT FAMILY SUMMARY

The following is God's formula for having a perfect family taken from Col. 3:18-21: Husbands **love** your wives! Wives **submit** to your husbands! Children **obey and honor** your parents! Fathers **do not provoke** your children!

DEDICATION OF CHILDREN

I vow to raise my children according to the Holy Word of God. I do hereby dedicate them to the Lord Jesus Christ to do with according to His Perfect Plan Of Life. I praise and thank God for my children. I pray that the children will be strong in spirit, filled with wisdom and grace, and that they will have favor with God and man. I ask these desires of my heart in the Name of The Lord Jesus Christ, my Lord, my Master and my Savior, Amen.

GENERAL DELIVERANCE OF CHILDREN

Husbands are often the most effective in commanding spirits to leave their wives, with the support of others. This is true with his children also. (Sit together as families during deliverance. A husband has special power and authority over his family that even I don't have as a deliverance minister.)

Children must be disciplined by their parents (Proverbs 13:23). The prayerful and judicious application of the rod can act as a deterrent to childish and foolish behavior (Proverbs 22:15). Parents many times prepare the way for deep-seated spirits of **Fear, Rejection and Conditional Love** to enter. God will turn the heart of the father (not the mothers) to the children (Malachi 4:6 and Col. 3:21). A child left to rear himself is a disaster going somewhere to happen (Proverbs 29:15).

Indwelling demons can be present because of **inheritance, curses, habitual sin, or legal holds or grounds from other sources**. The punishment should equal the offence. We provoke our children to wrath when we punish more severely than the offence justifies. The offence should be explained. Other ways to behave should be explored. Then show love; give a hug, approval, compliment on good behavior or improvement of conduct. (The book of Proverbs was a special comfort to me after Byron died because we had disciplined him; he was a well-behaved son.)

Scripture warns us to have nothing to do with fairy tales, fables, enchantments, charmers or such like: Tit. 1:14 (fables turn one from truth) and II Peter 1:16 (declares importance of truth). Children at a susceptible age may well be opened up to spirits of **Fear, Error, Perversity, Lying and Fantasy**. (God is ultimate truth and there is no fantasy in God or in His Word. Fantasy causes most of our young people's problems: drugs, drink, sex, etc.)

The truth is important to God and many, ignorantly, cause children to believe a lie in the guise of a friendly, jolly, phoney, called **Santa Claus**. This lie caused our daughter to doubt that her parents would tell her the truth. All **lies** come from the Devil (John 8:44). (God taught us to tell the truth in love, we practice tough love!)

The encyclopedia says that the origin of dolls is witchcraft and magic. Only witch doctors or medicine men were allowed to handle them. To this day, multitudes of idol (demon) worshippers use dolls in pagan religious ceremonies. Exodus 20:4 - No graven images and Jer. 48:10 - Lord places a curse on those that use deceit. (Pray and ask the Holy Spirit to show you what dolls to throw away; be cautious about any doll.)

The inventor of the first deck of cards evidently hated God and the Bible, and designed a message in the cards which was the exact opposite of the truth of Scripture. Jesus is supposed to be the joker. **Witches, psychics and Satan Worshippers** use playing cards for **divination, and to cast spells and curses**. It is time that Christians clean house and destroy the hidden works of darkness (I John 2:15-17, Romans 12:1-2, II Cor. 6:17-18 and I Timothy 6:12). (Playing card games can become addictive.)

By initiating young, interested believers into the battle for deliverance, they soon become seasoned soldiers, learning tactics of war in the battlefield. (We have taught small children to cast out demons; the demons hate to have to obey children! Earline Moody taught the first grade children were taught to war in the spirit.)

MINISTRY TO CHILDREN (EXCERPTS)

Since it has already been shown that demon spirits are able to gain entrance to a fetus and to children, it is obvious that there should be deliverance for them. Demons can be called out of children in the same way they are called out of older persons. There will be manifestations of the spirits leaving through the mouth and nose as in other deliverances. (They can also be cast out of the fetus in the womb.)

Ordinarily, children are quite easily delivered. Since the spirits have not been there very long, they are not as deeply embedded in the flesh. There are exceptions to this, as in the case of children who have been exposed to demonic attack through severe circumstances. The manifestations of the demons can be quite dramatic even in children. (It is fun to cast demons out of babies, watch demons manifest and watch them leave.)

A young Christian couple brought their three month old child for ministry. This was their first baby and they had disagreed as to how to discipline the child. The father and mother had a violent argument over the matter. **While they were having this argument, the child began to scream, and since that incident it was apparent that the child was suffering from tormenting spirits**. My wife held the child in her arms and began to command the troubling spirits to go in the name of Jesus. As the first spirit came out, the baby stiffened and cried out. Two other demons came out in the same way. Then the child grew quiet and relaxed, and was soon asleep.

Most children by the age of five or six can be given a simple explanation of what you are going to do before you begin the ministry. They need to know that you are not talking to them but to the spirits in them, otherwise they may be offended or frightened by words of command addressed to the evil spirits. Usually the children are quite cooperative. Since the children may feel more secure with a parent, it is often best for the parent to hold the child during the ministry. The deliverance minister must discern reactions in the child attributable to the spirits being stirred up. The spirits may cause the child to resist being held. He may cry or scream and show signs of great fear. The demons may try various tactics to make one think it is the child being hurt or wronged. The minister and/or parent will then become so sympathetic with the child that they will stop the ministry and the demons retain their hold. (Don't be fooled or become sympathetic to the demons!)

Especially in ministry with children, it is well to remember the fact that it is not the loudness of a command that moves the demon but the authority of the name and blood of the Lord Jesus Christ. The commands can be given with such calmness and matter-of-factualness that the child will scarcely realize what is taking place. (Speak quietly and softly; this infuriates the demons! Know your authority over the forces of evil.)

How do infants and children keep themselves free from the demons once they are delivered, since they are not competent to protect themselves? It is not the responsibility of the child but of his parents or guardians. I believe you will find in the Scripture that when Jesus ministered to children, one or both of the parents were present. **It is the responsibility of parents to be the spiritual guardians of their children**. (Very few parents do their job properly. We didn't due to ignorance of the Bible.)

CHILDREN AND DELIVERANCE (EXCERPTS)

Some people say that children do not need deliverance. I could not disagree more. Parents have a solemn responsibility to provide protection for their offspring in the matter of spiritual warfare. So many curses, legal holds, and other legal grounds can be inherited through the ignorance, curiosity, and/or willful disobedience of the parent. In addition, our society provides a climate for demon infestation. (We have not seen any parents that have protected their children completely or properly.)

Once one is alerted to the dangers of passing on weaknesses, infirmities and other unpleasant things to siblings, he should begin breaking curses, destroying legal holds and grounds, and binding inherited spirits. This is preparation for casting them out. The occult demons are tremendously powerful and tenacious, often staying in families for centuries. People afflicted with them are highly susceptible to psychic phenomena and influence. (Notice that the deliverance prayers are establishing the basis for casting out the demons.)

We have seen children (from babies to teens) receive significant deliverance in the church and at home. Parents are able to minister some of this to younger ones while the child is sleeping. There need be no fear created in the child about deliverance.

They will usually be able to handle the idea of casting out evil spirits better than many adults. (Adults have to overcome false religious teaching, ignorance of the Bible, and fear of deliverance.)

When a child is brought to us for prayer, we ask that one or both parents accompany them, preferably the father, since he has the most spiritual authority. Often I will talk briefly with the child, allaying any fears, with love for him. (We will not minister to the children without the parents present.)

Usually I ask if he sometimes does or says things he doesn't really want to do, things which get him into trouble. After an affirmative answer, I will mention that often ugly things called spirits get into a boy or girl and cause this sort of thing. I also talk with the child about asking the Lord

Jesus to come into his heart (Revelation 3:20) if he has not already done so. I then ask if he would like for those things to come out of him if they are there. **Children seldom want problem-causing things and usually readily consent to prayer**.

I pray for them, quietly taking authority over the spirits and commanding them to manifest and leave. If they are stubborn and the father is present, I will have him take authority and guide him in what to pray. **In practically every case this combined assault will rout the demons**. (The parents should enter into the deliverance of their children in church and at home.)

If parents wait until the child is grown up before attempting deliverance, they will discover the enemy has wasted no time and has burrowed in deeply, often scarring body and mind. They will work tirelessly to put a child in bondage, drag him out into the world, and enslave him with many sinful habits. An ounce of prevention here is certainly worth the proverbial pound of cure. (Full Gospel Christians are in general very demonized, not demon possessed, but simply have many demons!)

SUMMARY OF COMMENTS

1. Sit together as families during deliverance. A husband has special power and authority over his family that even we don't have as deliverance ministers.
2. The Book of Proverbs was a special comfort to me after Byron died because we had disciplined him; he was a well-behaved son.
3. God is ultimate truth and there is no fantasy in God or in His Word. Fantasy causes most of our young people's problems: drugs, drink, sex, etc.
4. God taught us to tell the truth in love; we practice tough love!
5. Pray and ask the Holy Spirit to show you what dolls to throw away; be cautious about any doll.
6. Playing card games can become addictive.
7. We have taught small children to cast out demons; the demons hate to have to obey children! Children in the First Grade were taught to war in the spirit.
8. Demons can also be cast out of the fetus in the womb.
9. It is fun to cast demons out of babies - watch demons manifest and watch them leave.
10. Don't be fooled or become sympathetic to the demons!
11. Speak quietly and softly; this infuriates the demons! Know your authority over the forces of evil.
12. Very few parents do their job properly.
13. We have not seen any parents that have protected their children completely or properly; we didn't.
14. Notice that the deliverance prayers are establishing the basis for casting out the demons.
15. Adults have to overcome false religious teaching, ignorance of the Bible and fear of deliverance.
16. We will not minister to the children without the parents present.
17. The parents should enter into the deliverance of their children in church and at home.
18. Full Gospel Christians are in general very demonized, not demon possessed, but simply have many demons!
19. The lie about Santa Claus caused our daughter to doubt that her parents would tell her the truth. All **lies** come from the Devil (John 8:44).

DEMONIC RELIGIOUS CULTS FOR THE YOUNG (EXCERPTS)

There is a strange hold that many weird cults have on thousands of ensnared young people which is through demonic control spirits. In the name of liberty, they have opened the door for terrible bondage (II Peter 2:19, 20).

Some of the most well-known are: Children of God; Unification, International Society of Krishna Consciousness; Forever Family; The Mission; The Process; Scientology; Love Israel; The Assembly; The Body; The Farm; The Way, etc.

Deeply craving and seeking peer approval, a disciplined life and a better world than the one they see, these youngsters do not realize how easily they can be deceived. Knowing the vulnerability of the group, unscrupulous promoters work zealously to exploit them and their unspoken cry, **I am important, please notice me**.

In the beginning the approach is always warm, friendly and accepting. Chanting is often used to focus attention and limit peripheral vision.

The cruelty, selfishness and egotism of the leaders is unbelievable. Many are Jezebellian women, some are charismatic witches. Others are vicious and unprincipled men, depraved and driven to all sorts of excesses.

Jesus said, **Ye shall know the truth and the truth shall set you free** (John 8:32). Paul admonished believers not to be entangled again in the yoke of bondage (Gal. 5:1). God's people are to be peculiar (I Peter 2:9; Tit. 2:14) but that peculiarity is to be found in the fact that they are zealous of good works and seek to honor God's name.

Proverbs 22:6 says train up a child, Prov. 23:13 says withhold not correction and Prov. 29:15 says rod and reproof bring wisdom. Rejection or withholding love, correction, praise or instruction will open a child to receive a counterfeit for the real love he or she needs. Even though a child would probably not realize it, his soul cries for love, discipline, training and instruction. They will find someone to do these things for them, even if what they find is a counterfeit.

DOLLS (EXCERPTS)

Dolls were believed to bring good luck to their owners, to make livestock give more milk, help win wars, and heal the sick. Only witch doctors or medicine men were allowed to handle them.

The **dictionary** defines a doll as a small carved or molded figure which served as a cult object or representation of a nursery story, cartoon or puppet character.

Both **World Book** and **Britannica** point out that dolls were buried with people and were supposed to be friends and servants in the spirit world.

Roman and Greek girls, in preparation for marriage, would leave their dolls on the altar of the temples of Artemis and Diana. To this day multitudes of idol (demon) worshippers use dolls in pagan religious ceremonies.

DOLLS IN TOLEDO, OHIO (EXCERPTS)

One night when my wife was complaining to me about the child's insolence, out of nowhere, I said **Her problems are those stinking doll babies, it's witchcraft**.

The next night while I was praying for someone's deliverance, she picked up an **encyclopedia** to check what it said about dolls! There it was: **origin in witchcraft and magic**.

DOLLS FOR BABY - SEVEN MONTHS OLD (EXCERPTS)

The Lord began to show us the legal grounds Satan held. It was in his dolls! He had received one for Christmas and a small plastic boy sailor doll at birth. The Lord also told my husband of various stuffed toys (in shapes of animals - whales, dogs and kangaroos), a plastic toy **Big Bird** and matching bib. These were thrown away and curses from them broken. **(Look for strange sicknesses or sicknesses that will not heal in children)**.

When the Lord commanded that **no graven images** were to be made, He wasn't being cruel and heartless. He knew the damage they could put upon people (Exodus 20:4). The Lord has also shown us that puppets are a deception and the Lord places a curse on those that use deceit (Jer. 48:10).

MARIONETTES, MARIOLATRY, MUMMERY, PUPPETRY & VENTRILOQUISM

List Of Scripture

Isa. 8:11-22 (Israel's **idolatrous** practices)
Isa. 8:19 (Wizards that **peep and mutter**)
Isa. 10:10-17(**Chirping** - chatter, peep, whisper)
Isa. 10:14 (Or opened the mouth or **peeped**)
Isa. 59:3 (Tongue hath **muttered** perverseness)

To Murmur (In Anger)

Imagine, mourn, mutter, roar, take away. See Strong's Concordance for murmur, **murmured**, murmurers, murmuring and murmurings.

Mariolatry

N. (Gr. Maria, Mary, and Latreia, worship.) **Worship of the Virgin Mary, regarded as carried to an idolatrous extreme:** opprobrious term.

Marionette

n. (probably from Ital. morio, **a fool or buffon**, but also said to be derived from the mariolettes, or little figures of the Virgin Mary), FANTOCCINI (from fantino, a child or PUPPETS (Fr. **poupee**, Lat. pupa, **a baby or doll**), the names given to figures, generally below life-size, suspended by threads or wires and imitating with their limbs and heads the movements of living persons. Used to teach worship of Mary in Europe. **(A demon told me that is name was poupee but I didn't recognize it. I thought the demon was trying to fool me. The woman was a Catholic.)**

And in a pamphlet of 1641, describing Bartholomew Fair, we read, **Hear a knave in a fool's coat, with a trumpet sounding or a drum beating, invites you to see his puppets. Hear a**

rogue like a wild woodman, or in an antic shape like an incubus, desires your company to view his motion.

The latter refers also to Pinketham, a **motion-maker**, in whose scenes the divinities of Olympus ascended and descended to the strains of music.

Likewise machines descending from above, double, with Dives rising out of hell and Lazarus seen in Abraham's bosom; besides several figures dancing jiggs, sarabands, and country dances, with the merry conceits of Squire Punch and Sir John Spendall.

Mummery

n.; pl. mummeries, (OFr. momerie, from momer, to mum.) 1. Performance by mummers. 2. Any show or ceremony regarded as pretentious or hypocritical.

Mumming seems to have been a survival of the Roman custom of masquerading during the annual orgies of the Saturnalia. The disguisyng and mummyng that is used in Christemase time, Langley writes in his synopsis of Polydore Virgil, **in the Northe partes came out of the feasts of Pallas, that were done with visars and painted visages, named Quinqatria of the Romaynes**. Aubanus, writing of mumming in Germany, says that **in the Saturnalia there were frequent and luxurious feastings amongst friends, presents were mutually sent, and changes of dress made; <u>that Christians have adopted the same customs</u>, which continue to be used from the Nativity to the Epiphany: that exchanges of dress too, as of old among the Romans, are common, and neighbors by mutual invitation visit each other in the manner which the Germans call mummery**.

Some were disguised as bears, others as unicorns, or wore deer's hide and antler's or ram's horns. **Mumming led to such outrages that Henry VIII issued a proclamation declaring the wearing of a mask or disguise a misdemeanor.** How about Mardi Gras in New Orleans?

They usually present on these four nights a rude drama called Galatian, which, in various versions, is common throughout the Lowlands of Scotland.

Puppetry

Puppet, n. (Fr. **poupee**; L. pupa, **a puppet**.) 1. A small figure that is a likeness of the human form; a doll. 2. Such a figure moved by attached strings or wires, or by the hands, in a puppet show. 3. A person whose actions, ideas, etc. are controlled by another.

Ventriloquism

n. (from L. ventriloquist, lit., one who speaks from the belly, from venter, belly, and loqui, to speak; and -ism.) the art or practice of speaking in such a way that the voice seems to come from some other source other than the speaker.

Thus, says Huxley, **If the ventriloquist desires to create the belief that a voice issues from the bowels of the earth, he imitates, with great accuracy, the tones of such a half-stifled voice, and suggests the existence of some one uttering it by directing his answers and gestures towards the ground**.

Ventriloquism, which is still a recognized form of conjuring entertainment, is of ancient origin.

Eurykles of Athens was the most celebrated of Greek ventriloquists, who were called after him Euryklides, and also Engastrimanteis (belly-prophets). It is not impossible that the priest of ancient times were masters of this art, and that to it may be ascribed such miracles as the speaking statues of the Egyptians, the Greek oracles, and the stone in the river Pactolus, the sound of which put robbers to flight. Many uncivilized races of modern times are adepts in ventriloquism, as the Zulus, the Maoris and the Eskimos. **It is well known in Hindustan and China, where it is practiced by traveling magicians.**

Comments

The above was taken from dictionaries and encyclopedias with the scripture from the Bible. The practices refer to **idolatrous and ungodly conduct**. Some of the key words researched are chirp, murmur, peep and mutter uttered by people practicing the occult or talking against God.

Marionettes is a part of the worship of the Virgin Mary rather than Jesus Christ. It is derived from the words fool and buffoon, incubus, divinities of Olympus, devils rising out of Hell, etc. **Mummery** is regarded as pretentious and hypocritical. It is described as contemptuous, mutter, annual orgies of the Saturnalia, unicorns, outrages, rude drama, etc. **Puppetry** is an imitation of life. It is described by religious puppet plays, voice throwing, etc.

Conclusion

God is total reality; there is no fantasy or play acting in God! There is no unreality in the Bible! Christians should not deal in any spiritual fantasy. **Fantasy is very simply a lie that is not from God.**

God does not need any human circus or side shows to sell and promote the Kingdom of God! All it takes is a straight forward application of the Bible with **signs, wonders and miracles following the true teaching of the Word of God** to attract people to church. Jesus said if you don't believe me then believe my miracles.

SATAN IN THE TOY STORE

How can a child be influenced to readily accept demons? Webster's defines fantasy as 1) imagination or fancy, especially wild, visionary fancy; 2) unreal mental image; illusion; phantasm; 3) whim; queer notion; caprice; 4) an imaginative poem, play, etc., and 5) in psychology, a mental image as in a day dream.

Movies - Star Wars, Dark Cauldrons, etc. aim to frighten, to deceive, to familiarize children with hideous characters, to entice children to accept evil as good, etc. For instance, consider E.T. He could heal, raise the dead, etc.; a mockery of Jesus and a horrible creature. **Woe to those who call evil good and good evil** (Isa.5:20).

Read Daniel 11:38; God of forces means munitions. The below games include force or munitions. In the games munitions is associated with occult, charms and magic.

Years ago God showed me the reason for Walt Disney movies, full of occult workings and such as E.T. It was to get the children to feel comfortable, even to love the better of the evil presented to them. Do you think it has worked?

In our work with people, we have found fantasy to be a major problem. Many people under 35 years old have a hard time living in a real world. Dwelling in fantasy has become to them the real world; the real world is fantasy. Fantasy costs in lost mental power, satisfaction of life and work.

Cartoons draw on Egyptology - Isis; mythology, witchcraft, occult, Smurfs, Dungeons & Dragons, Little People and Gremlins. The most violent block of T.V. time is Saturday morning.

Fairy Tales and Walt Disney movies are full of occult practices: Mary Poplins, Dark Cauldron, etc. Video games incite destruction and death.

Rock music and subliminal music is meant to operate on stimuli that exist below the threshold of the conscious mind. Its goal is to awaken the energy center (in the brain) and to expand mental awareness. Scientific instruments have proved it reaches its goal. Music is more powerful than drugs.

New Age Children's music is to incite rebellion and self elevation. Rock music leads young people into sexual perversions and violence.

Toys Having Either Occult Linkage, Actions Or Excessive Violence

SMURFS:(German word for demon) - Papa Smurf is a wizard who casts spells and mixes potions, and often refers to Beelzebub (Satan) in the cartoons. He practices sorcery and witchcraft. Wizards and witches were put to death in the Old Testament. Paying heed to them, however amusing or cute and innocent they seem to be, gives respectability to that which God forbids for He knows it leads to one opening up oneself to satanic bondage. Ignore and Renounce!

STAR WARS: The theme is based on a cosmic force taken from Zen Buddhism and Eastern religions. EMPIRE STRIKES BACK: Yoda is referred to as a Zen master. E.T. TOYS: E.T. levitates, uses mental telepathy, heals supernaturally, resurrected, imitation of the life of Jesus, operates in the occult.

DUNGEONS & DRAGONS: Fantasy game fought in the minds of the players. Teaches demonology, witchcraft, voodoo, murder, rape, blasphemy, suicide, assassination, insanity, sex perversion, homosexuality, Satan worship, barbarianism, cannibalism, sadism, demon summoning, necromancy and divination. Human sacrifice. Some game!!

RAINBOW BRITE AND SPRITES: Sprites are listed in the advanced D & D Monster Manual. New Age Movement uses rainbow symbol with the star. SHE-RA: Princess of power, magic power, female defender of the universe. RA is the name of Egyptian sun god. PEGASUS: Flying horse from D & D monster manual. New Age Movement uses it for astral flight/meditation.

UNICORNS: D & D Monster Manual; Medieval kings and popes used amulet made from horn; believed to have magical and healing powers. CARE BEARS: (Not Really???) Wear charms (amulets) to keep away evil spirits (occult symbols). Rabbit foot, rainbow with star (New Age symbol) horseshoe, four leaf clover. Latest character, wizard. HERSELF THE ELF: Elves are inferior spirit beings with great powers supposedly. Magical flowers.

MAGIC KIT: It's magic, spirit slate with mystery computer. Teaches how to become a magician. CABBAGE PATCH DOLLS: Creates soul tie with child; mockery of life and death, and natural emotions. CABBAGE PATCH PLAYMATES - (to promote illegitimacy) - Amulets Koosas - mysterious cuddly creature which brings good luck - adoptable - you name them. PUNK ROCK DOLL: Name and adopt, same as above.

GREMLINS: Violent, sadistic; use transformation (New Age concept), Cannibalism, and promotional scheme. From English word germane to vex. Kill and viciously attack people. CROSSBOWS & CATAPULTS: Designed from **Dark Ages**; Vikings vs. Barbarians, very violent. Fantasy. SWORD & SORCERY BATTLE GEAR: Fantasy, sorcery, occult, violence. G.I. JOE: Now adding occult characters to their ranks of regular army characters.

STARRIORS: Warrior robots kill for control of earth using chain saws, buzz saw, drills, spiked ream, vibrator chisel. SECRET WARS: Fight aliens with secret messages (occult); the 'Force', wild mutants and hideous creature transformation. OTHER WORLD: Similar to D & D. Violence with warlords, demons, dragons. BLACK STAR: Warlock with alien demon; similar to D & D. BLACKSTONE: Teaches magic.

MASTERS OF THE UNIVERSE: Evil lords of destruction, beast man, evil ocean warlord - sorcery. Trying to take the place of Jesus as protector of His creation. TRANSFORMER: New Age concept. The deceptive leader promotes peace through tyranny. Links up to Black Hole. Occult practice can change body into another form. SNAKE MOUNTAIN: Player becomes the snake and works the demon's jaws as he speaks. Experiment with demon power. ROBO FORCE: Evil Robot Empire, very violent, **He has killer instinct and a crusher hand**. Dictator and destroyer. GO BOTS: Alien robots? Transformation into vehicles. Confuse good and evil.

BOARD GAMES: These games open children to the influence of occult power, wizardry, violence, mind control and witchcraft: Thundar-Barbarian, Pandemonium, Magic 8 Ball, Monster Mansion, Krull (occult with sorcerer), Herself the Elf, Gremlins, Dragon Master, Mythical Cards, Dungeon, Ouija, Dark Towers, Magical Crystals, Dragon Lords, Towers of Night, Forest of Doom, Fires of Shadarr, Star Wars and Yoda, Fantasy Card Game, Hell Pits of Night-Fang, Rune Quest, Chivalry, Sorcery and Arduin-Grimoire.

SUMMARY OF TOYS

II Timothy 4:4 - **In the last days they will not endure sound DOCTRINE. They shall turn away their ears from hearing the truth; they shall turn unto FABLES and MYTHS!** Webster's Dictionary defines FABLES: fictitious narrative, legendary story of supernatural happenings, a narrative story in which animals SPEAK AND ACT LIKE HUMAN BEINGS. Beware Christian, these are the END TIMES!

THE CURSE OF THE BASTARD

A person begotten out of wedlock shall not enter into the assembly of the Lord; even until his tenth generation shall his descendants not enter into the congregation of the Lord (Deut. 23:2). This is the reason why bastards have so much trouble with their church relationships; they are cursed.

SINS OF THE ANCESTORS

Law Of Generations

Two genealogical studies prepared for non-religious purposes will clearly prove the law of generations: The Kallikak Family by H.H. Goddark, Macmillian Company and **A Study Of The Relation Of Crime, Pauperism, Disease, And Heredity In The 1900's by R.L. Ragsdale, G.P. Putnam and Sons** - Father, Martin Sr., origin was good English blood/middle class with both parents feeble-minded; from him came 41 matings, 222 feeble-minded children, and ONLY 2 normal children.

The Kallikak Family

First family has an honorable marriage; from it came 496 descendants, ALL NORMAL, 3 listed as degenerates, 2 alcoholics, and 1 sexually loose. All the legitimate children married into **better families** in their state and became: colonial governors, doctors, lawyers, judges, educators, traders, landowners, and respectable citizens. Among them was found: no feeble-mindedness, no illegitimate children, no immoral women, no epilepsy, no criminals, and no keepers of houses of prostitution. Of the 496 descendants, only 15 children died in infancy, 1 case of insanity (religious mania), 2 victims of habitual drunkenness, and 1 sexually loose.

At the close of the War of Independence, the father, Martin, Sr., went to a pub to celebrate the end of the war. There in an inebriated state he intercoursed a woman who was **loose and feeble-minded**. An illegitimate son, Martin, Jr., was born. Of that son, Martin, Jr., there were 480 descendants. Only 46 were found to be normal, 36 were illegitimate, 33 sexually immoral, 24 confirmed alcoholics, 3 epileptics, 82 died in infancy, 3 criminals, and 8 keepers of houses of **ill fame**. Of this large group some 1146 offspring were birthed; there were 262 feeble-minded, 197 considered normal, and 581 undetermined.

The Jukes Family

Father, Max, was a hunter, fisher, hard drinker, jolly and compassionate, adverse to steady work, and became blind (probably due to syphilis). Origin was middle class Dutch.

Of those 1200 descendants there were 280 paupers, 140 criminals, 250 arrests and trials, 140 years of imprisonment, 60 habitual thieves, 7 murderers, 50 common prostitutes, 40 syphilitic women, 400 men contracted syphilis, 40 wives contaminated, 440 total contaminated by syphilis, 300 children died prematurely, and 50 illegitimate births. In 75 years the family of 1200 members cost the state $1,308,000.00 in costs. Now let's study the influence of the sins from generation to generation:

First Generation: Max, blindness, probably due to the syphilis.
Second Generation: Effie, no information.
Third Generation: Name not recorded; harlot; married her cousin; not industrious.

Fourth Generation: 4 MALES -- illegitimate son; at 30 on relief; went to prison; able bodied, full health -- in poor house. ANOTHER SON -- at 22 on relief; at 44 breach of peace; jail at 49; in poor house rest of life. ANOTHER SON -- in poor house at 23 and remained there rest of life. ANOTHER SON -- at 24 on relief, assault and battery at 33, habitual drunk. DAUGHTER -- harlot, poor house at 23, kept brothel, contracted epilepsy, married second cousin. DAUGHTER -- harlot, birthed illegitimate son, a licentious vagrant, married second cousin. **NOTE:** In this generation all offsprings show profound stress with characteristics of the father.
Fifth Generation: 7 MALES, 10 FEMALES: MALE -- Laborer, syphilis, jail numerous times, petit liar, assault and battery, poor house most of life. MALE -- cohabited, killed at war. MALE -- at 21 on relief, jail vagrant, soldier in rebellion. MALE -- bricklayer, at 19 on relief, jail, married cousin. MALE -- at 7 in poor house, was abandoned. MALE -- soldier in rebellion, incurable syphilis. MALE -- not industrious, temperate. FEMALE -- harlot, illegitimate child. FEMALE -- harlot at 21. FEMALE -- deserted at 13. FEMALE -- deserted at 11, dead at 14. FEMALE -- deserted at 9. FEMALE -- harlot, incurable syphilis. FEMALE -- reputable character, **NOTE:** This is a female child given up for adoption. FEMALE -- died at young age. FEMALE -- harlot. FEMALE -- harlot, not industrious.
Sixth Generation: Nine Males; Fourteen Females: MALE -- on relief. MALE -- attempted rape, dangerous man, unmarried. MALE -- deserted at 8. MALE -- incurable syphilis, assault and battery, jail. MALE -- intemperate, lazy. MALE -- industrious, soldier at 21, good reputation, **NOTE:** a child deserted who was adopted . MALE - dwarf, double jointed. MALE -- intemperate, married cousin. FEMALE -- harlot. FEMALE -- reputable. **NOTE:** one of the children deserted then adopted. FEMALE -- died of syphilis. FEMALE -- harlot, could not read or write. FEMALE -- incurable syphilis, died of same. FEMALE -- harlot, incurable syphilis, incurable drunk, kept brothel. FEMALE -- incurable syphilis, harlot. FEMALE -- harlot incurable syphilis, lazy, kept brothel. FEMALE -- harlot, incurable syphilis, vagrant. FEMALE -- good reputation, **NOTE:** a child deserted, later adopted. FEMALE -- blind, on relief at 27 for rest of life. FEMALE -- harlot, relief at age 31.

Growth Of Sins

Note the profound growth of the sins of the forefathers as each generation progressed. You can see how it affected the 1200 descendents to the sixth generation.

The ONLY descendants listed as reputable and good citizens were three females and one male and they were among those children deserted who later were adopted into reputable families.

GENERAL LIST OF DEMONS TO CAST OUT

A good general list of demons to cast out of children is the **Schizophrenia-Paranoid Hands** list of demon families found on Pages 126 and 127, Chapter 21, Schizophrenia, **Pigs in the Parlor**. It can be used for mass or individual deliverance. Start with **Rejection**, then **Root of Bitterness**, then **Rebellion** families. After going through basic deliverance, **the three R's**, then start to cast out the other demon families (Schizophrenia-Paranoia).

Find out the child's problems **by talking to the parents (and the child if possible)**. After doing deliverance in paragraph above, then work on specific demon families identified for the individual. You can also use the previously listed names of demonic toys, movies, games and music as the names of demons in deliverance. **Very simply, there is a name of a demon for every evil practice that is contrary to the Holy Bible!**

MASS MINISTRY TO CHILDREN

1. Start with prayer. Use the **Short Prayer** and then **Moody's Prayers** on page twelve of **HOW TO DO DELIVERANCE.**
2. Break the curses on parents and children. Use **Curses on Children** in this lesson or **Prayer Against Biblical Curses** on page ten of **HOW TO DO DELIVERANCE.**
3. Break the soul ties on parents and children. Use **Prayer Against Soul Ties** on page ten of **HOW TO DO DELIVERANCE.**
4. Cast out the demons. Use list of demons as follows or as the Lord directs.
5. Start with **Basic Deliverance** on page nineteen of **HOW TO DO DELIVERANCE.**
6. Use **Schizophrenia and Paranoia** on page forty six of **LISTS OF DEMONS.**
7. Use **Abused Children** on page one of **LISTS OF DEMONS.**
8. Use **Children Drug Addicts** on page eight of **LISTS OF DEMONS.**
9. Use **Sexual Sin and Diseases** on page fifty of **LISTS OF DEMONS.**
10. Use **Common Demon Groupings** on page eleven of **LISTS OF DEMONS.**

REFERENCES

PIGS IN THE PARLOR by Frank Hammond
DEMOLISHING THE HOSTS OF HELL by Win Worley
A STUDY OF THE RELATION OF CRIME, PAUPERISM, DISEASE, AND HEREDITY IN THE 1900's by R.L. Ragsdale, G.P. Putnam and Sons
Tracts on demonic toys, movies, games and music written by Shirley Smith, 9700 Highway 107, Sherwood, Arkansas 72116

SECTION 14 - HOW TO DO DELIVERANCE PORTION

TABLE OF CONTENTS

PREFACE

General

The only way for deliverance to spread around the world is for many people to begin to practice deliverance. I encourage you to take the **Deliverance Manual**, begin to practice deliverance and to help others as you grow stronger. **God told us to help train an army to minister deliverance.**

Mass deliverance is simply deliverance for everyone that can hear your voice. You can use this lesson for your family or church. Normally we only work on one area of a person's life in a meeting and do not try to cover all areas at the same time.

There is nothing mysterious about deliverance; any Christian can cast out demons. As a teacher, I show you how to practice what I teach. The Bible is worthless unless you put it into practice.

Types Of Deliverance

Individual: This is a personal ministry to an individual - a one on one confrontation with the forces of evil. It is the most successful but the most time consuming. You can get very personal about a person's sins and deal with these sins in a Godly manner. An effective individual deliverance can easily take hours or days depending on the time available. If you are willing to take the time with people, you will see God do signs, wonders and miracles in their lives. The Bible says that the casting out of a demon is a miracle.

Small Group: this is a relatively personal ministry to a small group of people such as husband and wife, parents and children, concerned person bringing another for deliverance or small group sitting in a circle.

Large Group: this is a mass ministry to a large group of people such as a prayer group, church, camp or any other type of large audience. There is no limit to the number of people you can cast demons out of at the same time by the hearing of your voice.

Encouragement

Deliverance is the last battleground to freedom of the Christian. **The battle is the greatest and Satan will fight the hardest against this ministry.** You are fighting God's battles; you are cursed if you are unwilling to fight.

The benefits far outweigh having to go through the battle. **You will learn things about the spiritual world that can not be learned in any way other than being involved in deliverance. You will see many signs, wonders and miracles performed by God.** You will see peoples lives changed before your eyes and dramatically changed for the better. You will help your family as you are helping others; the fringe benefits are great!

Healing and deliverance go hand-in-hand. Many can not get healed without deliverance. **You will see many healings and miraculous healings by the Lord through praying for healing and casting out of demons of infirmities.**

Reason For Learning

The main reason we are teaching you how to do basic deliverance is that every Christian should be able to cast out demons at least in their own family. Later on God may lead you to have deliverance services in your prayer group or church. God told us to train an army for His use; you are part of that army!

Deliverance will assist in establishing family order and God's order. Every Christian should cast out demons. There are not many deliverance ministers to help people. Christians have many demons; proper deliverance takes a lot of time. Deliverance is a way of life; not a grand event.

Parents are the best persons to minister to their children; husband to wife and wife to husband. Parents need to protect their children and set the family free from demons.

Deliverance gives an understanding of God's and Satan's kingdoms that you will not get any other way. Deliverance allows you to see into the spiritual world by the manifestations of demons and angels.

Get involved! Study to show yourself approved by God. Seek God about deliverance. **Deliverance is a constant learning process.** Satan has spent thousands of years weaving a very complicated system to trap you and take you to Hell or cause you to live a miserable Christian life here on earth.

Deliverance Manuals

We have written nine different deliverance manuals in thirty-two years. The original **Deliverance Manual** took twenty years to write; a productive year of my life and a productive year of Earline's life. The other notebook manuals have been written since Earline went to be with The Lord. Given another thirty-two years, nine more manuals could be written. Satan has spent six thousand years in planning how to destroy the human race. We only have a short lifetime in learning how to combat the staggering amount of evil that we face.

Six Basic Steps To Your Deliverance

1. Identify your problems.
2. Forgive, pray and get yourself right with God.
3. Break the curses and soul ties on you and your descendents.
4. Cast out your demons.
5. Pray for healing of your soul and body.
6. Discipline your life by changing your way of thinking and acting.

These six steps would also apply to any person that you are ministering to. **It is easy to cast out demons but hard to discipline your life.**

LOOKING AT DELIVERANCE

Summary

1. Take the abundant life by force from Satan.
2. Forcefully drive out demons.
3. Hate sin and everything that God hates; hate Satan, demons and evil.

Take Heaven By Force

We forcefully drive demons out of Christians but we do not rail at demons.

Cursing Demons And Infirmities

The Psalms contain imprecations upon enemies and transgressors.

BASIC DELIVERANCE

Reason For Learning - The main reason we are teaching you how to do basic deliverance is that every Christian should be able to cast out demons at least in their own family.

General

1. Basic Deliverance consists of setting a person free from three common demon families: Rejection, Bitterness and Rebellion.

2. Typically a person becomes rejected, then becomes bitter and finally rebels (then come other problems).

3. The most important key in setting a person free from these families is to get the person to forgive anyone that has hurt him!

4. First, unforgiveness should be dealt with before the families of Rejection, Bitterness and Rebellion are cast out.

5. After basic deliverance, then other demon families can be attacked. For example, Cancer and Arthritis can come into a person thru the open door of bitterness. After basic deliverance, cast out the spirits of Cancer and Arthritis.

6. A person may have become demonized while in the womb by **sins of the ancestors** for causes other than rejection, bitterness and rebellion. If so, another approach is required.

7. The most important key in setting a person free from the sins of the ancestors is to get the person to **forgive his ancestors**, and ask God to forgive them and bless them if they are alive (parents are also ancestors).

8. After forgiveness for any hurt or sin, then any demonic ties should be broken. For example, curses of the ancestors passed down thru the generations, or soul ties caused by sexual sin or witchcraft control are demonic ties.

9. After **breaking curses and soul ties**, we ask God to restore the fragmented soul - mind, will and emotions. We ask God to send out angels to restore anything that the demons have stolen.

10. After **restoration of the fragmented soul**, we ask God to stir up the demons in the subconscious mind so that they can be identified and cast out.

11. The person can then be led in a general prayer of **salvation / deliverance** to God. There are many good prayers.

12. The leader should then pray and take authority over the demonic spirit world and ask God for help.

13. After the grounds for deliverance are established (taking away the legal rights before God for the demons to stay), then start casting out demons.

14. Use all the **weapons of the warfare in the Bible** against the demons. These include reading Scripture to the demons, exercising the Gifts of the Holy Spirit, causing the demons to reveal information against themselves, seeking discernment from God thru the Holy Spirit, praying to God in other tongues, asking Jesus for help, and any other methods that are helpful in gathering data, taking away legal rights and casting out. By all means, do what God tells you to do even if you do not understand it.

15. **Unforgiveness** - get the person to forgive others by an act of his will which God will honor. It may be very difficult for the person but God accepts their willingness to forgive.

16. **Unforgiveness** - Cancer or Arthritis can come into the person through the open door of unforgiveness which is bitterness.

17. Before any deliverance starts, a person should be given an opportunity to discuss his problems and background so that you can get to know the person spiritually and properly minister to him.

18. After deliverance is ended, a person should be counseled about how to walk out his deliverance and discipline his life.

19. It is good if teaching on basic deliverance or sins of ancestors precedes the deliverance.

20. After deliverance, anoint with oil and pray for any healing needed or for scars in the body where the demons left (inner healing).

CHILDREN'S DELIVERANCE

Summary

1. Sit together as families during deliverance. A husband has power and authority over his family that even we don't have as deliverance ministers.
2. The Book of Proverbs was a special comfort to me after Byron died because we had disciplined him; he was a well-behaved son.
3. God is ultimate truth and there is no fantasy in God or in His Word. Fantasy causes most of our young people's problems: drugs, drink, sex, etc.
4. God taught us to tell the truth in love; we practice tough love!
5. Pray and ask the Holy Spirit to show you what dolls to throw away; be cautious about any doll.
6. Playing card games can become addictive.
7. We have taught small children to cast out demons; the demons hate to obey children! Children in the First Grade were taught to war in the spirit.
8. Demons can be cast out of the fetus in the womb.
9. It is fun to cast demons out of babies - watch demons manifest and watch them leave.
10. Don't be fooled or become sympathetic to the demons!
11. Speak quietly and softly; this infuriates the demons! Know your authority over the forces of evil.
12. Very few parents do their job properly.
13. We have not seen any parents that have protected their children completely or properly; we didn't.
14. Notice that deliverance prayers are establishing the basis for casting out the demons.
15. Adults have to overcome false religious teaching, ignorance of the Bible and fear of deliverance.
16. We will not minister to the children without the parents present.
17. The parents should be active in the deliverance of their children in church and at home.
18. In general, Full Gospel Christians are very demonized, not demon possessed, but simply have many demons!
19. The lie about Santa Claus caused our daughter to doubt that her parents would tell her the truth. All **lies** come from the Devil.

General

Husbands are often the most effective in commanding spirits to leave their wives, with the support of others. **Children must be disciplined by their parents**. Parents many times prepare the way for deep-seated spirits of **Fear**, **Rejection** and **Conditional Love** to enter. Indwelling demons can be present because of **inheritance, curses, habitual sin, or legal holds or grounds from other sources**.

Scripture warns us to have nothing to do with fairy tales, fables, enchantments, charmers or such like: fables turn one from truth and importance of truth. Children at a susceptible age may well be opened up to spirits of **Fear, Error, Perversity, Lying and Fantasy. The truth is important to God** and many, ignorantly, cause children to believe a lie in the guise of a friendly, jolly, phoney, called **Santa Claus.**

The encyclopedia says that the origin of dolls is witchcraft and magic.

The inventor of the first deck of cards evidently hated God and the Bible, and designed a message in the cards which was the exact opposite of the truth of Scripture. **Witches, psychics and Satan worshippers use playing cards for divination, and to cast spells and curses.**

By initiating young, interested believers into the battle for deliverance, they soon become seasoned soldiers, learning tactics of war on the battlefield.

Ministry To Children

Demon spirits are able to gain entrance to a fetus and to children.

Ordinarily, children are quite easily delivered.

Most children by the age of five or six can be given a simple explanation of what you are going to do before you begin the ministry.

In ministry with children, it is well to remember the fact that it is not the loudness of a command that moves the demon but the authority of the name and of the blood of the Lord Jesus Christ.

It is the responsibility of parents to be the spiritual guardians of their children.

Once one is alerted to the dangers of passing on weaknesses, infirmities and other unpleasant things to siblings, the parent should begin breaking curses, destroying legal holds and grounds, and binding any inherited spirits.

When a child is brought to us for prayer, we ask that the parents accompany them, especially the father, since he has the most spiritual authority.

Children seldom want problem-causing things and usually readily consent to prayer.

In practically every case this combined assault with the parents will rout the demons.

MASS DELIVERANCE

Summary

1. Pray out loud one or more deliverance prayers selected for the meeting or appropriate for the teaching preceding deliverance.
2. Prayer Against Biblical Curses
3. Prayer Against Soul Ties
4. Prayer Against Occult and False Religions
5. Prayer Against Cursed Objects and Demon Infestation
6. Prayer to Loose Godly Spirits
7. One or all of the above prayers can be used in a mass deliverance meeting. Once the prayers have been prayed, call out the demons associated with the lists under each prayer.

How To Get Delivered

Relax and cooperate with the deliverance minister and workers.

Demonic Areas To Cover

It is not be possible to cover all areas of deliverance in one meeting.

Choose the prayer or prayers that are appropriate for the teaching or meeting.

Failure to hearken unto the voice of the Lord God, to observe to do all His commandments and His statutes; then all these curses shall come upon thee, and overtake thee. This verse says it all!

DELIVERANCE PRAYERS

Summary

1. Pray out loud for the most power in the spiritual world.
2. If you are working in personal deliverance, get the individual to pray about their specific problems and sins.
3. If you are working in mass deliverance, lead the group in praying form prayers.

General

There are **many good deliverance prayers** that have been written and printed in books and in loose-leaf form.

The **ideal prayer** is the one prayed by the individual to cover the specific area of that person's life that is being ministered to at that time.

BIBLICAL CURSES

Summary

1. God cursed the earth when Adam and Eve fell.
2. Biblical Curses apply to those or their descendents who have committed these sins.
3. Curses on Children can be used when specifically working with children.
4. Hex Signs and all associated with these symbols are demonic.

Blessings, Curses And Duration

Actually there are curses on the human race that go all the way back to Adam and Eve.

Very simply, we are **blessed for obeying** the Word of God and **cursed for disobeying** the Word of God.

God will supply all of your needs: **mental, physical, spiritual and material.** He can become your **Savior, Baptizer, Healer, Deliverer and Prosperer.** These things will only come to pass if you follow the Bible - **for every promise there is a condition.**

AIDS TO CASTING OUT DEMONS

Summary

Practice systematic mass and individual deliverance: basic then advanced. Work on one or more areas in mass or individual deliverance. **You can not cast out all of the demons at one time; Christians are very demonized!**

Pray deliverance prayers - break Biblical curses and soul ties - renounce occult and false religions - loose Godly Spirits - destroy or exorcise cursed objects - make positive confessions in Christ - read deliverance Scripture.

If the demon does not leave, find out what its legal right is. Get the person to forgive, repent or renounce. Ask God what it is, force the demon to tell you and/or ask the person what sin they or their ancestors committed to get them in that trouble.

Statements

Make positive confessions to God and to each other about living our life for Christ.

If The Demons Do Not Leave

No demon can resist the name of Jesus or disobey the Word of God when they are being used properly in deliverance. If this happens, then they have a **legal right before God to remain.**

You must **search out this legal right and remove it.** The most common ground is **unforgiveness.** Other common grounds are **sins of ancestors, anyone who had spiritual authority over that person,** and the **personal sins of that person.**

CASTING OUT DEMONS

Summary

1. Cast out demons associated with Basic Deliverance and then Advanced Deliverance found in the **Deliverance Manual**.
2. Cast out demons that the Holy Spirit, or patient and workers tell you about.

Basic Deliverance

Start with casting out families of demons that comprise basic deliverance: Rejection, Bitterness and Rebellion in that order.

Advanced Deliverance

After basic deliverance, go on to other demonic families.

Led By Holy Spirit

Be sensitive to the Holy Spirit and let Him lead you in the names and sequence of calling out demons!

DELIVERANCE SCRIPTURE

Summary

1. Read Scripture about deliverance out loud to the spiritual world.
2. Mark and/or underline the deliverance scriptures in your Bible for reference.
3. Memorize your favorite fighting verses to quote to the enemy.
4. Read Cleaning Your House verses found in the **Deliverance Manual** when exorcising a building.

Reading Scripture To Demons

It is very handy to have your Bible scriptures about deliverance underlined and marked with a "D" **so that you can read them** to loosen the hold of the demons when they are hard to cast out. It is even better to **memorize effective scripture verses** in fighting through to victory.

IDENTIFY GODLY / UNGODLY SPIRITS

Summary

1. **Discerning of Spirits,** Word of Knowledge and Word of Wisdom: three gifts of the Holy Spirit.
2. Names claimed by demons which describe their work: such as anger - to make angry.
3. Counterfeiting and imitating spirits of God (spirit of divination for Word of Knowledge).
4. Synonyms for evil spirits (Roget's Thesaurus).
5. Personality of demon (soul - mind, will and emotions); just like you are except it does not have a physical body.
6. Cause demons to manifest and identify their names and characteristics (spiritual warfare).
7. Detection by common symptoms or problems: emotional, mental, speech, sex, addictions, physical and religious (false religions, Christian cults, occult, spiritism, false doctrine).
8. The Bible contains many names of demons and angels.
9. Dictionaries, encyclopedias and medical books are a good source of names of demons.
10. Study false religions, carnal worldly practices, and effects of drugs, sex and power to identify demonic practices.

General

We **bind** the spirits (demons) of Satan and **loose** the spirits (angels) of God. **We cast the demons out of people, and God directs the angels to minister to our needs.**

Dictionary Of Classical Mythology

"A knowledge of the classics and an acquaintance with the **imaginary characters, places, and incidents of ancient mythology** which have been such an inspiring influence to writers of all ages adds greatly to ones enjoyment of literature, art and conversation. It is important, therefore, to present in dictionary form **the story of gods, goddesses, heroes, and heroines of the old Grecian and Roman literature.** It will lead to a better understanding of the countless references which are made from time to time in the literature of the day to classic subjects. It is a great wonderland of posy and romance, and forms a realm all its own, **the realm of antiquity's gods and demons and of prehistoric heroes.**"

It is talking about gods, goddesses and demons. **There is a demon behind every god and goddess worshiped by man!**

Idols Worshipped By Countries

The names of idols are the same as names of demons.

Taber's Cyclopedic Medical Dictionary

The following is Taber's definition of **multiple sclerosis:** "A chronic, slowly progressive disease of the **central nervous** system characterized by development of disseminated demyelinated glial patches called **plaques.** Symptoms and signs are numerous, but in later stages those of Charcot's triad (**nystagmus, scanning speech, and intention tremor**) are common. Occurs in the form of many clinical syndromes, the most common being the **cerebral, brain stem-cerebellar, and spinal.**

Characteristics of the disease tell you the symptoms of the disease and where it is located in the body. Demons will answer to their medical names, common names, symptoms or names they are given in the spiritual world.

Neurotic And Abnormal Personalities
(Psychoneurosis, Psychoneurotic And Psychopsychosis)

A study of psychology and psychiatry can be very helpful in deliverance.

Phobias

210 phobias are fears.

Using A Thesaurus In Deliverance

Because demons tend to <u>cluster</u> in family groupings, the thesaurus can be an amazingly helpful instrument to identify demons within a specific category.

The first false religion in the Bible can be traced back to **Nimrod, his wife, Semiramus, and her bastard child, Tammuz.** The Catholic religion is for those **who want to be religious.** The Masonic religion is for those **who want business success.** The Occult religion is for those **who want power, sex and drugs.**

NAMES OF DEMONS
Summary

1. The different names and lists of demons seems endless.
2. There is a name of a demon for any practice that is contrary to the Bible.
3. There is a name of a demon for any idol that is worshipped by man.
4. Choose the List of Demons in the **Deliverance Manual** that pertains to the area of ministry such as to children.
5. Common Demon Groupings in **Pigs In The Parlor** are families of demons that are commonly found. It is a good all around list to use.

CURSED OBJECTS
Summary

1. Be led by the Holy Spirit. Search your home and possessions for cursed objects; destroy the objects.
2. You can't destroy someone else's possessions. Anoint with oil and exorcise the object.
3. Follow the **Five Steps to Cleaning House**.
4. If you know of demonic prayers against your family, break the curses.
5. There is more power to speaking out loud than reading or praying silently.
6. Read Scripture for **Cleaning Your House** out loud in your home during the exorcism.

General

If you have a cursed object, you become cursed by God! Remove cursed objects from your being and from your home. Destroy by breaking, burning or at least throw them in the trash can.

Do not keep the cursed silver or gold of the object. If the cursed object belongs to someone else, anoint with oil and cast the demons out of it. Anoint your house with oil and drive out evil spirits from your house and possessions.

To Exorcise Inanimate Objects

In the case of objects dedicated to demons (such as idols and artifacts), the best course of action is to destroy them.

We suggest that two believers go on a mission such as this with Bible in hand.

Verbally denounce Satan, his power and demon hosts. Claim authority as a believer-priest using the name of Jesus Christ and the authority of His shed Blood.

Anoint the door lintel and window sills with olive oil.

Five Steps To Cleaning Your House

1. Five-way prayer of forgiveness - **you forgive your ancestors, descendants and others**; ask God to forgive and bless them. **Ask God to forgive you. You forgive yourself for sins against your body.** Ask forgiveness for spiritual adultery.
2. Break curses and soul ties from others and to others. Break curses of psychic prayers.
3. Remove objects from house or exorcise objects.
4. Anoint house with oil and drive evil spirits out.
5. Cast demons out of people that came in thru objects.

LEARN ABOUT DELIVERANCE

Summary

1. Get involved!
2. Study to show yourself approved by God.
3. Seek God about deliverance.
4. **Deliverance is a constant learning process.** Satan has spent six thousand years developing a very complicated system take you to Hell or cause you to live a miserable Christian life here on earth.

General

1. Get Experience - start casting out demons and get involved.
2. Study Bible - use a concordance and study Gospels mainly but do not neglect the rest of The Bible.
3. Fast and pray - seek the Lord about your problems.
4. Study deliverance books - learn as much as you can.
5. Study books on the mind, will and emotions.
6. Go to deliverance meetings - participate in teaching and ministry: mass, small groups and individuals.
7. Study Satan from a Christian viewpoint to see how he is trying to destroy you, your family and your church.
8. Emphasize practical methods - put the Bible to work.
9. Clean out your house - get rid of demonic objects.
10. Be persistent - keep after the demons in an area of your life until you are successful.

11. Learn to research a subject - use encyclopedias, dictionaries, medical and psychiatric books.
12. Learn the three phases of deliverance:
   1. How to Determine the Need for Deliverance
   2. How go Get Delivered
   3. How to Stay Delivered

PRACTICAL DELIVERANCE BOOKS

Summary

1. Study books and apply principles: Basic such as **Pigs In The Parlor**, Advanced such as eleven books written by Win Worley, and Mind such as **War On The Saints** (Unabridged Edition).
2. The seven deliverance manuals by Gene and Earline Moody are practical how-to-do-it books. The original manual is four books in one: **Basic Deliverance, Advanced Deliverance, Mass Deliverance** and **How To Do Deliverance**.

HOW NOT TO DO DELIVERANCE

Some Advice

For the person who wants God to use him or her for deliverance work among those oppressed by evil spirits, here is some advice:
1. The person ministering in the area of deliverance is in a position of all-out warfare with the forces of evil. Many have fallen by the wayside because of ignorance of Bible and deliverance, still having many demons within themselves, women and men ministering to the opposite sex by themselves, being lured by false doctrines, etc.
2. Demons can be very stubborn and highly seductive. Demons do not easily come out when they have a right before God to stay due to unconfessed sin, curses, soul ties, etc. They can lure the man or woman who is alone into a sex trap destroying the ministry, their family and others who are following that leader.
3. Effective weapons used against ministers are carelessness, pride, immorality, taking God for granted, spiritual weakness, and affliction of wife or husband where the minister refuses to yield to God.
4. Deliverance ministers should train their families and involve them in deliverance work. **Husband and wife should minister together as a team if feasible; this is a strong team.**
5. Unforgiveness is the biggest hindrance to answered prayer and to casting out demons. Unforgiveness between husband and wife is especially a hindrance.

Overall View Of Deliverance

Deliverance consists of about three equal parts: teaching, casting out and counseling.

Comments - Single men and women must be very careful in ministering deliverance. Satan wants to destroy your ministry by the appearance of sexual sin or by falling into that trap.

Deliverance Myths

There is much ignorance and many myths about deliverance. Unless the Church gets involved on a regular basis with deliverance, many Christians will continue to be defeated by Satan.

Battle Myths

There are many myths about Christian warfare. Satan is a worthy Adversary at what he does. He works twenty-four hours a day to destroy us. He will probably take about 98% of the world population and 75% of the church population to Hell with him. Because strait is the gate, and narrow is the way, which leadeth unto life, and few there be that find it.

The Woman Question

What should a woman do to protect herself in spiritual warfare?

Comments - Common teaching is that a Christian can not have a demon. Churches need demonstrations to show the manifestations to the congregations. It will be very difficult for a woman who has an unsaved husband to be effective in deliverance. They are not in agreement, woman is weaker vessel, she must go by herself, etc. A woman is much more effective when she is married and her husband is a believer who practices deliverance. Transference of spirits can not occur unless there is a crack in your armor.

Loudness Of Voice

Many people feel that if you shout or scream at demons that they will come out sooner. The contrary is true.

The formula for casting out demons is **And these signs** (signs, wonders and miracles) **shall follow them that believe** (Christians that believe the Bible)**; In my name** (Jesus Christ) **shall they cast out** (command out) **devils; they shall speak with new tongues.**

Laying Hands On Others

This is an area that is dangerous and caution must be exercised because of the potential harm to individuals and God's Kingdom. A good verse to ponder is **Lay hands suddenly on no man, neither be partaker of other men's sins: keep thyself pure.**

Comments - Some women want to be lord over the men in deliverance; they feel justified even if they are wrong. Men and women should not be in competition. Some deliverance does more harm than good if not done properly such as pulling out a person's eye to get rid of the demon. Their doctrine should be sound and according to the Bible.

Traveling Ministries

Suppose that a man or woman travels alone in the ministry. What are the pitfalls?

Private Ministry

A man should not minister to a woman alone and a woman should not minister to a man alone.

Comments - Pastors can lay hands on men or women improperly and open themselves up to demon attack. Women should lay hands on women and men on men in places where it would be inappropriate for the opposite sex to place their hands. One problem area is that women want to be counseled privately by their male pastor. A lot of mischief can happen behind closed doors leading to sex even in the church.

Deliverance Is Not A Parlor Game!

Deliverance is not a plaything to make the meeting interesting.

Deliverance Is Not A Grand Event!

Deliverance is a way of life probably until we die and God takes over our training.

You Can't Keep Your Cursed Objects And Stay Free!

If you persist in keeping your cursed objects, then you are cursed and the demons have a right to attack you, your family and what you have.

Fallen Deliverance Ministers

It is amazing to see the casualties among deliverance ministers.

Comments - When praying for someone in a group, the group needs to yield to the person that God has given the authority and discernment. Follow their leadership. Share a Word of Knowledge with the leader. There needs to be discipline and not confusion. Everybody does not have to call the demon out. You do not need crying, loudness, wildness, shouting and disorder. The group needs to pray, agree, give support and have unity. The Holy Spirit needs to be followed so that God's battle for the individual can be won. The leader should not fall for trying to take God's glory.

Difficulty In Driving Demons Out

Some demons come out easily and some demons take hours to drive out.

Agreement Between Husband And Wife

When husband and wife agree, there is great power before God.

Comments - Inner healing, visualization and related methods are excuses for not doing deliverance. It is necessary to cast out demons. If you only teach deliverance or only cast out demons or only counsel about deliverance, you will fail. To succeed, you must do all of these things. A lot of Christians quit along the way such as after salvation, baptism, healing; you need to follow through to freedom. Teach deliverance - minister by casting out - counsel afterwards.

Three-Fold Deliverance

The three arms of deliverance are teaching, ministering and counseling.

Comments - Christians have many demons including those in the five-fold ministry. It is fantasy to believe that all it takes is one session of deliverance for life. Demons are very common are there are multiplied billions; everyone can have their share. We cast about 10,000 demons out of one Christian man over a period of about a year. This helped show us how demonized Christians were.

SECTION 15 - HOW TO DO DELIVERANCE SUMMARY
ATTACK - ATTACK - ATTACK

CONTENTS

- 1. **SUMMARY**
- 2. **GENERAL**
- 3. **SHORT PRAYER**
- 4. **MOODYS' PRAYERS**
  - 1. **Sins of Ancestors, Curses, Soul Ties, Fragmented Soul and Subconscious Mind**
  - 2. **Taking Spiritual Authority Over The Meeting**
- 5. **MEDIUM PRAYER**
- 6. **LONG PRAYER**
  - 1. **Forgiveness**
  - 2. **General Confession**
  - 3. **Pride, Ego and Vanity**
  - 4. **Come to Jesus, The Deliverer**
  - 5. **Prince's Blood of Jesus**
  - 6. **Church's Command**
  - 7. **Restoring the Soul**
  - 8. **Warfare**
  - 9. **Soul Ties**
- 7. **REFERENCES**

7. BIBLICAL CURSES

- 1. **SUMMARY**
- 2. **BLESSINGS, CURSES AND DURATION**
- 3. **BIBLICAL CURSES**
- 4. **CURSES ON CHILDREN**
- 5. **SYMBOLS OF HEX SIGNS**
- 6. **REFERENCE**

8. AIDS TO CASTING OUT DEMONS

- 1. **SUMMARY**
- 2. **STATEMENTS**
- 3. **IF THE DEMONS DO NOT LEAVE**

9. CASTING OUT DEMONS

- 1. **SUMMARY**
- 2. **BASIC DELIVERANCE**
- 3. **ADVANCED DELIVERANCE**
- 4. **SPECIAL DELIVERANCE**
- 5. **LED BY HOLY SPIRIT**

10. DELIVERANCE SCRIPTURE

- 1. **SUMMARY**
- 2. **GENERAL**
- 3. **OLD TESTAMENT**
- 4. **NEW TESTAMENT**
- 5. **READING SCRIPTURE TO DEMONS**
  - 1. **General Verses for Spiritual Warfare**
  - 2. **Verses to Use Against the Ruler Demons**
- 6. **CLEANING YOUR HOUSE**
- 7. **REFERENCE**

11. HOW TO IDENTIFY GODLY AND UNGODLY SPIRITS

PREFACE

General

The only way for deliverance to spread around the world is for many people to begin to practice deliverance. I encourage you to take this guide, begin to practice deliverance and to help others as you grow stronger. **God told us to help train an army to minister deliverance.**

Mass deliverance is simply deliverance for everyone that can hear your voice. You can use this lesson for your family or church. Normally we only work on one area of people's lives in a meeting and do not try to cover all areas at the same time.

There is nothing mysterious about deliverance; any Christian can cast out demons. As a teacher, I am worthless if I can not show you how to practice what I teach. The Bible is also worthless to you unless you put it into practice.

TYPES OF DELIVERANCE

Individual

This is a personal ministry to an individual -a one on one confrontation with the forces of evil. It is the most successful but the most time consuming. You can get very personal about a person's sins and deal with these sins in a Godly manner. An effective individual deliverance can easily take three hours or more. If you are willing to take the time with people, you will see many signs, wonders and miracles take place in their lives.

Small Group

This is a relatively personal ministry to a small group of people such as husband and wife, parents and children, concerned person bringing another for deliverance or small group sitting in a circle.

Large Group

This is a mass ministry to a large group of people such as a prayer group, church, camp or any other type of large audience. There is no limit to the number of people you can cast demons out of at the same time by the hearing of your voice. Remember that the Bible says that the casting out of a demon is a miracle.

ENCOURAGEMENT

Deliverance is the last battleground to complete freedom of the Christian. **The battle is the greatest and Satan will fight the hardest against this ministry.** You are fighting God's battles; you are cursed if you are unwilling to fight.

The benefits far outweigh having to go through the battle. You will learn things about the spiritual world that can not be learned in any way other than being involved in deliverance. **You will see many signs, wonders and miracles performed by God.** You will see people's lives changed before your eyes and dramatically changed for the better. You will help your family as you are helping others; the fringe benefits are great!

Healing and deliverance go hand-in-hand. Many can not get healed without deliverance. **You will see many healings and miraculous healings by the Lord through praying for healing and casting out of demons of infirmities.**

SIX BASIC STEPS TO YOUR DELIVERANCE

1. Identify your problems.
2. Forgive, pray and get yourself right with God.
3. Break the curses and soul ties on you and your descendents.
4. Cast out your demons.
5. Pray for healing of your soul and body.
6. Discipline your life by changing your way of thinking and acting.

These six steps would also apply to any person that you are ministering to. **It is easy to cast out demons but hard to discipline your life.**

LOOKING AT DELIVERANCE

Summary

1. Take the abundant life by force from Satan.
2. Forcefully drive out demons.
3. Hate sin and everything that God hates; hate Satan, demons and evil.

TAKE HEAVEN BY FORCE

We are not **wrestling** against the Father, Son and Holy Spirit, but against Satan and his forces of evil. God has given us the abundant life but we have to take it by **force** from Satan! This is analogous to Israel; God gave them the promised land and then told them to take it by force (Eph. 6:12).

Two verses clearly illustrate this Bible principle: **Matt. 11:12,** Kingdom of heaven suffereth **violence** and the violent take it by **force** (abode of God is to be seized and the forces seized it). **Luke 16:16,** Kingdom of God is preached, and every man **presseth** into it (rule of Supreme Deity is preached and every man **forces** into it).

Some other good **fighting** verses are:

Psalm 57:6 They have digged a pit before me.
Isa. 54:17 No weapon formed against thee shall prosper.
Matt. 15:21-28 The woman fought for deliverance for her child!
II Cor. 10:3-6 Weapons of our warfare.
Eph. 6:10-18 Put on the whole armour of God.
Rev. 12:11 And they overcame him.

HOW TO TREAT DEMONS

Matt. 9:33Cast - to eject, drive out, pluck (dumb demoniac).
Matt. 9:34Casteth - thrust out, expel (dumb demoniac).
Matt. 17:18Rebuked - censure, admonish, tax upon (epileptic).
Mark 1:34Suffered - to send forth (sick or possessed with demons).
Luke 11:14Casting - put out, send away (demon that was dumb.)
Eph. 4:27Place - location, condition (Give no opportunity to the Devil.)
James 4:7Resist - oppose, withstand (Resist the Devil.)
II Pet. 2:11Railing - blasphemer, slanderous, profane, wicked (judgement).
I John 3:8Destroy - loosen, break up, put off (Destroy works of Devil.)
Jude 9Railing - vilification, evil speaking (reviling judgement).

As you can see from the above scripture, we forcefully drive demons out of Christians but we do not rail at demons. Luke 9:1 says we have **power and authority** (mastery, superhuman force, violence, control) and Luke 10:7 says the demons are **subject** (subordinate, obey) to Christians.

CURSING DEMONS AND INFIRMITIES

The Psalms contain imprecations (call down curses and evil) upon enemies and transgressors. For a good study, see **Strong's** or **Young's** Concordance for **curse, cursed, curses, cursest, curseth, cursing, accursed and cursedst**. The following verses describe the meaning of cursing:
Gen. 9:24-27Execrate - to abhor, loathe, detest (cursed younger son.)
Num. 22:6 & 23:8Blaspheme - perforate, bitterly curse (King of Moab asked Balaam, prophet, to curse Israel.)
Deut. 11:26-28; 27:15-26; 28:15-68 Blessing and curse, curses and more curses.
Judges 5:23Execrate - (Curse bitterly its inhabitants.)
II Sam. 16:10-12Vilification - revile, slander (curse David).
II Kings 2:23-25Despise - speak evil of (Cursed them in the name of the Lord.)
Job 3:1-10Contempt - vile (Cursed the day of his birth.)
Mark 11:21Doom - execrate, imprecate (fig tree which you cursed.)
Gal. 1:8-9Anathema - solemn curse, excommunicated (Let him be accursed.)

BASIC DELIVERANCE - FOR LEARNING

The main reason we are teaching you how to do deliverance is that every Christian should be able to cast out demons at least in their own family. Later on God may lead you to have deliverance services in your home or church. Every Christian is a minister, has a ministry, and has gifts given by The Holy Spirit. **God told us to train an army for His use; you are part of that army!**

The bottom line of deliverance is the casting out of demons. Deliverance will assist in establishing family order and God's order. Every Christian should cast out demons (**Mark 16:17**). There are not many **Deliverance Ministers** to help people. Christians have many demons; proper deliverance takes a lot of time. Deliverance is a way of life and not a grand event.

Parents are the best people to minister to their children; husband to wife and wife to husband. Parents need to set the family free from demons and protect their children.

Deliverance gives an understanding of God's and Satan's kingdoms that you will not get any other way. Deliverance allows you to see into the spiritual world by the manifestations of demons.

GENERAL

1. **Basic Deliverance consists of setting a person free from three common demon families: Rejection, Bitterness and Rebellion (also common to Schizophrenia).**
2. Typically a person becomes rejected, then becomes bitter and finally rebels (then come other problems).
3. The most important key in setting a person free from these families is to get the person to forgive anyone that has hurt him!
4. First, unforgiveness should be dealt with before the families of Rejection, Bitterness and Rebellion are cast out.
5. After basic deliverance, then other demon families can be attacked. For example, Cancer and Arthritis can come into a person thru the open door of bitterness. After basic deliverance, cast out the spirits of Cancer and Arthritis.
6. A person may have become demonized while in the womb by **sins of the ancestors** for causes other than rejection, bitterness and rebellion. If so, another approach is required.
7. Again, the most important key in setting a person free from the sins of the ancestors is to get the person to **forgive his ancestors**, and ask God to forgive and bless them if they are alive (parents are also ancestors).
8. After forgiveness for any hurt or sin, then any demonic ties should be broken. For example, curses of the ancestors passed down thru the generations, or soul ties caused by sexual sin or witchcraft control are demonic ties.
9. After **breaking curses and soul ties,** we ask God to restore the fragmented soul - mind, will and emotions. We ask God to send out angels to restore anything that the demons have stolen.
10. After **restoration of the fragmented soul**, we ask God to stir up the demons in the subconscious mind so that they can be identified and cast out.
11. The person can then be led in a general prayer of **salvation and deliverance** to God. There are many good prayers.
12. The leader should then pray and take authority over the demonic spirit world and ask God for help.
13. After the grounds for deliverance are established (taking away the legal rights before God for the demons to stay), then start casting out demons.
14. Use all the **weapons of the warfare in the Bible** against the demons. These include reading Scripture to the demons, exercising the Gifts of the Holy Spirit, causing the demons to reveal information against themselves, seeking discernment from God thru the Holy Spirit, praying to God in other tongues, asking Jesus for help, and any other methods that are helpful in gathering

data, taking away legal rights and casting out. By all means, do what God tells you to do even if you do not understand it.

15. **Unforgiveness** - get the person to forgive others by an act of his will which God will honor. It may be very difficult for the person but God accepts their willingness to forgive.

16. **Unforgiveness** - Cancer or Arthritis can come into the person later on.

17. Before any deliverance starts, a person should be given an opportunity to discuss his problems and background so that you can get to know the person and properly minister to him.

18. After deliverance is ended, a person should be counseled about how to walk out his deliverance and discipline his life.

19. It is good if teaching on basic deliverance or sins of ancestors precedes the deliverance.

20. After counseling, anoint with oil and pray for any healing needed or for scars in the body where the demons left (inner healing).

STEPS TO MINISTER DELIVERANCE

Initial Steps For An Individual

1. Find out about the person's problems and background.
2. Some discussion about how they got into trouble will be helpful.
3. Get the person to forgive others and lead them in a specific prayer about their problems.
4. Lead the person thru a prayer to break curses and soul ties, restore the fragmented soul, stir up the demons in the sub-conscious mind, and finally salvation and deliverance (Moodys' Prayers).

Steps For Basic Deliverance For Ministry To An Individual

1. Cast out the families of Rejection, then Bitterness and finally Rebellion.

Steps For Sins Of Ancestors For Ministry To An Individual

1. Start with basic deliverance of Rejection, Bitterness and Rebellion. Then go into other areas that have been identified and legal grounds established for casting out demons.

Steps For Basic Deliverance, Sins Of Ancestors or Other Topic for the Home Meeting

1. Teach on Basic Deliverance, Sins of Ancestors, or any other deliverance topic.
2. Take a refreshment and bathroom break of about 15 minutes.
3. Get each person to forgive others and lead them in a specific prayer about their problems.
4. Lead the group in a mass prayer about that topic, and include curses, soul ties, fragmented soul, subconscious mind, unforgiveness and salvation (Moodys' Prayers).
5. The leader will then pray and take authority over the demonic spiritual world, and ask God to send his forces and take charge of the deliverance.
6. Start the mass deliverance with basic deliverance and then go to any other topic.

Steps for Basic Deliverance, Sins of Ancestors or Other Topic for a Group

1. Teach on Basic Deliverance, Sins of Ancestors, or any other deliverance topic.
2. Lead the congregation in a mass prayer about that topic, and include curses, soul ties, fragmented soul, subconscious mind, unforgiveness and salvation (Moodys' Prayers).
3. The leader will then pray and take authority over the demonic spiritual world, and ask God to send his forces and take charge of the deliverance.
4. Start the mass deliverance with basic deliverance and then go to any other topic.

Final Steps

1. During mass deliverance, workers shall help individuals having trouble getting free.
2. After mass deliverance, work with individuals.
3. Counsel the person about how to walk out their deliverance and how to discipline their life.
4. Anoint with oil and pray for healing.

Variations

1. The above steps could be used over the phone, in the home, in a church service, at the altar, in the prayer room or wherever the opportunity presents itself in public or private.
2. The above procedures can be varied to fit the situation or at the direction of the Holy Spirit.

CHILDREN'S DELIVERANCE - SUMMARY OF COMMENTS

1. Sit together as families during deliverance. A husband has special power and authority over his family that even we don't have as deliverance ministers.
2. The Book of Proverbs was a special comfort to me after Byron died because we had disciplined him; he was a well-behaved son.
3. God is ultimate truth and there is no fantasy in God or in His Word. Fantasy causes most of our young people's problems: drugs, drink, sex, etc.
4. God taught us to tell the truth in love; we practice tough love!
5. Pray and ask the Holy Spirit to show you what dolls to throw away; be cautious about any doll.
6. Playing card games can become addictive.
7. We have taught small children to cast out demons; the demons hate to have to obey children! Children in the First Grade were taught to war in the spirit.
8. Demons can also be cast out of the fetus in the womb.
9. It is fun to cast demons out of babies - watch demons manifest and watch them leave.
10. Don't be fooled or become sympathetic to the demons!
11. Speak quietly and softly; this infuriates the demons! Know your authority over the forces of evil.
12. Very few parents do their job properly.
13. We have not seen any parents that have protected their children completely or properly; we didn't.
14. Notice that the deliverance prayers are establishing the basis for casting out the demons.
15. Adults have to overcome false religious teaching, ignorance of the Bible and fear of deliverance.
16. We will not minister to the children without the parents present.
17. The parents should enter into the deliverance of their children in church and at home.
18. Full Gospel Christians are in general very demonized, not demon possessed, but simply have many demons!
19. The lie about Santa Claus caused our daughter to doubt that her parents would tell her the truth. All **lies** come from the Devil (John 8:44).

GENERAL DELIVERANCE OF CHILDREN (EXCERPTS)

Husbands are often the most effective in commanding spirits to leave their wives, with the support of others. This is true with his children also. (Sit together as families during deliverance.

Children must be disciplined by their parents (Proverbs 13:23). The prayerful and judicious application of the rod can act as a deterrent to childish and foolish behavior (Proverbs 22:15). Parents many times prepare the way for deep-seated spirits of **Fear, Rejection and Conditional Love** to enter. God will turn the heart of the father (not the mothers) to the children (Malachi 4:6 and Col. 3:21). A child left to rear himself is a disaster going somewhere to happen (Proverbs 29:15). Indwelling demons can be present because of **inheritance, curses, habitual sin, or legal holds or grounds from other sources.**

The punishment should equal the offence. We provoke our children to wrath when we punish more severely than the offence justifies. The offence should be explained. Other ways to behave should be explored.

Then show love; give a hug, approval, compliment on good behavior or improvement of conduct. (The book of Proverbs was a special comfort to me after Byron died because we had disciplined him; he was a well-behaved son.)

Scripture warns us to have nothing to do with fairy tales, fables, enchantments, charmers or such like: Titus 1:14 (fables turn one from truth) and II Peter 1:16 (declares importance of truth). Children at a susceptible age may well be opened up to spirits of **Fear, Error, Perversity, Lying and Fantasy**. (God is ultimate truth and there is no fantasy in God or in His Word. Fantasy causes most of our young people's problems: drugs, drink, sex, etc.)

The truth is important to God and many, ignorantly, cause children to believe a lie in the guise of a friendly, jolly, phoney, called **Santa Claus. (This lie caused our daughter to doubt that her parents would tell her the truth. All lies come from the Devil, John 8:44. God taught us to tell the truth in love; we practice tough love!)**

The encyclopedia says that the origin of dolls is witchcraft and magic. Only witch doctors or medicine men were allowed to handle them. To this day, multitudes of idol (demon) worshippers use dolls in pagan religious ceremonies. Exodus 20:4 - No graven images and Jer. 48:10 - Lord places a curse on those that use deceit. (Pray and ask the Holy Spirit to show you what dolls to throw away; be cautious about any doll.)

The inventor of the first deck of cards evidently hated God and the Bible, and designed a message in the cards which was the exact opposite of the truth of Scripture. Jesus is supposed to be the joker. **Witches, psychics and Satan worshippers** use playing cards for **divination, and to cast spells and curses**. It is time that Christians clean house and destroy the hidden works of darkness (I John 2:15-17, Romans 12:1-2, II Cor. 6:17-18 and I Timothy 6:12). (Playing card games can become addictive.)

By initiating young, interested believers into the battle for deliverance, they soon become seasoned soldiers, learning tactics of war in the battlefield. (We have taught small children to cast out demons; the demons hate to have to obey children! First grade children were taught to war in the spirit.)

MINISTRY TO CHILDREN (EXCERPTS)

Since it has already been shown that demon spirits are able to gain entrance to a fetus and into children, it is obvious that there should be deliverance for them. Demons can be called out of children in the same way they are called out of adults. There will be manifestations of the spirits leaving through the mouth and nose as in other deliverances. (They can also be cast out of the fetus in the womb.)

Ordinarily, children are quite easily delivered. Since the spirits have not been there very long, they are not as deeply embedded in the flesh. There are exceptions to this, as in the case of children who have been exposed to demonic attack through severe circumstances. The manifestations of the demons can be quite dramatic, even in children. (It is fun to cast demons out of babies, watch demons manifest and watch them leave.)

A young Christian couple brought their three-month old child for ministry. This was their first baby and they had disagreed as to how to discipline the child. The father and mother had a violent argument over the matter. **While they were having this argument, the child began to scream, and since the incident it was apparent that the child was suffering from tormenting spirits**. My wife held the child in her arms and began to command the troubling spirits to go in the name of Jesus. As the first spirit came out, the baby stiffened and cried out. Two other demons came out in the same way. Then the child grew quiet and relaxed, and was soon asleep.

Most children by the age of five or six can be given a simple explanation of what you are going to do before you begin the ministry. They need to know that you are not talking to them but to the spirits in them, otherwise they may be offended or frightened by words of command addressed to the evil spirits. Usually the children are quite cooperative. Since the children may feel more secure with a parent, it is often best for the parent to hold the child during the ministry. The deliverance minister must discern reactions in the child attributable to the spirits being stirred up. The spirits may cause the child to resist being held. He may cry or scream and show signs of great fear. The demons may try various tactics to make one think it is the child being hurt or wronged. The minister and/or parent will then become so sympathetic with the child that they will stop the ministry and the demons retain their hold. (Don't be fooled or become sympathetic to the demons!)

Especially in ministry with children it is well to remember the fact that it is not the loudness of a command that moves the demon but the authority of the name and of the blood of the Lord Jesus Christ. The commands can be given with such calmness and matter-of-factualness that the child will scarcely realize what is taking place. (Speak quietly and softly; this infuriates the demons! Know your authority over the forces of evil.)

How do infants and children keep themselves free from the demons once they are delivered, since they are not competent to protect themselves? It is not the responsibility of the child but of his parents or guardians. I believe you will find in the Scripture that when Jesus ministered to children, one or both of the parents were present. **It is the responsibility of parents to be the spiritual guardians of their children**. (Very few parents do their job properly.)

CHILDREN AND DELIVERANCE (EXCERPTS)

Some people say that children do not need deliverance. I could not disagree more. Parents have a solemn responsibility to provide protection for their offspring in the matter of spiritual warfare. So many curses, legal holds, and other legal grounds can be inherited through the ignorance, curiosity, and/or willful disobedience of the parents. In addition, our society provides a climate for demon infestation. (We have not seen any parents that have protected their children completely or properly; we didn't.)

Once one is alerted to the dangers of passing on weaknesses, infirmities and other unpleasant things to siblings, he should begin breaking curses, destroying legal holds and grounds, and binding any inherited spirits. This is preparation for casting them out. The occult demons are tremendously powerful and tenacious, often staying in families for centuries. People afflicted with them are highly susceptible to psychic phenomena and influence. (Notice that the deliverance prayers are establishing the basis for casting out the demons.)

We have seen children (from babies to teens) receive significant deliverance in the church and at home. Parents are able to minister some of this to younger ones while the child is sleeping. There need be no fear created in the child about deliverance.

They will usually be able to handle the idea of casting out evil spirits better than many adults. (Adults have to overcome false religious teaching, ignorance of the Bible, and fear of deliverance.)

When a child is brought to us for prayer, we ask that one or both parents accompany them, preferably the father, since he has the most spiritual authority. Often I will talk briefly with the child, allaying any fears, with love for him. (We will not minister to the children without the parents present.)

Usually I ask if he sometimes does or says things he doesn't really want to do, things which get him into trouble. After an affirmative answer, I will mention that often ugly things called spirits get into a boy or girl and cause this sort of thing. I also talk with the child about asking the Lord Jesus to come into his heart (Revelation 3:20) if he has not already done so. I then ask if he would like for those things to come out of him if they are there. **Children seldom want problem-causing things and usually readily consent to prayer**.

I pray for them, quietly taking authority over the spirits and commanding them to manifest and leave. If they are stubborn and the father is present, I will have him take authority and guide him in what to pray. **In practically every case this combined assault will rout the demons**. (The parents should enter into the deliverance of their children in church and at home.)

If parents wait until the child is grown up before attempting deliverance, they will discover the enemy has wasted no time and has burrowed in deeply, often scarring body and mind. They will work tirelessly to put a child in bondage, drag him out into the world, and enslave him with many sinful habits. An ounce of prevention here is certainly worth the proverbial pound of cure. (Full Gospel Christians are in general very demonized, not demon possessed, but simply have many demons!)

REFERENCES

Pigs In The Parlor - Ministry to Children
Demolishing The Host Of Hell - Children & Deliverance

MASS DELIVERANCE - SUMMARY

1. Get the people to pray out loud one or more **Deliverance Prayers** selected for the meeting or appropriate for the teaching preceding deliverance.
2. **Prayer Against Biblical Curses**
3. **Prayer Against Soul Ties**
4. **Prayer Against Occult And False Religions**
5. **Prayer Against Cursed Objects And Demon Infestation**
6. **Prayer To Loose Godly Spirits**
7. One or all of the above prayers can be used in a mass deliverance meeting. Once the prayers have been prayed, call out the demons associated with the lists under each prayer.
8. Call out the list of demons associated with the teaching such as **Sexual Sin and Diseases**.

HOW TO GET DELIVERED

Relax and cooperate with the deliverance minister and workers. There is nothing to be afraid of. God never gives a spirit of fear; all fear is from Satan. We have not lost a deliveree in about twenty-five years of ministry.

Demons are like air. They are usually expelled by the exhaling of breath. This can be by yawning, coughing, deep breathing or gentle exhaling of breath. Demons can have nests in the body which have substance. They are usually expelled by blowing the nose or coughing up phlegm. Don't feel bad when this happens.

For instance, it is beautiful to see a cancer vomited out of a person during deliverance. I sat at his feet and watched Win Worley deliver a woman from cancer at Lake Hamilton Bible Camp. Paper towels and waste cans may be provided for this reason.

Demons can temporarily take over your body and manifest their characteristics. They can look through your eyes, cause the body to assume grotesque shapes, temporarily paralyze the body, throw the body on the floor and cause it to squirm around, and talk using your voice.

Deliverance is the casting out of demons from your body. Prayer is the infilling of the Holy Spirit. Leave the air passages open so that the spirits can leave.

Do not pray, pray in tongues or chant. Chanting is the repetition of a word or phrase such as saying Jesus repeatedly.

Decide that you want to get rid of the demons within your body. You no longer agree with them and they no longer will be your pets. **Exercise your mind and will to be delivered.** If the demons do not leave, command them, by name, to go; do this verbally, out loud, for more power.

Do not hold back or be embarrassed. As they come up and out of your chest, let them go even if you have to spit or whatever. It is all right even if they take over some part of your body. If you have too much pride to let the demons manifest to get delivered, you give the demons a right to stay. **God hates pride; it is an abomination to Him!**

Deliverance workers should move around quietly. Provide paper towels to those who need them. Lay hands on those who are having trouble, agree with them, and command the demons to come out.

Do not start a conversation with the person during mass deliverance. This interrupts the flow of the deliverance and you then have your own private meeting.

Deliverance is not prayer. You command the demons to go in The Name of Jesus Christ. He will not cast the demons out. He has given us that authority and He expects us to use it.

Babies and children generally get delivered easily. Babies can even get delivered in the womb. Women generally manifest more than men do. Women usually get into and out of spiritual trouble more quickly than men. Men generally get delivered by the simple exhaling of the breath. The more a person is in bondage, the greater the manifestations will be.

Deliverance is dynamic and exciting. It is wonderful to see people getting set free from demon bondage. Jesus Christ is glorified when Satan is defeated by Christians here on earth.

Families should sit together. Husbands are the most effective in casting demons out of their family because they are given spiritual authority over it.

It is not the loudness of a command that moves the demon but the authority of the name and blood of the Lord Jesus Christ. You must know your authority or the demons will recognize your weakness. By initiating young, interested believers into the battle for deliverance, they soon become seasoned soldiers, learning tactics on the battlefield.

DEMONIC AREAS TO COVER

It is not be possible to cover all areas of deliverance in one meeting. You may want to only cover one area at a meeting such as Sexual Sin and Diseases. Mass deliverance at some time should cover the following areas: deliverance prayers, Biblical curses, soul ties, occult and false religions, cursed objects and loosing Godly spirits.

DELIVERANCE PRAYERS

Deliverance Prayers are found in the next chapter. **Choose the prayer or prayers that are appropriate for the meeting.** These are prayers to use before starting to cast out demons.

PRAYER AGAINST BIBLICAL CURSES

I forgive my ancestors and anyone else that has cursed me. I ask that God forgive me and them. I break curses placed on me or my descendants from uttering a wish of evil against one; to imprecate evil, to call for mischief or injury to fall upon; to execrate, to bring evil upon or to; to blast, vex, harass or torment with great calamities. I break these curses in Jesus' name. I break the curses back to ten generations or even to Adam and Eve on both sides of my family, and destroy legal holds and legal grounds that demons have to work in my life. I break curses that follow in the name of the Lord Jesus Christ.

In the Name of Jesus Christ, I now rebuke, break, loose myself and my children from evil curses, charms, vexes, hexes, spells, jinxes, psychic powers, bewitchment, witchcraft and sorcery, that have been put upon me or my family line from persons or from occult or psychic sources, and I cancel connected or related spirits and command them to leave me. I thank you, Lord, for setting me free. **But it shall come to pass, if thou wilt not hearken unto the voice of the Lord thy God, to observe to do all His commandments and His statutes which I command thee this day; that all these curses shall come upon thee, and overtake thee.**

Mistreating God's Chosen People, Willing Deceivers, Adultery, Harlotry and Prostitution, Disobedience to Bible, Idolatry, Keeping Cursed Objects, Refusing To Fight For God, House of Wicked, Not Giving To Poor, Stealing, Swearing Falsely By God, Failing To Give Glory to God, Robbing God of Tithes, Dishonoring Parents, Hearkening to Wives Rather Than God, Making Graven Images, Cheating People Out of Property, Taking Advantage of Blind; Oppressing Strangers, Widows and Orphans; Bestiality, Incest With Sister or Mother, Murder Secretly or For Hire, Pride, Putting Trust In Man, Doing The Work of God Deceitfully, Rewarding Evil For Good, Abortion or Causing Unborn To Die, Having Bastards, Murdering Indirectly, Striking Parents, Kidnapping, Cursing Parents, Not Preventing Death, Sacrificing to Gods, Witchcraft, Turning Someone Away From God, Following Horoscopes, Rebelling Against Pastors, Losing Virginity Before Marriage, False Prophets, Rape, Not Disciplining Children, Teaching Rebellion Against God, Cursing Rulers, Refusing To Warn Sinners, Defiling The Sabbath, Sacrificing Humans, Seances and Fortune Telling, Intercourse During Menstruation, Homosexuals and Lesbians, Necromancers, Blaspheming Lord's Name, Being Carnally Minded, Oral and Anal Sex, Children Rebelling, Nonproductivity, Fugitive and Vagabond, Improper Family Structure, Destruction of Family Priesthood, Refusing To Do The Word of God, Family Disorder, Failure and Poverty, Any Sin Worthy of Death, Touching God's Anointed, Perversion of Gospel, Loving Cursing, Choosing That Which God Delights Not In, Looking To World For Help, Stubbornness and Rebellion, Offending Children Believing Christ, Adding To or Taking Away From Bible, **and all Biblical Curses not listed Above.**

PRAYER AGAINST SOUL TIES

Father, I break and renounce evil soul ties that I have had or may have had with lodges, adulterers, close friends, husbands, wives, engagements, cults and binding agreements between buddies.

Forgive me for developing soul ties with anyone. I forgive those who would control me. I renounce these evil soul ties, break them and wash them away with the shed blood of the Lord Jesus Christ. I break evil soul ties with the following:

1. Beasts
2. Anyone I Have Had Sex With Outside of Marriage
3. Divorced Mates
4. By Incest, Rape, Fornication, Adultery, Homosexuality, Bestiality, Lesbianism
5. Bloodless Religions, Religious Cults
6. Blood Brothers and Sisters By Rites
7. Witchcraft, Occult, Satan Worship
8. Fortune Tellers, Mediums

9. Psychiatrists, Social Workers, Psychologists, Mental Institutions
10. Finally, I break any agreement with anyone that forms an evil soul tie.

PRAYER AGAINST OCCULT AND FALSE RELIGION

Lord, I now confess seeking from Satan the help that should only come from God. I now confess occultism and false religions as sin. Lord, I now repent and renounce these sins and ask you to forgive me. I renounce Satan and his works: I hate his demons; I count them my enemies. In the Name of Jesus Christ I now close the door on occult practices, and I command such spirits to leave me in the Name of Jesus Christ.

In the Name of Jesus Christ, I now renounce, break and loose myself and my children from psychic powers or bondages and bonds of physical or mental illness, upon me or my family line, as the results of parents or any other ancestors. I thank you Lord, for setting me free.

In the Name of Jesus Christ, I now renounce, break and loose myself from demonic subjection to my mother, father, grandparents, or any other human beings, living or dead, that have dominated me in any way, and I thank you, Lord, for setting me free.

I forgive my ancestors and ask that You would forgive me for participating in occult and false religion. I renounce all fortune telling, magic practices and spiritism, cults and false teachings, and Satan worship. I break every curse and soul tie brought about by psychic heredity, occult contacts and religious cults. I now break any demonic hold on my family line due to supernatural experiences apart from God including the following forbidden practices and all that they entail:

Enchantments, Wizardry, Necromancy, Witchcraft, Observer of Times, Fortune Telling, Consulting With Familiar Spirits, Occult Practices, Spiritism, Sorcery, Magic Practices, Son or Daughter Passing Through Fire, Divination, Charmers, False Religious Cults **and any other Occult or False Religious Practice.**

PRAYER AGAINST CURSED OBJECTS AND DEMON INFESTATION

Lord Jesus, I ask that you forgive me for having cursed objects in my home. Show me by the Holy Spirit what to destroy:

1. Books and objects identified with anything related to Satan's Kingdom.
2. Sinful activities of former residents that left curses.
3. Knocking or noisy ghosts and apparitions (poltergeist).
4. Owl and frog images of all types.
5. Witch's mask and fetishes used by witch doctors.
6. Objects and literature that pertain to false religions, cults, the occult and spiritism.
7. Graven images of gods (demons).
8. Objects dedicated to demons (idols and artifacts).
9. Ouija boards or other occult paraphernalia.
10. Prayers and worship to demons bring curses on home.
11. Mexican sun gods; idols, incense; Buddhas; hand carved objects from Africa or the Orient; anything connected with astrology, horoscopes, fortune telling, etc.; books or objects associated

with witchcraft, good luck charms or cult religions (Christian Science, Jehovah's Witnesses, metaphysics, etc.); rock and roll records and tapes.
12. Jewelry given to a person by someone in witchcraft, hex signs, ancient geometric and mystical motifs, jewelry designed to bring good luck and act as talisman to chase evil.
13. Egyptian ankh, Polynesian tikkis of gods, broken cross (peace symbol), chais, African jujus, Italian horn, protectors from the evil eye, hand with index and little fingers pointing up, crosses, clovers, stars, wishbones, lucky coins, mystic medals, horseshoes, religious fetishes and statues.
14. Products with cryptic curses (hidden, secret, occult curses).
15. Puppets, cult objects or representations. Dolls used for witchcraft and magic.

PRAYER TO LOOSE GODLY SPIRITS

Lord Jesus Christ, we ask that you direct the angels to minister to our needs. We loose warring angels, ministering angels, the Holy Spirit and the Seven-Fold Spirit of God. We loose legions of angels including the following Godly spirits:

Spirit of Wisdom, Poor in Spirit, Spirit of God, Spirit of Your Father, Spirit of the Lord, Strong in Spirit, Right Spirit, Spirit of Truth, Holy Spirit, Spirit of Life, Broken Spirit, Spirit of Adoption, Spirit of Princes, Fervent in Spirit, Faithful Spirit, Spirit of Meekness, Humble Spirit, Spirit of Faith, Excellent Spirit, Spirit of Jesus Christ, Spirit of Man, Eternal Spirit, Patient in Spirit, Meek and Quite Spirit, Spirit of the Ruler, Spirit of Glory, Spirit of Judgment, Spirit of Prophecy, Spirit of Understanding, Spirit of Elijah, Spirit of Counsel/Might, Contrite Spirit, Spirit of Knowledge, Good Spirit, New Spirit, Spirit of Deep Sleep, Spirit of Holy Gods, Spirit of Living Creature, Spirit of Grace and Supplication, Spirit of Holiness, Spirit of Christ, Spirit of Grace, Quickening Spirit, Free Spirit **and all other Godly Spirits.**

DELIVERANCE PRAYERS - SUMMARY

1. Pray out loud for the most power in the spiritual world.
2. If you are working in personal deliverance, get the individual to pray about their specific problems and sins.
3. If you are working in mass deliverance, lead the group in praying the form prayers.
4. A good selection of prayers to use in and meeting is the **Moodys' Prayers.**
5. You can choose to use the **Short Prayer**, **Medium Prayer** or **Long Prayer**, or the **Moodys' Prayers.**

GENERAL

There are many good deliverance prayers that have been written and printed in books and in loose-leaf form. Some of these prayers are general and some have been written for specific subjects.

The ideal prayer is the one prayed by the individual, being ministered to at that time, to cover the specific areas of that person's life that are in sin (personal deliverance). **The next best prayer** is the form prayer which the person or group repeats after the deliverance leader or reads from the printed prayer.

The following prayers have been used many times by us and others. They have produced good results. One side benefit is that the people can see what is wrong and evil in their lives by what is contained in the prayers. These prayers can be used for individuals, small groups or large groups equally well.

SHORT PRAYER

Lord Jesus Christ, I believe you died on the cross for my sins and rose again from the dead. You redeemed me by your blood and I belong to you, and I want to live for you. I confess all my sins, known and unknown, I'm sorry for them all. I renounce them all. I forgive all others as I want you to forgive me. **(Pause to allow forgiveness of others as The Holy Spirit leads.)** Forgive me now and cleanse me with your blood. I thank you for the blood of Jesus Christ which cleanses me now from all sin. And I come to you now as my deliverer. You know my special needs--the thing that binds, that torments, that defiles; that evil spirit, that unclean spirit. I claim the promise of your word, 'Whosoever that calleth on the name of the Lord shall be delivered.' I call upon you now. In the name of the Lord Jesus Christ, deliver me and set me free. Satan, I renounce you and all your works. I loose myself from you, in the Name of Jesus. I command you to leave me right now in Jesus' Name. Amen!

This is my favorite prayer because it is short and effective. The first part is **salvation** and the last part is **deliverance.** You can pause and let the people forgive others as the Holy Spirit leads them.

MOODYS' PRAYERS

Sins of Ancestors, Curses, Soul Ties, Fragmented Soul and Subconscious Mind

I forgive my ancestors **(upwards)**, descendants **(downwards)**, and anyone else **(outwards)** that has sinned against me or hurt me **(those outside of me)**. I ask you to forgive them for their many sins and mistakes. I remit their sins, sever demonic ties, and set myself free. **I ask God to bless them with spiritual blessings, bring them into truth, and meet their needs out of His Riches in Glory through Christ Jesus.** I ask that God will forgive me **(Godwards)** for my many sins, and I forgive myself **(inwards)** for sins against my body.

I now take authority over Satan and all the forces of evil according to the Holy Bible, the complete Word of God, and command that you obey it. **In the Name of Jesus Christ, I command these things to be done.**

I break curses, charms, spells, jinxes, psychic powers, hexes, vexes and demonic ties that bind. I break soul ties caused by witchcraft, sorcery, bewitchment or sexual sins. Lord Jesus, restore my fragmented soul: mind, will and emotions; send your angels out to recover anything that Satan has stolen from me. Lord Jesus, stir up the demons in my subconscious mind so that they can be identified and cast out. **I pray in the blessed name of Jesus Christ: My Lord, Master and Savior, and command the forces of evil to obey in the Name of Jesus Christ. Amen.**

Taking Spiritual Authority Over The Meeting

Satan, we come against powers, principalities, evil forces in this world and spiritual wickedness in high places. We come against demons inside or outside of anyone present, over this city, state, nation and world, in Hell or out of Hell. The Bible says, **Behold, I give unto you power to tread on serpents and scorpions, and over all the power of the enemy: and nothing shall by any means hurt you.** We intend to exercise that power to set ourselves free. Satan, we come against you by the power and blood of Jesus Christ, by the Word of God, by the name of Jesus, by the authority of the believer, in the unity of our spirits. Satan, we tell you that we sit in heavenly places with our Christ Jesus. We are over you, your fallen angels, your demons and forces of evil. We command you to line up in rank and file and order, and come out quickly. We bind the power that you have and loose ourselves from you in the name of Jesus.

Lord Jesus Christ, we ask that you would send the gifts of the Holy Spirit as needed to minister to the needs of the people and to accomplish what you want done here today. We are careful to give you the glory, honor, praise and credit for everything that is said or done. We ask these things in the blessed name of Jesus Christ, our Lord and Master and Savior. And we take authority over Satan according to the whole Word of God. For it's in Jesus name we pray. Amen!

MEDIUM PRAYER

Thank you, Lord, for dying for my sins, for your glorious resurrection, and for making me a new creature in Christ by faith in your precious blood. Dear Lord, I have a confession to make:

1. I have sought supernatural experience apart from you.
2. I have disobeyed your Word.
3. I want you to help me renounce these things and cleanse me in body, soul and spirit in Jesus' name.
4. I renounce witchcraft and magic, both black and white.
5. I renounce Ouija boards and other occult games.
6. I renounce séances, clairvoyance and mediums; ESP, second sight, and mind reading.
7. I renounce fortune telling, palm reading, tea-leaf reading, crystal balls, Tarot and other card laying.
8. I renounce astrology and interest in horoscopes.
9. I renounce the heresy of reincarnation and healing groups involved in metaphysics.
10. I renounce hypnosis under any excuse or authority.
11. I break curses placed on me from occult sources, in Jesus' name.
12. I renounce curiosity about either future or past, and which is outside Thy Will.
13. I renounce water witching or dowsing, levitation, body lifting, table tipping, psychometry and automatic writing.
14. I renounce astral projection and other demonic skills.
15. I renounce literature I have ever read in these fields and vow that I will destroy such books in my own possession.
16. I now break, in the name of Jesus Christ, psychic heredity, and demonic holds upon my family line as a result of the disobedience of any of my ancestors. I also break bonds of physical or mental illness, in Jesus' name.
17. I also break demonic subjection to my mother, father, grandparents or any other human being.
18. In the name of Jesus Christ I renounce the psychic and occult.
19. I renounce cults that deny the Blood of Christ.
20. I renounce philosophies that deny the Divinity of Christ.
21. I call upon the Lord to set me free.
22. Lord, I have another confession to make. I have not loved, but have resented certain people. I call upon you, Lord, to help me forgive them. I do now forgive (**Here we pause for several minutes while each person puts the names in the prayer which the Lord brings to mind, either of persons living or dead.)**
23. I do now forgive myself.
24. I renounce evil spirits that bind or torment me and I call upon the Lord to set me free.

LONG PRAYER

Forgiveness

Lord, I have a confession to make: I have not loved, but have resented certain people and have unforgiveness in my heart, and I call upon you, Lord, to help me forgive them. I do now forgive **(name them, both living and dead)** and ask you to forgive them also, Lord. I do now forgive and accept myself, in the name of Jesus Christ.

General Confession

Lord Jesus Christ, I believe that you are the Son of God, that you are the Messiah come in the flesh to destroy the works of the Devil. You died on the cross for my sins and rose again from the dead. I renounce unbelief and doubt as sin. I confess my sins and repent. I ask you to forgive me. I believe that your blood cleanses me from sin.

Pride, Ego And Vanity

Father, I come to you in the Name of Jesus Christ. **These six things doth the Lord hate: yea, seven are an abomination unto him: a proud look, a lying tongue, hands that shed innocent blood, a heart that deviseth wicked imaginations, feet that be swift in running to mischief, a false witness that speaketh lies, and he that soweth discord among brethren.** Father, I renounce these and turn away from them. I humble myself before you and come to you as a little child.

Come To Jesus, The Deliverer

I come to you, Jesus, as my Deliverer. You know my problems **(name them)**, the things that bind, that torment, that defile and harass me. I now loose myself from dark spirits, from evil influences, from satanic bondages and from spirits in me that are not the Spirit of God. I command such spirits to leave me now in the Name of Jesus Christ.

Prince's Blood Of Jesus

Through the Blood of the Lord Jesus Christ, I am redeemed out of the hand of the Devil. My sins are forgiven. I am justified, made righteous, just as if I'd never sinned. I am made holy, set apart to God. My body is a temple for the Holy Spirit, redeemed, cleansed, sanctified. **The Blood of Jesus Christ, God's Son,** cleanses me continually from sin. Therefore Satan has no part in me, no power over me. I renounce Satan, loose myself from him, command him to leave me, in the Name of the Lord Jesus Christ!

Church's Command

In the name of the Lord Jesus Christ, I command Satan and his demons to loose my mind. I ask you to send angels to break, cut and sever fetters, bands, ties and bonds, whether they be by word or deed. I ask you to loose the Seven-Fold Spirit of God: Spirit of the Lord, Fear of the Lord, Counsel, Might, Wisdom, Knowledge, and Understanding into me and my family.

Restoring The Soul

You can insert the name of the person or persons that you are praying for, rather than your name in the prayer:

Father, I come to you in the name of Jesus Christ. I ask you to send angels to gather and restore my soul to its rightful place in me. I ask for you to send your angels to unearth and break earthen vessels, bonds, bands and bindings that have been put upon my soul, willingly or unawares. I ask you to have them free my soul from bondage by whatever means is required. I agree and say Father, that the Lord Jesus Christ is powerful and effective to do this.

Father, I ask you to send your angels to gather and restore the pieces of my fragmented mind, will and emotions to their proper place. Bring them into their original positions perfectly as you planned them when you formed Adam and Eve in the Garden of Eden.

I have the power and authority of Jesus Christ that has been delegated to me. In the authority of Jesus Christ, I break, cast out and return to the sender, the power of curses upon my head and soul.

Warfare

Heavenly Father, I bow in worship and praise before you. I cover myself with the Blood of the Lord Jesus Christ as my protection. I surrender myself completely and unreservedly in every area of my life to you. I take a stand against the workings of Satan that would hinder me in my prayer life. I address myself only to the true and living God, and refuse involvement of Satan in my prayer. Satan, I command you, in the Name of the Lord Jesus Christ, to leave my presence with your demons. I bring the Blood of the Lord Jesus Christ between us. I resist the endeavors of Satan and his wicked spirits to rob me of the will of God. I choose to be transformed by the renewing of my mind. I pull down the strongholds of Satan.

Soul Ties

Father I break and renounce evil soul ties that I have had or may have had with (lodges, adulterers, close friends, husbands, wives, engagements, cults, binding agreements between buddies). I renounce these evil soul ties, break them and wash them away with the shed blood of the Lord Jesus Christ.

REFERENCES

Pigs In The Parlor - Short Prayer
Out In The Name Of Jesus - Medium Prayer
Hegewisch Baptist Church - Long Prayer

BIBLICAL CURSES
Summary

1. God cursed the earth when Adam and Eve fell.
2. **Biblical Curses** apply to those or their descendents who have committed these sins.
3. **Curses on Children** can be used when specifically working with children.
4. **Hex Signs** and all associated with these symbols are demonic.

Blessings, Curses And Duration

Exodus 20:1-5 Curse of idol worship extends to **fourth generation** of great grandchildren.
Deut. 23:2 Curse of the bastard extends to **tenth generation** of descendants.
Deut. Ch. 28 Blessings are for obeying and curses for disobeying the Holy Bible; **verses 1-14: blessings, 15-44: curses and 45-68: wrath of God**.

Exodus 20:1-5 & Ezekiel 18:1-9 God showed Earline that this was the curse of idol worship brought on her by her **Indian ancestors** which caused her and her family **heart trouble**. He also showed her how to break the curse.

Notice how a family can be cursed to the fourth or tenth generation by the ancestors. **Actually there are curses on the human race that go all the way back to Adam and Eve.** Blessings can go from generation to generation if not broken by sin. Curses can also go from generation to generation if not broken by prayer.

Very simply, we are **blessed for obeying** the Word of God and **cursed for disobeying** the Word of God. Blessings and curses are promises from God which will either bring His favor or down the wrath of God on your family .

God will supply your needs: **mental, physical, spiritual and material**. He can become your **Savior, Baptizer, Healer, Deliverer and Prosperer**. These things will only come to pass if you follow the Bible - **for every promise there is a condition**. If you do not meet the condition, you will not receive the promise!

There is probably a curse for every scripture that is disobeyed. Sixty-six curses are listed which follow:

Biblical Curses (Excerpts)

1. Those who curse/mistreat Jews (Deut. 27:26; Gen. 27:29; 12:3; Num. 24:9).
2. Those willing deceivers (Jos. 9:23, Jer. 48:10; Mal. 1:14; Gen. 27:12).
3. An adulterous woman (Numbers 5:27).
4. Disobedience of Lord's commandments (Deut. 11:28; Dan. 9:11; Jer. 11:3).
5. Idolatry (Jer. 44:8; Deut. 29:19; Ex. 20:5; Deut. 5:8-9).
6. Those who keep or own cursed objects (Deut. 7:25; Jos. 6:18).
7. Those who refuse to come to the Lord's help (Judges 5:23).
8. House of the wicked (Prov. 3:33).
9. He who gives not to the poor (Prov. 28:27).
10. The earth by reason of man's disobedience (Isa. 24:3-6).
11. Jerusalem is a curse to nations if Jews rebel against God (Jer. 26:6).
12. Thieves and those who swear falsely by the Lord's Name (Zech. 5:4).
13. Ministers who fail to give the glory to God (Mal. 2:2; Rev. 1:6).
14. Those who rob God of tithes and offerings (Mal. 3:9; Haggai 1:6-9).
15. Those who hearken unto their wives rather than God (Gen. 3:17).
16. Those who lightly esteem their parents (Deut. 27:16).
17. Those who make graven images (Deut. 5:8; 27:15, Ex. 20:4).
18. Those who willfully cheat people out of their property (Deut. 27:17).
19. Those who take advantage of the blind (Deut. 27:18).
20. Those oppressing strangers, widows, fatherless (Deut. 27:19; Ex. 22:22-24)
21. Him who lies with his father's wife (Deut. 27:20; Lev. 18:8).
22. Him who lies with his sister (Deut. 27:22).
23. Those who smite their neighbors secretly (Deut. 27:24).
24. Those who take money to slay the innocent (Deut. 27:24).

25. Him who lies with any beast (Deut. 27:21; Ex. 22:19).
26. Adulterers (Job 24:15-18).
27. The proud (Psalm 119:21).
28. Those who trust in man and not the Lord (Jer. 48:10).
29. Those who do the work of the Lord deceitfully (Jer. 48:10).
30. Him who keeps back his sword from blood (Jer. 48:10; I Kings 20:35-42).
31. Those who reward evil for good (Prov. 17:13).
32. Illegitimate children (Deut. 23:2).
33. Children born from incestuous unions (Gen. 19:36-38).
34. Murderers (Exodus 21:12).
35. To murder indirectly (Exodus 21:14).
36. Children who strike their parents (Exodus 21:15).
37. Kidnappers (Exodus 21:16; Deut. 24:7).
38. Those who curse their parents (Exodus 21:17).
39. Those who cause the unborn to die (Exodus 21:22-23).
40. Those who do not prevent death (Exodus 21:29).
41. Those involved in witchcraft (Exodus 22:18).
42. Those who sacrifice to false gods (Exodus 22:20).
43. Those who attempt to turn anyone away from the Lord (Deut. 13:6-9).
44. Those who follow horoscopes (Deut. 17:2-5).
45. Those who rebel against pastors (Deut. 17:12).
46. False prophets (Deut. 18:19-22).
47. Women who keep not their virginity until they are married (Deut. 22:13-21)
48. Adulterers (Deut. 22:22-27).
49. Parents who do not discipline their children, but honor them above God (I Sam. 2:17, 27-36).
50. Those who curse their rulers (I Kings 2:8-9; Ex. 22:28).
51. Those who teach rebellion against the Lord (Jer. 28:16-17).
52. Those who refuse to warn them that sin (Ezek. 3:18-21).
53. Those who defile the Sabbath (Ex. 31:14; Num. 15:32-36).
54. Those who sacrifice human beings (Lev. 20:2).
55. Participants in séances and fortune telling (Lev. 20:6).
56. Homosexual and lesbian relationships (Lev. 20:13).
57. Sexual intercourse during menstruation (Lev. 20:18).
58. Necromancers and fortune tellers (Lev. 20:27).
59. Those who blaspheme the Lord's name (Lev. 24:15-16).
60. Those who are carnally minded (Romans 8:6).
61. Sodomy (oral and anal sex) (Gen. 19:13, 24-25).
62. Rebellious children (Deut. 21:18-21).
63. Possibly from murder, nonproductivity, a fugitive, vagabond (Gen. 4:11; Matt. 5:21-22, Jesus' statement on hatred equals murder, John 3:15).
64. Possible curse upon improper family structure - destruction of family priesthood (Mal. 4:6) with special attention given to the relationship between father and children.
65. The curse causeless shall not come (Prov. 26:2).
66. Any sin worthy of death is also cursed by God (Deut. 21:22-23).

Curses On Children

1. Children born from incestuous unions (Gen. 19:36-38).

2. Curse of idol worship extends to **fourth generation** of great grandchildren (Exodus 20:1-5).
3. Children who strike their parents (Exodus 21:15).
4. Those who curse their parents (Exodus 21:17).
5. Iniquity of fathers on children (Exodus 34:6-7).
6. Children wandered for forty years (Numbers 14:18 & 33).
7. Idol worship (Deut. 5:9-10).
8. Rebellious children (Deut. 21:18-21).
9. Curse of the bastard extends to **tenth generation** of descendants (Deut. 23:2).
10. In son's days evil will come on his house (I Kings 21:19).
11. The iniquity of the father upon the children (Jer. 32:18).

Symbols Of Hex Signs (Excerpts)

Remove these symbols from your person and possessions:

1. Six Petal Rosette and Lucky Stars - these are your lucky stars.
2. The Irish Shamrock Hex - good luck, fast life, good fortune and fidelity.
3. Tulip - faith, hope and charity.
4. Unicorn - virtue and piety.
5. Fertility.
6. Twelve Petal Rosette - that each month of the year be joyous ones.
7. The Distelfink - the bird of happiness always near you and good fortune.
8. Your Lucky Stars - lucky stars that guide your heart.
9. Love and Romance - rosette and hearts of love and romance.
10. Eight Pointed Star - star and rosette to bring abundance and goodwill.
11. Friendship.
12. There is a symbol for each of the above listed hex signs.

REFERENCE

Annihilating The Host Of Hell! - Book 1 - Biblical Curses

AIDS TO CASTING OUT DEMONS

Summary

Practice systematic deliverance: basic then advanced then special deliverance - mass and individual deliverance. Work on one or more areas of a person's life at a time or in mass deliverance. **You can not cast out all of the demons at one time; Christians are very demonized!**

Pray deliverance prayers - break Biblical curses and soul ties - renounce occult and false religions - loose Godly Spirits - destroy or exorcise cursed objects - make positive confessions in Christ - read deliverance Scripture.

If the demons do not leave, find out what their legal right is and remove it. Ask God what it is, force the demon to tell you and/or ask the person what sin they or their ancestors committed to get them in that trouble.

Statements

Make positive confessions to God and to each other about living our life for Christ. Some of these types of statements follow:

1. We forgive everyone that has hurt or sinned against us, and we pray for our enemies.
2. We exercise honesty - humility - repentance - renunciation - forgiveness - prayer - warfare.
3. We seize the Kingdom of Heaven and take it by force from Satan.
4. We overcome Satan by the Blood of the Lamb, by our testimony for Jesus Christ, and **we love not our lives unto death.**
5. We send back every fiery dart and demon attack that has been sent against us. We give no opportunity to the Devil.
6. We cast out the demons and their works. We eject, drive out, pluck out, thrust out, expel, rebuke, censure, admonish, send away, put out, loosen holds, break up nests, and put off works of demons.
7. We have power, authority, mastery, superhuman force and control over all the works of the enemy; you must obey and subordinate yourselves to our commands.
8. We resist, despise, have contempt for, speak doom to, abhor, loathe, detest and hate sin and evil, Satan, fallen angels, demons and everything that God hates,
9. We break the power of cursed objects, hex signs, demonic toys and games, and objects infested by demons.
10. We put on the Whole Armor of God and cover ourselves with the Blood of Jesus Christ. **We accept Jesus Christ is our Lord, Master and Savior!**
11. We close doorways for Satan in the occult, addictions, sexual impurities, demonic healing, demonic religions, rock music, inheritances and any others known or unknown.

If The Demons Do Not Leave

No demon can resist the name of Jesus or disobey the Word of God when they are being used properly in deliverance. If this happens, then they have a **legal right before God to remain.**

You must **search out this legal right and remove it.** The person being ministered to must do their part! Generally, the right to remain has to do with what other people have done to that person or what that person has done to himself. The most common ground is **unforgiveness.** Other common grounds are **sins of ancestors or anyone who had authority over that person,** or the **personal sins of that person.**

CASTING OUT DEMONS

Summary

1. Cast out demons associated with **Basic Deliverance**, then **Advanced Deliverance** and then **Special Deliverance**.
2. Cast out demons that the Holy Spirit or the people tell you about.

Basic Deliverance

Start with casting out families of demons that comprise basic deliverance: Rejection, Bitterness and Rebellion in that order.

Rejection	**Bitterness**	**Rebellion**
Fear of Rejection	Resentment	Self-Will

Self-Rejection	Hatred Unforgiveness Violence Temper Anger Retaliation Murder	Stubbornness Disobedience Anti- Submissiveness

Advanced Deliverance

After basic deliverance, go on to other demonic families. The list of names of demons seems to be endless. There is a name of a demon for everything that is contrary to the Word of God. Call the demon out by his characteristic or personality. Demons will answer to their medical names, common names, spiritual names or physical symptoms.

Special Deliverance

Caution: The following list was made for those that have been involved in Satan worship. They are very demonized and will require personal deliverance as the demons may tear their bodies when coming out. **These demons are particularly associated with Satan worship:**

I now command controlling spirits to come out of me as follows:

Soul: Mind - Will - Emotions
Conscious - Subconscious - Unconscious
Body: Physical - Brain - Sexual Organs

I now command special demons to manifest and come out or leave as your name is called:

Wer Beasts: Vampires - Werewolves - Zombies
Manifestations: Changelings - Incubi/Succubi - Dopple Gangers
Objects: Familiar Objects - Fetish - Talisman - Amulets - Marks - Hagstones - Biofeedback
Curses: Spells - Incantations - Hexes - Vexes

I now command demons associated with the above practices to come out as well as the following demonic families:

Demons: Son of Satan, Mind Control, Death, Occult, Magic, Witchcraft, Drugs, Child Abuse, Fornication, Demonic Healing, Eastern Religions, Demonic Inheritance, Demonic Games, Rock Music, Voodoo, Familiar and Guiding Spirits, Forces and Powers

Led By Holy Spirit

Be sensitive to the Holy Spirit and let Him lead you in the names and sequence of calling out demons!

DELIVERANCE SCRIPTURE

Summary

1. Read **Deliverance Scripture** out loud to the spiritual world.
2. Mark and/or underline the Scriptures in your Bible for reference.

3. Memorize your favorite fighting verses to quote to the enemy.
4. Read **Cleaning Your House** verses when exorcising a house or building.

General

The following is a partial list of scripture about deliverance. Once you learn to recognize deliverance, you can find scripture throughout the Bible that tells about how demons work in people's lives and what God thinks about how we should handle deliverance.

Old Testament

Ex. 20:2-5; **Lev.** 20:6, 27; **Deut. 5:7-9;** 7:25-26; 18:9-14; **I Sam.** 15:23; 16:14-18, 23; **I Chron.** 21:1; **Job** 1:6-12; 2:4-7; 12:16; 30:3-8; **Psalms 18:2;** 149:5-9; **Isa.** 14:4-23; 58:6-7; 61:1-3; **Ezek.** 20:7, 30, 43; **Dan.** 10:12-13; **Joel 2:32**; **Zech.** 3:1-2

New Testament

Matt. 4:23-24; 5:23-24; 7:22-23; 8:16-17, 28-33; 10:1, 7-8; 12:22-29, 43-45; 15:22-28; 16:18-19; 17:14-21; 18:18-20; **28:18-20**; **Mark 1:23-27; 5:2-20; 7:25-30; 9:17-29;** 16:15-20; **Luke 4:33-36,** 38-41; 6:17-18; **8:26-39; 9:1-2;** 10:17-20; **11:14-26;** 13:11-16; **John 8:31-32,** 44; **14:12-14**; **Acts** 1:8; 5:3-4, 15-16; 8:5-7; 10:38; 19:11-19; **Rom.** 1:21-32; 16:20; **I Cor.** 5:4-5; **II Cor.** 10:3-6; 11:13-15; 12:7; **Gal.** 5:19-21; **Eph.** 1:19-23; 2:1-3; 3:10; 4:8-10, 26-27; 6:10-18; **Phil.** 1:28; 2:9-11; **Col.** 1:13-17; 2:15, 18-19; 3:5-8; **I Thes.** 2:18; **II Thes.** 2:7-12; **I Tim.** 1:18-20; 4:1-3; **II Tim.** 2:24-26; 3:1-6; **Heb.** 4:12; 12:14-16; **James** 1:5-8; 2:19; 3:14-16; 4:6-8; **I Pet.** 1:13-14; **I John** 3:8; 4:18; **Rev.** 12:7-11; 16:13-14; 20:1-3, 7-10.

Reading Scripture To Demons (Excerpts)

It is very handy to have your Bible scriptures about deliverance underlined and marked with a **D so that you can read them** to loosen the hold of the demons when they are hard to cast out. It is even better to **memorize effective scripture verses** in fighting through to victory.

General Verses for Spiritual Warfare

James 4:7	Prov. 18:10	II Cor. 10:3-5
Eph. 6:10-18	Rev. 12:11	I John 4:4-14
Luke 10:19	Mark 16:17	

Verses to Use Against the Ruler Demons

Hate

I John 4:16b, 19-21	I John 3:14	Psalm 60:4
Son of Sol. 2:4	Luke 10:27	Matt. 22:37-39
Prov. 10:12	I Thes. 4:8	Phil. 2:1-2
Eph. 3:16-19	I Cor. 13:4-8a	Gal. 5:22-23

Pride

Prov. 16:18-19	Prov. 3:34	Prov. 13:10
Prov. 16:16-17a	Prov. 14:3	Prov. 15:25
Prov. 16:5	Prov. 21:23-24	Prov. 28:9
Prov. 19:1, 23	II Tim. 3:1-2	Phil. 2:5-8
James 4:10	I Peter 5:6	

Self-Pity

Nehemiah 8:10	Phil. 3:4; 4:13	Psalm 33:1
Psalm 34:1-3	Psalm 50:23	Psalm 104:33-34
Phil. 4:11, 13, 19	I Tim. 6:6	I Thes. 5:18

Fear

Psalm 56:3	Psalm 46:1-2	Psalm 107:2
II Tim. 1:7	Is. 44:2b-3	I John 4:18
Heb. 13:6	Josh. 1:9	

Fear of Man

Prov. 29:25	Josh. 1:5	Josh. 10:8

Rebellion

Prov. 17:11	I Sam. 15:23	Jer. 28:16
Jer. 29:32	II Tim. 3:1-3	Eph. 5:21
Phil. 2:5-8	Phil. 2:14	I Thes. 5:18
Rom. 12:1-2	Rom. 13:1-2	

Lust

II Tim. 2:22	I Cor. 6:9-10	I Cor. 6:17-20
I Cor. 3:16-17	Eph. 5:3	Lev. 19:2
Heb. 12:14	I Peter 2:11	Isaiah 52:11
Matt. 5:8, 27-28	Heb. 13:4	Titus 1:15

Unbelief

Mark 11:23-24	Luke 1:45	John 8:31-32
John 7:38	John 6:29	Acts 27:25
Heb. 11:1	I Peter 1:6-7	Gal. 2:20
Mark 16:17-18		

Rejection

John 3:16	Eph. 1:4-6	Heb. 13:5b
I John 4:16, 19	I Thes. 3:12-13	I Thes. 5:15-18
Phil. 2:1-11	John 15:7-12	John 6:37
John 4:10	Psalm 23	Psalm 91:1-2
Psalm 55:22	Psalm 16:5-8	

CLEANING YOUR HOUSE

These are verses to read out loud while you exorcise your house of demons:

Num. 23:8, 23 Can only curse if God curses (notice that God curses.)
Deut. 21:23 Anyone hanged is accursed of God.
Deut. 32:5 Have corrupted themselves.
Josh. 6:18 Those who keep or own cursed objects (you are cursed.)
II Sam. 7:29 Blessing of the Lord.
Gal. 3:13 Christ has redeemed us from the curse (must be applied.)

Col. 2:14-15 Blotting out ordinances against us.
Rev. 12:11 Overcome by word of testimony.
Rev. 22:3 No more curse in Heaven.

REFERENCE

Out In The Name Of Jesus - Reading Scripture to Demons

HOW TO IDENTIFY GODLY AND UNGODLY SPIRITS
HOW TO RECOGNIZE EVIL SPIRITS (EXCERPTS)

1. **Discerning of Spirits,** Word of Knowledge and Word of Wisdom: three gifts of the Holy Spirit.
2. Names claimed by demons which describe their work: such as anger - to make angry.
3. Counterfeiting and imitating spirits of God (spirit of divination for Word of Knowledge).
4. Synonyms for evil spirits (Roget's Thesaurus).
5. Personality of demon (soul - mind, will and emotions); just like you are except it does not have a physical body.
6. Cause demons to manifest and identify their names and characteristics (spiritual warfare).
7. Detection by common symptoms or problems: emotional, mental, speech, sex, addictions, physical and religious (false religions, Christian cults, occult and spiritism, false doctrine).
8. The Bible contains many names of demons and angels.
9. Dictionaries, encyclopedias and medical books are good sources of names of demons.
10. Study false religions, carnal worldly practices, and effects of drugs, sex and power to identify demonic practices.

THE SPIRITS OF GOD AND SATAN (EXCERPTS)

1. **Beloved, believe not every spirit, but try the spirits whether they are of God** (I John 4:1).
2. We can bind and loose spirits.
3. Therefore, we are safe in assuming that for every ministering spirit of the Lord, there will be one, and often many satanic counter spirits.
4. Loosing spirits from the Lord.

GENERAL

1. We **bind** the spirits (demons) of Satan and **loose** the spirits (angels) of God. We cast the demons out of people and God directs the angels to minister to our needs.
2. Godly spirits commonly mentioned are spirit, Spirit of God, Spirit of the Lord, Holy Spirit (human spirit, angels and Holy Spirit).
3. Ungodly spirits commonly mentioned are evil spirits, demons and devils. There is actually only one Devil, Satan; demons are the correct terminology. There are millions of fallen angels and billions of demons.
4. The following are lists of godly and ungodly spirits found in the Bible. You can identify many more after you have been in deliverance awhile. Ungodly spirits generally are found grouped in families. Where you find one demon, you frequently find a family of demons with the same characteristics with one demon as the leader (strong man or ruler demon).

DICTIONARY OF CLASSICAL MYTHOLOGY

"A knowledge of the classics and an acquaintance with the **imaginary characters, places, and incidents of ancient mythology** which have been such an inspiring influence to writers of all ages adds greatly to ones enjoyment of literature, art and conversation. The people outside literary and educational pursuits have sufficient opportunity or leisure to acquire or keep up a knowledge of this popular branch of learning. It is important, therefore, to present in dictionary form the story of **gods, goddesses, heroes, and heroines of the old Grecian and Roman literature**. It will lead to a better understanding of the countless references which are made from time to time in the literature of the day to classic subjects. It is a great wonderland of posy and romance, and forms a realm all its own, **the realm of antiquity's gods and demons and of prehistoric heroes**."

Notice the highlighting and what it says to you. It is talking about gods, goddesses and demons. There is a **demon** behind every god and goddess worshiped by man!

You are seeing products with these names more and more today. Is this innocent or deliberate? The definitions of these names can be found in unabridged dictionaries. We recommend that you purchase one for spiritual research.

IDOLS WORSHIPPED BY COUNTRIES

The names of idols are the same as names of demons. There is a demon behind every idol that is worshipped by man. Notice that there are male and female gods and goddesses. Satan has something for everyone. Temple prostitutes included male homosexuals, female lesbians and female prostitutes.

TABER'S CYCLOPEDIC MEDICAL DICTIONARY

The following is Taber's definition of **multiple sclerosis**: "A chronic, slowly progressive disease of the **central nervous** system characterized by development of disseminated demyelinated glial patches called **plaques**. Symptoms and signs are numerous, but in later stages those of **Charcot's triad (nystagmus, scanning speech, and intention tremor)** are common. Occurs in the form of many clinical syndromes, the most common being the **cerebral, brain stem-cerebellar, and spinal**. A history of remissions and exacerbations is diagnostic. **Etiology is unknown and there is no specific therapy." (This means that the doctors don't know what causes the disease and how to cure it).**

Notice the underlined words. **They tell you the symptoms of the disease and where it is located in the body.** With this information, you can pray for healing and enter into spiritual warfare more effectively. The symptoms can be called out as names of demons such as plaques, Charcot's triad, nystagmus, scanning speech and intention tremor. **Demons will answer to their medical names, common names, symptoms or names they are given in the spiritual world.**

We worked with a woman in deliverance who had this disease by using the above method. We would get manifestations as we called out the demons by their medical names. She was delivered and healed. **The key is forgiving your ancestors and anyone in spiritual authority over you for their sins and asking for forgiveness for your sins that opened the door to the disease.**

NEUROTIC AND ABNORMAL PERSONALITIES
THE THREE P'S FAMILIES
PSYCHONEUROSIS, PSYCHONEUROTIC AND PSYCHOPSYCHOSIS

These lists of demons help you to understand those you are ministering to who have these personalities. A study of psychology and psychiatry can be very helpful in identifying names of demons. The method of treatment can also open the door to demons. **The medical profession identifies the names of demons but they don't know about casting them out.**

PHOBIAS

Phobias are fears. There are 210 phobias recognized by psychiatrists.

USING A THESAURUS IN DELIVERANCE (EXCERPTS)

1. Because demons tend to cluster in family groupings, the thesaurus can be an amazingly helpful instrument to identify demons within a specific category.
2. When the spirit is forced to manifest, his name, located in the thesaurus, becomes a tool to uncover his supportive network of demons.
3. This method has been tried in the laboratory of experience and many times has been the key to a breakthrough in cases where the demons have a particularly stronghold on the individual.

SOURCE AND BRANCHES OF FALSE RELIGIONS

Source

The first false religion in the Bible can be traced back to **Nimrod, his wife, Semiramus, and her child, Tammuz**. From this source branched out other false religions. The Catholic religion is for those **who want to be RELIGIOUS**. The Masonic religion is for those **who want BUSINESS SUCCESS**. The Occult religion is for those **who want POWER, SEX AND DRUGS**. This is true of anyone who follows a bloodless religion without the blood of Jesus Christ and has not had a born-again experience with Jesus Christ: Lord, Master and Savior.

Prayer

I break curses back to the false religion of Nimrod. I forgive anyone who is Catholic, Masonic or Occult. I break curses coming from these sources. I command those spirits to leave me in the Name of Jesus Christ. Amen.

REFERENCES

1. **Pigs In The Parlor** - 3 R's (Root of Bitterness, Rebellion and Rejection) and **53 Common Demon Groupings.**
2. **Demolishing The Hosts Of Hell**, Names Claimed By Demons (1300 Demons) and Using a Thesaurus in Deliverance.
3. **Roget's Thesaurus** - Synonyms (names of demons).
4. **Battling The Hosts Of Hell** - Names of Demons.
5. **Conquering The Hosts Of Hell** - The Spirits of God and Evil Spirits Mentioned or Implied in Scripture
6. **Education Book Of Essential Knowledge, An Addition Of Webster's Encyclopedic Dictionary**, Consolidated Book Publishers, U.S.A.
7. **Unger's Bible Dictionary** by Merril F. Unger, Moody Press, Chicago
8. **Taber's Cyclopedic Medical Dictionary**, F.A. Davis, Co., Philadelphia, PA

9. **Psychology Made Simple**, by Abraham P. Sperling, Made Simple Books, Double Day and Company, Inc., Garden City, New York

NAMES OF DEMONS

Summary

1. The different names and list of demons seems endless.
2. There is a name of a demon for any practice that is contrary to the Bible.
3. There is a name of a demon for any idol that is worshipped by man.
4. Choose the **List of Demons** that pertains to the area of ministry such as to children.
5. **Common Demon Groupings** are families of demons that are commonly found. It is a good all around list to use.

Lists Of Demons

The following are the titles of different lists of demons which are found in the **Mass Deliverance Manual** written by Gene and Earline Moody:

Abused Children (Deliverance for the Subconscious Mind)
Ahab and Jezebel (The Curse of Ahab and Jezebel)
Bad Habits of Thinking and Reacting
Baldness - Beards - Hair
Bastards (The Curse of the Bastard)
Biblical Curses
Catholic Spirits
Charismatic Witchcraft
Children Drug Addicts
Children's Deliverance
Christian Fantasy - Lies not Truth
Christmas - Pagan or Christian Holiday?
Classical Mythology (How to Identify Godly and Ungodly Spirits)
Common Demon Groupings (How to Minister Basic Deliverance)
Cursed Objects (Cleaning Your House)
Cursing Others and Being Cursed
Drugs and Medicines
Drunkenness and Gluttony
Effeminacy - Sins of Sodom
Fears Of (How to Identify Godly and Ungodly Spirits)
Good Homemakers
Grief and Bitterness (Deliverance from Grief and Bitterness)
Hate, Vengeance, Envy and Strife
Holidays
Humanism
Idols Worshipped by Countries (How to Identify Godly and Ungodly Spirits)
Indians (Indian Curses)
Infirmity, Weakness, Sickness, Disease (Body - Cured and Healed by Deliverance)
Ingratitude (An Attitude of Gratitude)
Lies, Deceit and Flattery
Maintaining Your Deliverance from Evil Spirits

Mass Deliverance Supplement
Mind (The Mind: Freeing - Restoring - Protecting)
Occult (Forbidden Practices of the Occult)
Passive Mind (Passive Mind - The Devil's Workshop)
Perfecting Love
Psychoneurosis (The Neurotic Personalities)
Psychoneurotic (The Delinquent Personalities)
Psychopsychosis (The Pathologic Personalities)
Rape
Rebellion
Religious Error (Spirits of Religious Error)
Respect, Fear and Nervousness
Satan, Fallen Angels and Demons (Learn About the Real Enemy -Satan and Followers)
Schizophrenia and Paranoia (Schizophrenia)
Schizophrenia and Related Diseases (How to Identify Godly and Ungodly Spirits)
Scripture (Deliverance Scripture)
Selected Topic Studies
Self (How to be Miserable)
Sexual Harassment - Abuse - Assault - Violence
Sexual Sin and Diseases (Sexual Diseases, Impurities and Demons)
Toys and Games (Children's Deliverance)
Ungodly Spirits (How to Identify Godly and Ungodly Spirits)
Valentine's Day (What's Wrong with Valentine's Day?)
Ungodly Spirits (How to Identify Godly and Ungodly Spirits)
Valentine's Day (What's Wrong with Valentine's Day?)
When Demonization of Christians is Denied (Can a Christian Have a Demon?)
Witchcraft (Winning over Witchcraft)
Women's Inheritance (Our Inheritance from Woman's Viewpoint)
Women's Weaknesses (From Eve to Jezebel - Women's Weaknesses)

General List Of Demons To Cast Out Of Children

A good general list of demons to cast out of children is the **Schizophrenia - Paranoid Hands** list of demon families found in Chapter 21, **Pigs In The Parlor**. It can be used for mass or individual deliverance.

Start with **Rejection, then Root of Bitterness, then Rebellion** families. After going through basic deliverance, **the three R's,** then start to cast out the other demon families (Schizophrenia-Paranoia).

Find out the child's problems **by talking to the parents (and the child if possible).** After doing deliverance in paragraph above, work on specific demon families identified for the individual.

You can also use the names of demonic toys, movies, games and music as the names of demons in deliverance. Very simply, there is a name of a demon for every evil practice that is contrary to the Holy Bible!

Common Demon Groupings

A good general list of demons to cast out of families and to use in mass deliverance is Common Demon Groupings from **Pigs in the Parlor** as follows:

Bitterness
Resentment
Hatred
Unforgiveness
Violence
Temper
Anger
Retaliation
Murder

Rebellion
Self-will
Stubbornness
Disobedience
Anti-Submissiveness
Inadequacy
Strife
Contention
Argument
Quarreling
Fighting
Distrust
Control
Possessiveness
Dominance
Witchcraft
Daydreaming
Retaliation
Destruction
Spite
Hatred
Sadism
Hurt
Cruelty
Passivity
Sensitiveness
Self-Awareness
Fear of Man
Fear of Disapproval
Perfection
Persecution
Unfairness

Accusation
Judging
Criticism
Faultfinding
Lethargy
Rejection
Fear of Rejection
Self-Rejection
Despondency

Insecurity
Inferiority
Self-Pity
Loneliness
Timidity
Shyness
Insomnia
Ineptness

Jealousy
Envy
Suspicion
Disgust
Selfishness
Worry
Withdrawal
Pouting
Dread
Fantasy
Pretension
Unreality
Tension
Escape
Indifference
Stoicism
Excitement
Sleepiness
Alcohol
Drugs
Sexual Impurity
Lust
Pride
Vanity

Passivity
Funk
Indifference
Listlessness

Depression
Despair

Discouragement
Defeatism
Dejection
Hopelessness
Suicide
Death

Morbidity

Heaviness
Gloom
Burden

Anxiety
Fear

Apprehension

Nervousness

Headache
Nervous Habits
Restlessness

Insomnia
Roving

Fantasy Lust
Masturbation

Fear of Judgment
Fear of Condemnation
Fear of Accusation
Fear of Reproof
Sensitiveness
Anger
Mental Illness
Insanity
Madness
Mania
Retardation
Senility
Schizophrenia
Paranoia
Hallucinations
Frustration
Paranoia
Jealousy
Envy
Suspicion
Distrust
Persecution
Fears
Grief
Confusion
Frustration
Incoherence
Forgetfulness
Sadness
Doubt
Unbelief
Skepticism
Tiredness
Death
Indecision
Procrastination
Compromise
Confusion
Forgetfulness
Indifference
Inheritance
Self Deception
Self-Delusion
Self-Seduction
Pride
White Magic
Mind Binding

Ego
Frustration
Criticism
Irritability
Intolerance
Harlotry
Rape
Competition
Driving
Argument
Pride
Ego

Impatience
Agitation
Urantia
Intolerance
Resentment
Criticism
Mormonism
False Burden
False Responsibility
False Compassion

Sorrow
Heartache
Heartbreak
Crying

Cruelty

Fatigue
Handwriting Analysis
Weariness

Infirmity
(May include
any disease
or sickness)

Water Witching
(Physical)
(Emotional)
(Mental)
(Curses)

Hyperactivity

Homosexuality
Lesbianism
Adultery
Fornication
Incest

Exposure
Frigidity

Cults
Jehovah's Witnesses
Christian Science
Rosicrucianism
Theosophy

Subud
Latihan
Unity

Bahaism
Unitarianism
(Lodges, societies and social agencies using the Bible & God as a basis but omitting the blood atonement of Jesus Christ)

Occult
Ouija Board
Palmistry

Automatic Handwriting Laziness
ESP
Hypnotism
Horoscope
Astrology
Levitation
Fortune Telling

Tarot Cards
Pendulum
Witchcraft
Black Magic

Conjuration

Confusion
Fear of Man
Fear of Failure
Occult Spirits
Spiritism Spirits
Blasphemy
Mind Idolatry
Intellectualism
Rationalization
Pride
Ego
Belittling
Fears (All Kinds)
Phobias (All Kinds)
Hysteria

Fear of Authority
Lying
Deceit
Caffeine
Pride
Ego
Vanity
Self-Righteousness
Haughtiness
Importance
Arrogance
Frustration
Affectation
Theatrics
Playacting
Sophistication
Pretension
Self-Hatred
Self-Condemnation

Restlessness
Driving
Pressure

Cursing
Ritualism
Course Jesting
Gossip
Criticism
Backbiting
Mockery
Fear of Lost
Railing
Etc.
Addictive & Compulsive
Nicotine
Alcohol
Drugs

Medications
Gluttony
Taoism
Gluttony
Nervousness
Compulsive Eating
Resentment
Etc.
Idleness
Self-Pity
Self-Reward

Self Accusation
Greed
Discontent

Incantation
Fetishes
Etc.

Religious

Formalism
Legalism
Doctrinal Obsession
Fear of God
Fear of Hell
Salvation
Religiosity

Spiritism
Seance
Spirit Guide
Necromancy

False Religions
Buddhism

Hinduism
Islam
Shintoism
Confucianism

Covetousness
Stealing
Kleptomania
Material Lust

CURSED OBJECTS

Summary

1. Be led by the Holy Spirit and search your home and possessions for cursed objects; then destroy the objects.
2. You can't destroy someone else's possessions. So, anoint with oil and exorcise the object.
3. Follow the **Five Steps to Cleaning House**.
4. If you know of demonic prayers against your family, break the curses.
5. There is more power in the spoken word.
6. Read Scripture for **Cleaning Your House** out loud in your home during the exorcism.

General

If you have a cursed object, you become cursed by God! Remove cursed objects from your being and from your home; destroy by breaking, burning or at least throw them in the trash can. Do not keep the cursed silver or gold of the object. If the cursed object belongs to someone else and you can not throw it away, then anoint with oil and cast the demons out of it. Anoint your house with oil and cast out evil spirits from your house and possessions.

To Exorcise Inanimate Objects (Excerpts)

In the case of objects dedicated to demons (idols, artifacts, etc.), the best course of action is to destroy them. However, it is well to check secondhand cars, homes and apartments also because if the former owners had ouija boards, or other occult paraphernalia, or were involved in serious bondage to sin, then there is every reason to suspect that evil spirits could be lingering behind. These spirits can and will cause trouble to the new owners.

Keep in mind that any prayers offered to anyone or anything other than God the Father, Son and Holy Spirit constitute prayers and/or worship to demons. Very often these are answered in the form of curses, for demons can and do respond to those who request of them. **(If you know of demonic prayers against your family, break the curses placed against you.)**

We suggest that two believers go on a mission such as this with Bible in hand. These should be destroyed. Look for little Mexican sun gods, idols, incense, Buddhas, hand carved objects from Africa or the Orient, Ouija boards, anything connected with astrology, horoscopes, fortune telling and so on. Books or objects associated with witchcraft, good luck charms, or the cult religions (metaphysics, Christian Science, Jehovah's Witnesses, etc.), rock and roll records and tapes fall in the category of things which have been often loaded with evil spiritual power.

Verbally denounce Satan and his power, and of his demon hosts and claim authority as a believer-priest because of the name of Jesus Christ and the authority of His shed Blood. **(There is more power in the spoken word.)**

Some Scripture which has proven useful in this includes: Rev. 12:11; 22:3; Col. 2:14-15; Gal. 3:13; Deut. 21:23; 32:5; Num. 23:8, 23; II Sam. 7:29. **(Read out loud in the house.)**

The door lintel and window sills should be anointed by touching them with olive oil. Other things such as statues have been so anointed in Jesus name and many times the demonic power is checked or destroyed. Any specific areas of demonic activity or influence of which you are aware should be denounced by name (Prov. 3:33). **(This should be done for objects that you don't own and can not destroy.)**

FIVE STEPS TO CLEANING HOUSE
Worshipping Other Gods Is Spiritual Adultery

1. Five-way prayer of forgiveness - **you forgive your ancestors, descendants and others**, ask God to forgive and bless them. **Ask God to forgive you; you forgive yourself for sins against your body**. Also ask forgiveness for spiritual adultery.
2. Break curses and soul ties from others and to others; break curses of psychic or Catholic prayers.

3. Clean out house of those objects or exorcise objects.
4. Anoint house with oil and drive evil spirits out of house.
5. Cast demons out of people that came in thru curses from objects.

Prayer

Lord, I come to you about cursed objects and demon infestation in my possessions and home, and in me. I forgive my ancestors, descendants and others who have had spiritual influence over me. I ask you to forgive and bless them, especially with salvation. Please forgive me and I forgive myself for spiritual adultery. I forgive those who have cursed me; forgive me for cursing others. I break the curses and demonic soul ties including psychic and Catholic prayers. I will clean out my house of cursed objects or exorcise objects that I don't own. I will anoint my house with oil and drive the evil spirits out of the house. Show me cursed objects, demon infestation and spirits that need to be cast out of people. In Jesus Name I pray. Amen.

REFERENCES

Battling The Hosts Of Hell, How to Exorcise Inanimate Objects
Conquering The Hosts Of Hell, Notes on Witchcraft, Symbols and Accursed Objects

LEARN ABOUT DELIVERANCE

Summary

1. Get involved!
2. Study to show yourself approved by God.
3. Seek God about deliverance.
4. **Deliverance is a constant learning process.** Satan has spent thousands of years weaving a very complicated system to trap you and take you to Hell, or cause you to live a miserable Christian life here on earth.

General

1. **Get Experience** - start casting out demons and get involved. Head knowledge of deliverance is insufficient! You can memorize The Bible and go to Hell!
2. **Study Bible** - use a concordance and study Gospels mainly.
3. **Fast and pray** - seek the Lord about your problems.
4. **Study deliverance books** - learn as much as you can.
5. **Study books on the mind, will and emotions.**
6. **Go to deliverance meetings** - participate in teaching and ministry: mass, small groups and individuals.
7. **Study Satan from a Christian viewpoint** - to see how he is trying to destroy you, your family and your church.
8. **Emphasize practical methods** - put the Bible to work.
9. **Clean out your house** - get rid of demonic objects.
10. **Be persistent** - keep after the demons in an area of your life until you are successful.
11. **Learn to research a subject** - use encyclopedias, dictionaries, medical and psychiatric books.
12. **Learn the three phases of deliverance** - How to Determine the Need for Deliverance, How go Get Delivered, and How to Stay Delivered.

PRACTICAL DELIVERANCE BOOKS
SUMMARY

1. Buy, study and follow the Basic, Advanced and Mind books; start with Basic.
2. **Deliverance Manual** is a practical how-to-do-it book.

Basic - Pigs In The Parlor - Frank and Ida Mae Hammond, Impact Books.

Advanced - Battling The Hosts Of Hell; Conquering The Hosts Of Hell; Demolishing The Hosts Of Hell; Annihilating The Hosts Of Hell, Volumes I and II; Eradicating The Hosts Of Hell; Smashing The Hosts Of Hell; The Alcoholic Syndrome; Grappling with the Host of Hell; Freedom from the Hosts of Hell; and **Harassing The Host of Hell**, eleven books (and fifty booklets covering particular topics) by Win Worley, Hegewisch Baptist Church, Highland, Indiana.

Mind - War On The Saints - Unabridged Edition, Jessie Penn-Lewis & Evans Roberts, Thomas E. Lowe, LTD.

REFERENCES

The above listed books have been freely referred to in this booklet. They are classics in the field of deliverance. Every Christian should have a copy of these books. We strongly recommend that you purchase a copy of each book; then use them to set you, your family and your church free.

DELIVERANCE MANUAL

Gene and Earline Moody wrote the **Deliverance Manual** which is actually four books in one: **Basic Deliverance, Advanced Deliverance, Mass Deliverance** and **How To Do Deliverance**. These are practical lessons of how to do deliverance.

HOW NOT TO DO DELIVERANCE
Some Advice

For the person who wants God to use him or her for deliverance work among those oppressed by evil spirits, here is some advice:

1. The person ministering in the area of deliverance is in a position of all-out spiritual warfare with the forces of evil. Many have fallen by the wayside because of ignorance of Bible and deliverance, still having many demons within themselves, women and men ministering to the opposite sex by themselves, being lured by false doctrines, etc.
2. Demons can be very stubborn and highly seductive. Demons do not easily come out when they have a right before God to stay due to unconfessed sin, curses, soul ties, etc. They can lure the man or woman who is alone into a sex trap destroying the ministry, their family and others who are following that leader.
3. Effective weapons used against ministers are carelessness, pride, immorality, taking God for granted, spiritual weakness, and affliction of wife or husband where the minister refuses to yield to God.
4. Deliverance ministers should train their families and involve them in deliverance work. **Husband and wife should minister together as a team if possible.**
5. Unforgiveness is the biggest hindrance to answered prayer and to casting out demons. Unforgiveness between husband and wife is especially a hindrance.

OVERALL VIEW OF DELIVERANCE

Deliverance consists of about three equal parts: teaching, casting out and counseling. Christians generally either do not get involved or only get involved slightly. Because of this, there are weaknesses in the ministry of deliverance. Deliverance will not be completely successful unless there is a balance in the church of teaching, ministry and counseling.

The biggest weakness is trying to cover deliverance by just casting out demons without proper teaching or counseling. Here, many Christians only go after the surface demons and do not go after the root causes of why the person got into sin in the first place.

The second biggest weakness is not walking out the deliverance. After the demons are cast out, a person must change their ways of thinking and acting, and discipline their life or they will let the demons come back into them. A person needs extensive counseling to help them do this and they must decide to change their lives.

The third biggest weakness is the lack of teaching on deliverance. There is a large body of knowledge about deliverance but you hear little practical teaching come from the pulpit.

Comments

Single men and women must be very careful in ministering deliverance. Satan wants to destroy your ministry by the appearance of sexual sin or by falling into that trap.

DELIVERANCE MYTHS

There is much ignorance and many myths about deliverance. Deliverance is the most misunderstood part of the Christian life. Many deliverance workers and ministers do not realize how demonized they and the Christian body are. Sometimes they fall by the wayside because they do not continue to purge their bodies of demons. **Unless the Church gets involved on a regular basis with deliverance, many Christians will continue to be defeated by Satan.**

This is the sequence that God used in our ministry: **first** - ourselves, **second** - other Christians, **third** - five-fold ministers, and **finally** - other deliverance ministers. **Everyone needs deliverance.**

When the young Christian starts to cast out demons, he will make statements like, **You are completely free of demons.** Jesus never told anyone in the Bible that they were completely free of demons.

Comments

Common teaching is that a Christian can not have a demon. Churches need demonstrations to show the manifestations to the congregations. Transference of spirits can not occur unless there is a crack in your armour related to that spirit.

BATTLE MYTHS

There are many myths about Christian warfare. Satan is a good Devil, a worthy Adversary, at what he does; he works twenty-four hours a day to destroy us. He will probably take about 98% of the world population and 75% of the church population to Hell with him. **Because strait is**

the gate, and narrow is the way, which leadeth unto life, and few there be that find it. (Matt. 7:14).

I am sure you realize that the following are false statements: All we need to have in the church is token deliverance. I can keep my cursed objects without causing any harm. We can get all of our demons cast out in one grand event.

THE WOMAN MINISTER

Questions

The Bible says that the woman is the weaker vessel (1 Peter 3:7). What are the pitfalls of the following:

1. Should a man minister to a woman alone in deliverance? (possible sexual sin)
2. Should a woman minister to a man alone in deliverance? (possible sexual sin)
3. What about a woman minister who travels with another woman? (possible lesbianism)
4. What about a woman who ministers by herself that is either married or unmarried? (possible danger to unprotected female)
5. What about a woman who ministers that is married and her husband is unsaved or saved, and will not travel with her? (husband possibly not in agreement or acting as a covering; woman has to travel by herself)

Comments

1. **Earline and I ministered as a husband and wife team. What were the advantages of this method?** (she protects me against women; I protect her against men)
2. It will be very difficult for a woman who has an unsaved husband to be effective in deliverance. They are not in agreement, woman is weaker vessel, she must go by herself, and other problems at home. A woman is more effective when she is married and her husband is a believer who practices deliverance and they are in agreement.
3. Everyone should be involved in deliverance: children and adults, male and female, young and old.
4. Women who are in the five-fold ministry should do deliverance. It should be done in situations where she has protection: in open church with congregation or in her office. The deliverance team should be present to assist and protect her.
5. I will do everything I can do to support women pastors and ministers to do what GOD has called them to do. I have no problem with submitting to a woman in leadership.
6. The woman is a greater target than a man for rape, sexual abuse and other dangers even though men are being raped and sodomized today. The woman needs to be more careful than a man but the man needs to be careful too.
7. The woman is not inferior in anyway to a man but is simply weaker as GOD made her. GOD did not make any mistakes when he formed Eve as a woman.
8. GOD made the man to protect, provide, honor, love and cherish the woman and not to take advantage of her in anyway.

LOUDNESS OF VOICE

Many people feel that if you shout or scream at demons that they will come out sooner. The contrary is true. If the demons feel that you don't know your authority or how to cast out demons, they will feel that you are in a weak position and will resist leaving.

The formula for casting out demons is Mark 16:17, **And these signs** (signs, wonders and miracles) **shall follow them that believe** (Christians that believe the Bible)**; In my name** (Jesus Christ) **shall they cast out** (command out) **devils; they shall speak with new tongues.**

An analysis of this verse reveals that you must believe the Bible in what it says about casting out demons, you cast them out in the Name of Jesus, and signs will follow your ministry. Even children can cast out demons in the Name of Jesus. **I charge you by Jesus Christ to cast out demons if you are a Christian.**

LAYING HANDS ON OTHERS

This is an area that is dangerous and caution must be exercised because of the potential harm to individuals and God's Kingdom. A good verse to ponder is I Tim. 5:22, **Lay hands suddenly on no man, neither be partaker of other men's sins: keep thyself pure.**

It is not necessary to lay hands on someone to cast out demons. In some cases it is better not to lay hands on the person being ministered to. **This is especially true when casting out sexual demons from the opposite sex.** You need to be led by the Holy Spirit in what to do.

If you have sexual demons within you, they will interact with the sexual demons in the other person. They will stir up emotions in either or both individuals. This is especially true between the opposite sex, or between homosexuals, or between lesbians.

We have observed men laying hands on women, and women laying hands on men improperly. The safest way is to lay hands on the top of the head. Next in safeness is to lay hands on the shoulder. Many times God heals by the lengthening of legs and straightening of the back. In this instance it is safe to hold a persons shoes and pray for them. In between the head and shoulders, and the feet is the danger zone of eroticism (sexual arousal). This is the area that stirs up sexual feelings.

I like to get a woman to help me lay hands on another woman. I may ask her to lay hands on the chest or stomach to assist in driving out the demons. The husband is the best person to lay hands on the wife in these areas.

The way a person ministers to others reveals what is going on inside them. If they have sexual demons, they will try to love on the opposite sex to get gratification.

Suppose that a person has latent homosexual or lesbian demons that they are not aware of. Then, they will want to love on men and boys, or women and girls. They may want to lay hands on their sexual organs and to kiss them to get rid of the homosexual or lesbian demons. This actually invites these type of demons to attack the person being ministered to and satisfies the demons within the person doing the ministering. Ministers have that tendency if they are not careful.

Comments

Some women want to be lord over the men in deliverance; they feel justified even if they are wrong. Men and women should not be in competition. Some deliverance does more harm than good if not done properly such as pulling out a person's eye to get rid of the demon. **Their doctrine should be sound and according to the Bible.**

TRAVELING MINISTRIES

Suppose that a man or woman travels alone in the ministry. This person could be single or married. If married, the mate is not traveling with that person. Sexual pressures and loneliness may build up in the traveling minister. There may be an unconscious desire to love on the person being ministered to; this satisfies the unfulfilled desire within the minister. This is extremely dangerous and has caused divorces and loss of ministries.

Outside of the desire to live, sex is the greatest drive in mankind. The big three used to destroy a person's relationship with God are money, sex and power. Sex is a playground for Satan and he has used it to destroy multitudes of Christians, ministers and churches. **Fornication or adultery is on the pathway to Hell.**

The Bible clearly states that the woman is weaker than the man. A woman traveling alone is more vulnerable than a man traveling alone. The woman is also subject to being raped or molested. However, it is now getting to the point where men are being raped too.

Suppose that the woman is a lesbian or has lesbian tendencies, is manly or has manly qualities, or has problems with rejection and not being loved. Traveling with another woman may lead to a lesbian relationship. If a woman looks like, acts like or dresses like a man, then she is a candidate for this problem. This applies to the woman who tries to act like a man in the ministry.

PRIVATE MINISTRY

A man should not minister to a woman alone and a woman should not minister to a man alone. What frequently happens is that the couple ends up in bed having sex. Suppose that the minister is a man of God. Many women will come to him with their problems of a serious nature. He may feel sorry for them and try to comfort them and minister to their emotions. **If he does not go about this ministry in a proper way, then he is on the abbess of destruction which can lead to Hell.**

Suppose that the minister is a woman of God. She may feel that she is strong and not subject to the temptations of mortal woman. Due to her lack of a man, she may go overboard in ministering to the man and make a fool out of herself. She may feel that she can minister to the man in her motel room which is the ideal setup for Satan's mischief.

Husband and wife can protect each other from the opposite sex. You should ask yourself this question, **How am I opening myself up to sexual attack?**

Comments

Pastors can lay hands on women improperly and open themselves up to demon attack. Women should lay hands on women and men on men in places where it would be inappropriate for the opposite sex to place their hands. One problem area is that women want to be counseled privately by their male pastor. A lot of mischief can happen behind closed doors leading to sex even in the church.

DELIVERANCE IS NOT A PARLOR GAME!

Deliverance is not a plaything to make the meeting interesting. It is deadly serious and can make the difference between life and death, or a victorious life here and in the hereafter. We should not practice token deliverance in our meetings or churches.

DELIVERANCE IS NOT A GRAND EVENT!

Deliverance is a way of life probably until we die and God takes over our training. Christians are very demonized and require years for cleansing and retraining so that the demons are not let back in.

You can't keep your cursed objects and stay free! If you persist in keeping your cursed objects, then you are cursed and the demons have a right to attack you, your family and what you have. Don't expect the demons to let you alone when you give them a right before God to torment you.

FALLEN DELIVERANCE MINISTERS

It is amazing to see the casualties among deliverance ministers. These should be the strongest of Christians and the most knowledgeable of the Word. They are trapped by not confessing sin, not crucifying the flesh and not casting out demons in their lives. They are trying to help others when they need help themselves. They are immature and do not know the Word of God or much about deliverance. They have received a measure of deliverance but need much more.

It is also amazing to see these fallen men and women get into false doctrine. A big problem is their pride, ego and vanity. They want to be Number One or have the Preeminence. They want others to tell them how great they are. A common problem is being overweight and indulging themselves on food rather than the food of the Word. Most can not take constructive criticism and are very sensitive about their weight.

We all pay for our mistakes in the here-and-now and in the here-and-after. These people are not open minded and will not change. Therefore, their organizations suffer from their bad decisions of judgement in the mental, physical, spiritual and material realms.

Comments

When praying for someone in a group, the group needs to yield to the person that God has given the leadership, authority and discernment. God may tell the leader to use someone that God has given a revelation to. Share a Word of Knowledge, Word of Wisdom and Discerning of Spirits with the leader. Everyone works together in the unity of The Spirit. The Holy Spirit needs to be followed so that God's battle for the individual can be won.

There needs to be discipline and not confusion. Everybody does not have to call the demon out. You do not need crying, loudness, wildness, shouting and disorder. The group needs to pray, agree, give support and have unity. The leader should not fall for trying to take God's glory.

DIFFICULTY IN DRIVING DEMONS OUT

Some demons come out easily and some demons take hours to drive out. A worthless command is, **All demons come out of this person or everyone in the congregation or everyone in the world now in the Name of Jesus.**

Another worthless statement is, All of your demons are gone. How do you know that all of their demons are gone? Can you see into the body and soul of the person? If Jesus didn't say this, how can you?

AGREEMENT BETWEEN HUSBAND AND WIFE

Agreement

When husband and wife agree, there is great power before God. When husband and wife disagree, there is weakness before God. In the deliverance ministry, they need to support each other. They can not be careless, take God for granted, or not do the things that a Christian must do.

They need to train the children about the battle. Satan will attack the children of a couple that minister in deliverance.

Comments

Inner healing, visualization, etc. is a cop-out for not doing deliverance. If you do deliverance, then inner healing is not required. If you only teach deliverance or only cast out demons or only counsel about deliverance, you will fail; to succeed you must do all of these things. A lot of Christians quit along the way such as after salvation, baptism, healing, prosperity; you need to follow through to freedom. Teach deliverance, minister by casting out demons and counsel afterwards.

THREE-FOLD DELIVERANCE MINISTRY

Three Areas Of Deliverance

The three areas of deliverance are teaching, ministering and counseling. If they ever get around to it, the church usually wants to cast out the demons and get this messy subject over with so that they can go on to more glorious services.

Suppose the man is a drunk. Then, they will try to cast out drunkenness and not find out why the man became a drunk. This is surface or token deliverance: dealing with the surface demons and not the root causes. If you don't deal with the reasons why the person became an alcoholic, then he will probably let the demon back in. It is difficult to dig out the root causes and is time consuming, requires discernment and must have the power of God.

Those who don't believe in deliverance say that all a Christian has to do it to crucify the flesh. In a sense they are right; you must crucify the flesh to be successful in deliverance. You can't get your pet demon cast out and go back and do the same thing again. Examples: smoking - the demon is cast out and the person goes out and buys a pack of cigarettes again; gluttony - the demon is cast out and the person goes and eats three pieces of pie.

Teaching and counseling must be continuing. You don't just bring in the deliverance minister once a year and that takes care of everything, or you minister to a person and you don't need to talk to that person again. This is the same problem that a new Christian faces after salvation - the need for continual feeding and growth.

Comments

Christians have many demons including those in the five-fold ministry. It is fantasy to believe that all it takes is one session of deliverance for life. Demons are very common and there are multiplied billions so that everyone can have their share.

We cast about 10,000 demons out of one man over a period of about a year. We used to ask the demon what his name was, and how many demons he controlled. Then we would write down this information and systematically cast out the demons. **This showed us how demonized Christians are.**

Most of the people we have worked with are Full-Gospel Christians. You are like a mansion with many rooms; every room needs to be cleaned. Search out and destroy every problem that is ungodly and you can't control so you can follow God.

Deliverance is not for the unwilling or the heathen; it is a waste of time. You can intercede, pray and war for them. Don't cast out demons from the non-Christian; you are doing them a disservice. Try to get them to accept Christ before deliverance.

The best way to do deliverance is face-to-face; the next best way is phone line to phone line. You can cast out demons across the world on the phone. If the person is willing and will submit to your leadership, then deliverance can be effective over the phone. There is no distance in God and He is everywhere at once.

Your mate needs to agree with you and both need to walk the Christian walk. There must be good communications and openness between mates who are in deliverance. Allow your wife to have her say and do not become bitter against her.

LIST OF DEMONS TO USE WITH HOW NOT TO DO DELIVERANCE

You can use Lists of Demons found in the lessons: **Bad Habits of Thinking and Reacting, Charismatic Witchcraft, Drunkenness and Gluttony, and Ingratitude.**

The following are characteristics of those in this lesson: hate, vengeance, envy, strife, rejection, bitterness, rebellion, selfishness, Ahab, Jezebel, ignorance, false doctrines, seduction, soul ties, alluring, carelessness, pride, immorality, taking God for granted, spiritual weakness, unforgiveness, cursed objects, sexual demons, homosexuality, lesbianism, eroticism, demonic sexual feelings, demonic kissing, sexual pressures, loneliness, divorce, separation, love of money, manly women, effeminate men, inability to give or receive love, token deliverance, immaturity, ego, vanity, overweight, drunkenness, smoking.

REFERENCES

Deliverance Manual by Gene and Earline Moody (unless otherwise noted).
Pigs In The Parlor - Fifty-Three Common Demon Groupings.
Demolishing The Hosts Of Hell, Names Claimed By Demons.
Roget's Thesaurus - Synonyms.
Battling The Hosts Of Hell - Names of Demons.
Conquering The Hosts Of Hell - The Spirits of God and Evil Spirits Mentioned or Implied in Scripture.

Education Book Of Essential Knowledge, An Addition Of Webster's Encyclopedic Dictionary, Consolidated Book Publishers.
Unger's Bible Dictionary by Merril F. Unger, Moody Press.
Taber's Cyclopedic Medical Dictionary, F.A. Davis Co.
Psychology Made Simple by Abraham P. Sperling, Double Day and Company.

SECTION 16 - SELECTED PRAYERS

CONTENTS

6. **Black Infirmity**

MOODYS' PRAYERS

Sins Of Ancestors, Curses, Soul Ties, Fragmented Soul & Subconscious

We forgive our ancestors **(upwards)**, descendants **(downwards)**, and others **(outwards)** that have sinned against GOD and hurt us **(those outside of us)**. We ask you to forgive them for their sins and mistakes. We remit their sins, sever demonic ties, and set ourselves free. **We ask GOD to bless them with spiritual blessings, bring them into truth and meet their needs out of His Riches in Glory through CHRIST JESUS.** We ask that GOD forgive us **(Godwards)** for our sins, and We forgive ourselves **(inwards)** for sins against our body.

We ask You to send the gifts of THE HOLY SPIRIT to minister to the needs of the people and accomplish what you want done. We are careful to give you the glory, honor, praise and credit for what is said and done. **These things we ask in the blessed NAME OF JESUS CHRIST: LORD, MASTER AND SAVIOR.**

We command the forces of evil to obey in THE NAME OF JESUS CHRIST. We take authority over Satan and the forces of evil according to the HOLY BIBLE, the complete WORD OF GOD and command that you obey it. We break curses, charms, spells, jinxes, psychic powers, hexes, vexes and demonic ties that bind. We break soul ties caused by witchcraft, sorcery, bewitchment and sexual sins. Restore our fragmented souls: minds, wills and emotions; send your angels out to recover what Satan has stolen from us. Stir up the demons in our subconscious minds so that they can be identified and cast out.

Taking Spiritual Authority Over The Meeting

Behold, I give unto you power to tread on serpents and scorpions (fallen angels and demons), **and over all the power of the enemy: and nothing shall by any means hurt you** (Luke 10:19). We come against powers, principalities, evil forces in this world and spiritual wickedness in high places. We come against demons inside or outside of anyone present, over this city, state, nation and world, in Hell or out of Hell. We come against you by THE POWER AND BLOOD OF JESUS CHRIST, by THE WORD OF GOD, by THE NAME OF JESUS, by the authority of the believer, in the unity of our spirits, to set ourselves free. We sit in heavenly places over Satan, fallen angels, demons and forces of evil. We command you to line up in rank, file and order, and come out quickly. We bind the power that you have and loose ourselves from you in THE NAME OF JESUS CHRIST of Nazareth. We take authority over Satan and the kingdom of evil according to THE WHOLE WORD OF GOD.

BASIC DELIVERANCE

Prayer

ALMIGHTY GOD, I forgive those who have rejected me, been bitter against me and have rebelled against me. Please forgive me for rejection, bitterness and rebellion against others.

In THE NAME OF JESUS CHRIST I command the spirits to come out of the Unconscious, Subconscious and Conscious Mind. I command the families of Rejection, Bitterness and Rebellion, and other families to come out of me and bring their works with them as your name is called:

LIST OF DEMONS FOR BASIC DELIVERANCE

Basic Deliverance

Rejection: Fear of Rejection, Self Rejection.
Bitterness: Resentment, Hatred, Unforgiveness, Violence, Temper, Anger, Retaliation, Murder.
Rebellion: Self Will, Stubbornness, Disobedience, Anti-Submissiveness.
Diseases: Cancer, Arthritis and diseases that come in through Bitterness.

Rejection

Feelings of being Rejected, Refused, Repudiated, Declined, Denied, Rebuffed, Repelled, Renounced, Discarded, Thrown Away, Excluded, Eliminated and Jettisoned.

Rejection, Poor in Spirit, Pride - Ego - Vanity, Double Mindedness, **Fear of Rejection, Self Rejection,** Roots of Rejection, Ahab Jezebel Complex, Destruction of Family Priesthood, Dominance, Homosexuality, Lesbianism, Rebellion, Withdrawal, Overpermissive, Too Harsh, Lying, Guilt, Distrust, Inability to Communicate, Witchcraft Control, Ugliness, Schizophrenia, Anger, Rejection from the Womb, Smoking, Drinking, Dementia Praecox, Instability, Agony, Inability to Give or Receive Love, Insecurity, Inferiority, Fantasy, Unreality, Sexual Perversion, Frustration

Passive-Aggressive Behavior, Lack of Confidence, Repression, Co-Dependency, Ignominy, Disappointment & Guilt, Anti-Social Disorder, Vexation, Introversion, Inhibition, Lashing Out, Abuse of Self & Others, Dysfunction, Projection, Addictions, Sex for Love, Depression, Emotional Instability, Anger, Bitterness, Intense Emotional Pain, Shame, Anxiety, Over-Compensation, Negativism, Dejection, Sadness / Crying, Work-A-Holism, Eating Disorder, Over-Sensitivity, Fear, Afraid to be Alone, Hysteria, Mistrust, Humiliation, Grief, Intensive Emotional Pain, Over-Protection, Overweight, Oppression, Eating disorders, Suicide, Isolation, Betrayal, Torment, Emotional Trauma, Feelings of Rejection, Phobia, Loneliness, Emptiness, Neurosis, Grandiosity, Abandonment, Social Isolation, Emotional Victimization, Deception, Psychological Victimization, Denial, Hopelessness, emotional Callousness, Murder, Bashfulness, Disrepute, Disesteem, Discredit, Worthlessness, Insignificance, Disgrace, Emotional / Psychological Rape, Perversions, Need for Approval / Validation, Dishonor, Suspicions, Post-traumatic Stress Disorder, False / Non-Expectations, Discrimination, Segregation, Exile, Eviction, Scorn, Shun, Ignore / Neglect, Insecurities, Disapproval, Repudiation, Comparison, Favoritism, Dysfunctions, Feeling of Not Being Wanted, Nobody Loves Me Syndrome, Justification of Inappropriate Word / Behavior, **Sabotage of Relationships / Organization / Self / Purpose / Destinies**, Low Self-Worth, **Self: Pity, Depreciation, Consciousness, and Fulfilling Prophecy**.

Bitterness

Feelings of being Bitterly Cursed, Rebellious, Sharp, Acrid, Embittered, Poisoned, Violent, Provoked, Vexed, Grieved, Sorrowing, Bitter Herb, Calamity, Bile, Venom, Angry, Chafed, Most Bitter and Provoked.

Bitterness, Resentment, Hatred, Unforgiveness, Violence, Temper, Anger, Retaliation, Murder, Root of Bitterness, Failure To Forgive, Arthritis, Schizophrenia, Mind Binding, Memory Loss, Recall, Broken Relationships.

Rebellion

Feelings of being Disobeyed, Transgressed, Violated, Disregarded, Defied, Infringed, Shirked, Resisted, Mutiny, Rebelled and Revolted.

Rebellion, Greed, **Disobedience,** Lying, **Self-will,** Hate, **Stubbornness,** Evil Plotting and Planning, **Anti-submissiveness,** Evil Control of Others, Destruction, Unrighteous Judgement, Subversion, Rock Music, Resistance, Christian Rock, Interference, Deceit, Friction, Trickery, Repulse, Betrayal, Defiance, Pride, Aggressiveness, False Love, Scorn, Arrogance, Sorcery, Conniving, Seduction, Confusion, Sullen Masculine Women, Taking Tranquilizers, Effeminate Men, Taking Drugs, Insecurity, Restless, Frustration, Witchcraft, Depression, Unholy Sex, Doubt.

Haughtiness, Independence, Segregation, Wrath, Separatism, Obstinacy, Insubordination, Defensiveness, Vanity, Strife, Conceit, Loftiness, Non-Compliance, Contempt, Recalcitrance, Unruliness, Waywardness, Rejection of Authority, Defiance, Sedition, Disdain, Selfishness, **Self: Centeredness, Importance, Righteousness and Protection.**

Schizophrenia

Inward

INSECURITY, INFERIORITY
LUST: Fantasy Lust, Perverseness (2)
REJECTION: Fear Of Rejection, Self Rejection, Fear Of Judgment (1)
SELF ACCUSATION: Compulsive Confession (3)
JEALOUSY, ENVY **(PARANOIA)**
SELF PITY
FALSE COMPASSION: False Responsibility (4)
DEPRESSION: Despondency, Despair, Discouragement, Hopelessness, SUICIDE
GUILT: Condemnation, Unworthiness, Shame
PERFECTION: Pride, Vanity, Ego, Intolerance, Frustration, Impatience, Anger
UNFAIRNESS
WITHDRAWAL, FANTASY, DAYDREAM, UNREALITY, VIVID IMAGINATION, Pouting
SELF AWARENESS: Timidity, Shyness
LONELINESS
SENSITIVENESS
TALKATIVENESS: Nervousness, Tension
FEARS: People, Insanity, Germs, Other

Outward

CONFRONTATION: Suspicion, Distrust, Persecution, Fears **(PARANOIA)** (5)
ACCUSATION TOWARD OTHERS: Projection (6)
REBELLION: Disobedience, Anti-Submissiveness
SELF WILL, SELFISHNESS, STUBBORNNESS (7)
SELF DELUSION, SELF DECEPTION, SELF SEDUCTION (8)
PRIDE, UNTEACHABLENESS, JUDGMENTAL, CONTROL & POSSESSIVENESS
BITTERNESS: RESENTMENT, UNFORGIVENESS, MEMORY RECALL, ANGER, RETALIATION

HATRED, VIOLENCE, MURDER

General

Schizo, Damnable Seed, a commanding ruler: Double Mindedness; **(Mental Illness)**, **(Rejection)** - Lust, Fantasy Lust, Perverseness, Jealousy, Paranoia, Self-pity, Depression, Suicide, Guilt, Pride, Vanity, Loneliness, Fears, Attention Seeking, Inferiority, Harlotry, Rejection, Unfairness, Withdrawal, Fantasy, Daydreaming, Timidity, Self Awareness, Shyness, Sensitivity, Chattering, Nervousness, Vivid Imaginations, Fear Of Germs, Frustration, Impatience, Inordinate Affection For Animals, Intolerance, Insanity, Self-Rejection, Self-Accusation, Tension, Fear Of People, Compulsive Confession, Envy, Fear Of Judgment, False Compassion, Fear Of Rejection, False Responsibility, Despondency, Despair, Discouragement, Hopelessness, Condemnation, Unworthiness, Shame, Perfection, Ego. **(Rebellion)** - Fear, Accusation, Rebellion, Selfishness, Pride, Hatred, Resentment, Violence, Murder, Memory Recall Loss, Disobedience, Paranoia, Suspicion, Distrust, Persecution, Confrontation, Self Will, Projection, Stubbornness, Anger, Root Of Bitterness, Judgmental, Self-Deception, Self-Delusion, Self-Destruction, Unteachableness, Control, Possessiveness, Unforgiveness, Retaliation, False Beliefs, Anti-Submissiveness, mental and spiritual spirits.

Comments

1. Keeps one from giving and receiving love - both GOD's and Man's.
2. Weds one to the world for love.
3. Makes one tell all seeking attention, punishment and correction.
4. Includes inordinate affection for animals.
5. With honesty at all costs - seeking evidence for suspicions.
6. Keeps one from looking at self. Projects one's own faults into others.
7. Weds one to selfish desires.
8. Both mental & spiritual. Seductive: to temporally mislead, decoy.
   Delusion: a misleading of the mind, false belief, fixed misconception.
   In psychiatry: a false belief regarding self - common in paranoia.

BASTARDS AND INCEST

Prayer

ALMIGHTY GOD, I forgive my ancestors for creating bastards and committing incest. Please forgive me for the same sins. I break the curses of the bastard and incest on me and my descendents. I command the following spirits of sexual sins and diseases to come out of me in THE NAME OF JESUS CHRIST: (Use the OVERALL LIST OF DEMONS for sex.)

Comments

At least 25 infectious organisms are transmitted through sexual contact. The eight most common include: **Curable (Bacterial) STD's:** Chalamydia, Gonorrhea, Syphilis and Trichomoniasis. **Incurable (Viral) STD's:** Genital Herpes, Human Papilloma Virus (HPV), Hepatitis B and Human Immunodeficiency Virus (HIV) / AIDS. Other diseases are caused by STD's. We curse the bacterial and viral organisms since the Christian has repented.

MAIN LIST OF SEXUAL DEMONS

Soul Ties

Unnaturally Close Friendships, Blood Covenants, Covenants, Promises, Allegiances

Lust

Inordinate Affections: Excessive, Disorderly, Unregulated, Immoderate
Obscene: Carnal and Voluptuous Senses and Appetites
Rock, Country, Blue Grass, Melancholy Music
Poetry, Art, Literature and Media
Lust, Passions, Fantasy Lust
Worship of Sex
Divers Lusts, Lust of Eyes, Lust of Flesh
Lustfulness
Vain Imaginations
Unrestrained Passions and Lusts
Material Lust
Food Lust
Sex Dreams
Burning with Lust

Selfishness

Selfishness, Lovers of Pleasure, Loss of Self Confidence
Self: Conceit, Protection, Pity, Reward, Awareness, Condemnation, Hatred, Gratification, Other spirits in the Self Family

Sex With Demons

Succubus, Incubus, Fondling Hands, Caressing Hot Lips, Occult Sex, Sex Orgies
Satan Worship

Pornography

Pornography, Child Pornography, X-Rated Movies, Obscene Jokes, **Pornographic Channels, Pictures and Books**

General

Fornication
Adultery (Also Marriage To Divorced Person)
Masculine Women, Lesbianism
Effeminate Men, Homosexuality
Evil Concupiscence
Lasciviousness, Lewdness, Lewd Emotions
Filthy Language: Obscenity, Blasphemy, Profanity
Masturbation
Abortion, Murder, Killing, Death
Ahab, Jezebel
Exposure, Uncleanness, Perversion
Pride, Ego, Vanity
Sexual Fantasies and Activities, Flirting
Nymphomania, Masochism
Immorality, Prostitution, Harlotry, Whore, Whoredom
Incest, Bastard

Rape, Fondling, Voyeurism
Bad Dreams, Bestiality
Deviation, Depravity
Frigidity, Impotence
Rage, Fear, Anxiety, Debilitating Guilt, Menopause
Manic Depression, Schizophrenia, Exhibitionism, Dementia
Domination, Control, Promiscuity
Shame, Insecurity, Hurt, Victim, Suicide
Cruelty, Hardness, Hate, Harshness, Unscrupulousness
Insanity, Degenerate Mind, Carnal Mind
Idolatry
Distrust, Lost Respect for Mate, Deceit
Undisciplined
Enmity Towards God, Works of Darkness, Mockery
Spiritually Dwarfed Manhood and Womanhood
Defiled, Degraded, Violated
Sexual Bargaining, Married Prostitute and Pimp
Fear of Homosexuality and Lesbianism
Love of Sex, Power and Money
Child and Adult Sexual Molestation
Abnormal and Deviate Sex and Impurities
Depraved Manners, Morals and Character
Subliminal Messages, Sub-audio Suggestions
Alcohol and Drugs
Ignorance, Irresponsibility, Boredom
Doubt, Condemnation, Pressure
Lewdness, Uncleanness, Sexual Liberty
Whore, Prostitute, Harlot, Sex Slave
Enviousness, Jealousy, Cheating
Deficient Thinking
Evil Companionship and Conversation
Useless, Putrid
Lack of Concern, Indifference
Masturbation
Paraphiliac, Rape, Bestiality, Exhibitionism, Fetish Objects
Debilitating Guilt
Abusers of themselves with mankind: Catamites, Arsenokoites and Sodomites; Oral and Anal Sex, and other related demonic families of sexual sins and diseases

ABNORMAL SEXUAL BEHAVIOR

Abnormal

Homosexuality, Bisexual, Transsexual, Transvestite, Gay, Lesbian, Masturbation, Bisexuality, Prostitution, Voyeurism, Exhibitionism, Fetishism, Sexual Fetishism, Zoophilia, Sexual Sadism, Sexual Masochism, Necrophilia, Klismaphilia, Lewdness, Telephone Scatologia, Urophilia, Apotemnophilia, Coprophilia, Coprophagia, Pedophilia, Toucheurism, Frotteurism, Sexual Asphyxia, Rape, Gerontophilia, Pyromania, Bestiality, Air Embolism, Aspiration of Semen

Homosexual

Buggery / Anal Intercourse
Occasional / Exploratory Homosexual
Situational / Deprivation Homosexual
Facultative / Latent Homosexual
Peer / Compulsive Homosexual
Bondage, Flagellation, Weapon Worship, Going in Drag, Fairy Hawk, Fairy Flats, Dream Boat, Dirt, Gay Dirt, Dykes, Butch, Ma'chis'mo, and other related demons and their works.

CHARISMATIC WITCHCRAFT

Prayer

ALMIGHTY GOD, please forgive me for practicing charismatic witchcraft. I break the power of the ruler demons over my family and organization. I break demonic ties, bonds and caps. I break soul ties to pastors, religious leaders and any Christian who has been trying to control me. I break curses placed on me by submitting my will to others. I break curses brought by charismatic witchcraft and control. I break the curse of Jezebel and Ahab. I renounce false gifts given by Satan. I drive out demonic works and associated spirits of witchcraft and mind control as follows in THE NAME OF JESUS CHRIST:

Rejection by Christian brothers, sisters, pastors
Rejection of deliverance and Lake Hamilton Bible Camp
Rejection by husband, wife, mother, father, children
Rejection between deliverance workers, pastors
Rejection in womb, of self, of others
Hurts and deep hurts by Christians
Touch me not, inability to give or receive love, conception in lust

False doctrine, hearsay
False preachers, teachers, evangelists, prophets, apostles
False tongues, prophecy, interpretation, demonic gifts
False religions, religious cults, eastern religions
False love, sweetness, sentimentality
False prosperity, love of money, think and grow rich, money by faith
False positive thinking, metaphysical faith, soulish faith
False charismatic movement, false partial gospel
False shaking, quaking, crying, putting on a show
False cooperating, discipleship

Charismatic witchcraft, witches, warlocks
Domination, control, manipulation, dictatorial
Mind control, blanking, blocking, binding, confusion
Witchcraft, occult, antichrist, familiar spirits, divination
Jezebel, Ahab, passivity, destruction of family priesthood, lukewarmness

Commanding angels for riches, imaging, visualization
Greed, covetousness, mammon
Financial poverty of workers, pastors, churches, camps

A different gospel, another Jesus
Apostate religion, almost fooling the very elect
Spirit of error, spirit of the world,, aborted spirit
Ruler demons over workers, pastors, families, churches, camps
Soul ties and curses from control

Despondency, despair, defeat, hopelessness, morbidity
Strife, contention, bickering, quarreling among brethren
Inability to work with other Christians
Denominational spirits, separation, infighting
Spiritual pride, ego, vanity, pre-eminence, haughtiness
Self idolatry, we are gods, worship of man, fear of man

Mormonism, Jehovah Witnessism, bloodless religions
Catholicism, occult, Masonry, religious demons
Evil eye, third eye, Masonic eye, all seeing eye

Christian fantasy, falseness, false love
Playacting, theatrics, affectation, pretension
Hypocrisy, lying, deceit, deception, delusion, compromise

BODY CURED AND HEALED

Deuteronomy 28 Diseases

ALL DISEASES OF EGYPT AND, EVERY SICKNESS AND EVERY PLAGUE IN BOOK OF LAW: confusion, destruction, perishing, plague, pestilence, sickness, death, consumption (wasting disease), fever, inflammation (blood poisoning), extreme burning (high fever), madness (encephalitis), pestilence,, eye trouble from dust, asthma, emphysema, heart trouble, botch (skin ulcers and boils), itch, scurvy, pellagra, beriberi, psoriasis, madness, blindness, astonishment of heart (terror, amazement), tumors, hemorrhoids, eye and heart fail waiting for their return, destruction (crushed), madness, boils, ulcers (from top of head to sole of feet), impetigo, eczema, astonishment, destruction, distress, wonderful plagues, plagues on children, long chronic illness, no rest, fearful, terror, blindness, depression, heaviness, fear of death, no assurance, fretting and worry always, constant danger

Biblical Diseases

Ague, Blains, Boils, Blemish, Blindness, Botch, Broken-Handed, Broken-Footed, Bruises, Canker, Crook-Backed, Dropsy, Dwarf, Emerods, Flat Nose, Flux, Gangrene, Halt, Impotent, Infirmity, Inflammation, Issue, Itch, Lameness, Leprosy, Lunacy, Madness, Maimed, Murrain, Palsy, Pestilence, Scab, Scale, Scurvy, Sores, Wen, Withered, Worms, Wounds

Princes, Kings & World Rulers

Accident, Accident Prone, Bone Breaker, Back Breaker, Traumatic Shock

Paralysis

Crippling, Deformity, Atrophy, Depression, Discouragement, Hopelessness, Despair, Suicide, Death, Affliction, Spinal Cord Scar Tissue

Roots Of Infirmity

Shame and Embarrassment, Rebellion & Idolatry, Grief, Troubled Will in Conflict, Resentment & Envy, Disobedience, Curse of Jezebel, Vanity & Pride, Curse of the Law, Acupuncture & Acupressure, Witchcraft & Occult, Envy & Jealousness, Hypnotism & Demonism, Taoism & Pantheism, Reincarnation, Astrology, Psychic Healing, Spiritualistic Healing, Hate, Metaphysical Healing, Occult Healing

Ailments

Kidney Stones, Kidney Failure, Kidney Infection, Kidney Panic, Tooth Decay, Christian Science Healing, Traumatic Shock, Leukemia, Cancer of Bone, Traumatic Death, Tuberculous of Bone, Acne, Carbuncles, Skin Cancer, Menstrual Cramps, Diarrhea, Colitis, Cancer of Bowels, Eye Trouble, Bowel Upset, Cancer, Hernia, Heart Disturbances, Melancholy (sadness), Scalp Ailments, Falling Hair, Restlessness, Inability to Sleep, Aimlessness, Futility, Pestilence, Consumption (T.B.), Fever, Inflammation, Botch (boils), Madness, Emerods (Hemorrhoids), Blindness, Encephalitis, Schizophrenia, De la Touretts Syndrome, Polio, Huntington's Cholera, Muscular Sclerosis, Stroke, Scab (measles, small pox), Spinal Meningitis, St. Vita's Dance, Blasting (prevents growth), Scoliosis, Brutishness (unteachable ignorance), Female Cancer (uncontrollable body odor), Heart Attack (astonishment of heart), Venereal Disease (inflammation of a fungus infection in sex organs)

ORGANS AND SYSTEMS

We thank you for healing our bodies as the spirits are cast out. We command the spirits to come out of each organ and system of the body in THE NAME OF JESUS CHRIST:

BLOOD Cells And Platelets, Plasma, Bone Marrow, Spleen, Thymus
CARDIOVASCULAR Heart, Blood Vessels (circulatory, conduction, impulse conducting, portal, vascular)
DIGESTIVE Mouth, Esophagus, Stomach, Small And Large Intestines, Rectum, Anus, Liver, Gallbladder, Pancreas, Appendix (gastrointestinal, alimentary)
ENDOCRINE Thyroid, Parathyroid, Adrenal, Pituitary, Pancreas, Stomach, Pineal, Ovaries, Testes
HEMATOLOGIC (hematopoietic)
IMMUNE
INTEGUMENTARY
ORGANS (chromaffin, cytochrome, hypophyseoportal, microsomal ethanol oxidizing, reticuloendothelial)
LYMPHATIC (lymphoreticular)
MUSCULSOKELETAL Muscles, Tendons, Ligaments, Bones, Joints (muscular, estrapyramical motor)
NEUROLOGIC (brain, spinal cord, nervous, autonomic, central, parasympathetic, peripheral, sympoathetic, vasomotor, vegetative, visceral efferent)
PULMONARY
RENAL
MALE REPRODUCTIVE Penis, Prostate, Seminal Vesicles, Vasa Deferentia, Testes (genital)
FEMALE REPRODUCTIVE Vagina, Cervix, Uterus, Fallopian Tubes, Ovaries (genital)
RESPIRATORY Nose, Mouth, Pharynx, Larynx, Trachea, Bronchi, Lungs (pulmonary)

SKELETAL (haversian, osseous)
SKIN (integumentary)
SUBSYSTEMS
URINARY Kidneys, Ureters, Bladder, Urethra (urologic, urogenital)
Amen

SPIRITUAL ROOTS OF DISEASE

General

Various: genetically inherited disease, manic depression, paranoid schizophrenia, Jungian psychology
Depression: anxiety attacks, use of Prozac and other drugs
Bitterness: anger, hatred, unforgiveness, resentment, retaliation, violence, murder

Specific

Various: scoliosis, sciatica, epilepsy, attention deficit disorder, immune system, Chrons' Disease, ulcerative colitis, diabetes (autoimmune disease), lupus, multiple sclerosis, rheumatoid arthritis, autism, Parkinson's Disease, addictions, masturbation, Alzheimer's Disease, cholesterol, shingles and hives, rosacea, acne, ovarian cysts, breast cysts, systolic acne, endometriosis, herpes, viruses, osteoporisis, spondylolysis, degenerative disc disease, alcoholism, psoriasis, skin diseases, sinus infections, PMS, fibromyalgia, sleep disorders, multiple personality disorder, migraines, allergies, mitral valve prolapse, reflux, CFS (chronic fatigue syndrome), parasites, irritable bowel syndrome, colic, flu, Sjogren's Syndrome, panic attacks, phobias, hypoglycemia, hyperglycemia (diabetes), hypothyroidism (Hashimoto's Disease), hyperthyroidism (Graves' Disease)
Cancer: colon, skin, liver, breast, ovarian, uterine, Hodgkin's Disease, leukemia, prostate
Arthritis: involving inflammation of the joints, osteoarthritis
Nonbacterial Inflammation: interstitial cystitis, prostatitis
Cell Wall Rigidity: asthma, angina pectoris, hypertension (high-blood pressure), toxic retention
Addictive Personality: weight, anorexia and bulimia

Fear, Anxiety And Stress

MCS/EI: multiple chemical sensitivities / environmental illness, power of the tongue
Endocrine System
Limbic System: general adaptation syndrome (GAS), general adaptation syndrome of fear, anxiety and stress
Cardiovascular System: angina (pain), high-blood pressure (hypertension), heart arrhythmias, mitral valve prolapse (heart valve disease), coronary artery disease, strokes, diseases of heart muscle from inflammation, aneurysms, varicose veins, hemorrhoids, thrombophlebitis (vein inflammation)
Muscles: tension headaches, muscle contraction backache
Connective Tissue Disease: rheumatoid arthritis
Related Inflammatory Diseases of Connective Tissue: prostatitis, interstitial cystitis
Pulmonary System: asthma (called hypersensitivity reaction), hay fever
Immune System: immunosuppression or deficiency, autoimmune diseases
Gastrointestinal System: ulcers, irritable bowel syndrome (IBS), diarrhea, constipation, nausea and vomiting, ulcerative colitis, malabsorption (leaky gut)
Genitourinary System: diuresis, impotence, frigidity
Skin: eczema, neurodermatitis, acne

Endocrine System: diabetes mellitus, amenorrhea
Central Nervous System: fatigue and lethargy, Type A Behavior, overeating, depression, insomnia

Sexually Transmitted Diseases

Related Venereal Diseases: Insanity, Endocarditis, Staggering Gait, Weil's Disease, Soft Chancroid, Heart Disease, Granuloma Inguinal, Ulcerative Lesions, Yaws, Bejel, Mumps, Pinta, Venereal Lympogranuloma, Relapsing Fever, Tropical Ulcer, Rat-Bite Fever
Gonorrhea: Pelvic Inflammatory Disease, Blindness, Oral and Anal Sex, Anal Gonorrhea, Pelvic Inflammatory Disease (PID)
Chlamydia: Urethritis, Cervicitis, Epididymitis, Pelvic Inflammatory Disease, Conjunctivitis, Sterility, Nonspecific Urethritis, Rectal Infections, Infertility
Genital Warts: Human Papilloma Viruses (HPV), Cervical Cancer, Penile Warts
Acquired Immune Deficiency Syndrome: AIDS, HIV, ARC, PCP, Pneumonia, Meningitis, Herpes Simplex, Intravenous Drug Users, Addicts, Hemophilia, Homosexual and Bisexual Men and Sex Partners, Blood Transfusions, Candidiasis, Viral Infections, Kaposi's Sarcoma
Syphilis: Homosexual and Bisexual Men and Sex Partners, Heterosexuals, Chancre (Shanker), Paralysis, Senility, Blindness, Congenital Syphilis
Genital Herpes: Cervical Cancer, Prostatic Cancer
Vaginitis: Fungal Vaginitis, Hemophilus, Gardnerella
Other Sexually Transmitted Diseases: Body Lice and Mites, Vaginal and Urinary Tract Infections
Hepatitis: Viral Hepatitis, Homosexuality, Liver Cancer
Intestinal Parasites: Spirochetal Infections

Sexual Dysfunctions And Injuries

Premature Ejaculation, Impotence, Retarded Ejaculation, Erectile Dysfunction, Anorgasmia, Dyspareunia, Prolapse, Endometriosis, Ovarian Tumors, Vaginisumus, Accidents, Structural Damage, Deformities, Hormonal Abnormality

Black Infirmity

infirmity, high blood pressure, heart disease, arthritis, lupus, cancer, stroke, hardening of arteries, mental illness, worry, pandemonium, anxiety, pharmakeia

SECTION 17 - DELIVERANCE WARFARE PRAYERS WITH LISTS

Biblical Curses

I forgive my ancestors and anyone else that has cursed me. I ask that God forgive me and them. I break any curses placed on me or my descendants from uttering a wish of evil against one; to imprecate evil, to call for mischief or injury to fall upon; to execrate, to bring evil upon or to; to blast, vex, harass or torment with great calamities. I break these curses in Jesus' name. I break the curses back to ten generations or even to Adam and Eve on both sides of my family, and destroy every legal hold and every legal ground that demons have to work in my life. I break curses that follow in the name of the Lord Jesus Christ.

In the Name of Jesus Christ, I now rebuke, break, loose myself and my children from any and all evil curses, charms, vexes, hexes, spells, jinxes, psychic powers, bewitchment, witchcraft and sorcery, that have been put upon me or my family line from any persons or from any occult or psychic sources, and I cancel all connected or related spirits and command them to leave me. I thank you, Lord, for setting me free. **But it shall come to pass, if thou wilt not hearken unto the voice of the Lord thy God, to observe to do all His commandments and His statutes which I command thee this day; that all these curses shall come upon thee, and overtake thee.**

Mistreating God's Chosen People, Willing Deceivers, Adultery, Harlotry and Prostitution, Disobedience to Bible, Idolatry, Keeping Cursed Objects, Refusing To Fight For God, House of Wicked, Not Giving To Poor, Stealing, Swearing Falsely By God, Failing To Give Glory to God, Robbing God of Tithes, Dishonoring Parents, Hearkening to Wives Rather Than God, Making Graven Images, Cheating People Out of Property, Taking Advantage of Blind, Oppressing Strangers, Widows and Orphans, Bestiality, Incest With Sister or Mother, Murder Secretly or For Hire, Pride, Putting Trust In Man, Doing The Work of God Deceitfully, Rewarding Evil For Good, Abortion or Causing Unborn To Die, Having Bastards, Murdering Indirectly, Striking Parents, Kidnapping, Cursing Parents, Not Preventing Death, Sacrificing to Gods, Witchcraft, Turning Someone Away From God, Following Horoscopes, Rebelling Against Pastors, Losing Virginity Before Marriage, False Prophets, Rape, Not Disciplining Children, Teaching Rebellion Against God, Cursing Rulers, Refusing To Warn Sinners, Defiling The Sabbath, Sacrificing Humans, Seances and Fortune Telling, Intercourse During Menstruation, Homosexuals and Lesbians, Necromancers, Blaspheming Lord's Name, Being Carnally Minded, Oral and Anal Sex, Children Rebelling, Nonproductivity, Fugitive and Vagabond, Improper Family Structure, Destruction of Family Priesthood, Refusing To Do The Word of God, Family Disorder, Failure and Poverty, Any Sin Worthy of Death, Touching God's Anointed, Perversion of Gospel, Loving Cursing, Choosing That Which God Delights Not In, Looking To World For Help, Stubbornness and Rebellion, Offending Children Believing Christ, Adding To or Taking Away From Bible, **and all Biblical Curses not listed Above.**

Soul Ties

Father, I break and renounce evil soul ties that I have had or may have had with lodges, adulterers, close friends, husbands, wives, engagements, cults and binding agreements between buddies.

Forgive me for developing soul ties with anyone. I forgive those who would control me. I renounce these evil soul ties, break them and wash them away with the shed blood of the Lord Jesus Christ. I break all evil soul ties with the following:

1. Beasts
2. Anyone I Have Had Sex With Outside of Marriage
3. Divorced Mates
4. By Incest, Rape, Fornication, Adultery, Homosexuality, Bestiality, Lesbianism
5. Bloodless Religions, Religious Cults
6. Blood Brothers and Sisters By Rites
7. Witchcraft, Occult, Satan Worship
8. Fortune Tellers, Mediums
9. Psychiatrists, Social Workers, Psychologists, Mental Institutions
10. Finally, I break any agreement with anyone that forms an evil soul tie.

Occult and False Religion

Lord, I now confess seeking from Satan the help that should only come from God. I now confess occultism and false religions as sin. Lord, I now repent and renounce these sins and ask you to forgive me. I renounce Satan and his works: I hate his demons; I count them my enemies. In the Name of Jesus Christ I now close the door on occult practices, and I command such spirits to leave me in the Name of Jesus Christ.

In the Name of Jesus Christ, I now renounce, break and loose myself and my children from psychic powers or bondages and bonds of physical or mental illness, upon me or my family line, as the results of parents or any other ancestors. I thank you Lord, for setting me free. In the Name of Jesus Christ, I now renounce, break and loose myself from demonic subjection to my mother, father, grandparents, or any other human beings, living or dead, that have dominated me in any way, and I thank you, Lord, for setting me free.

I forgive my ancestors and ask that You would forgive me for participating in occult and false religion. I renounce all fortune telling, magic practices and spiritism, cults and false teachings, and Satan worship. I break every curse and soul tie brought about by psychic heredity, occult contacts and religious cults. I now break any demonic hold on my family line due to supernatural experiences apart from God including the following forbidden practices and all that they entail:

Enchantments, Wizardry, Necromancy, Witchcraft, Observer of Times, Fortune Telling, Consulting With Familiar Spirits, Occult Practices, Spiritism, Sorcery, Magic Practices, Son or Daughter Passing Through Fire, Divination, Charmers, False Religious Cults **and any other Occult or False Religious Practice.**

Ungodly Spirits

Lord Jesus, I forgive my ancestors and ask that you forgive me for the following families of ungodly spirits and command that they come out as their name is called:

Spirit of Infirmity or Weakness, Spirit of Antichrist, Spirit of Fear, Deaf Spirit, Perverse Spirit, Dumb Spirit, Sorrowful Spirit, Blind Spirit, Spirit of Slumber, Foul Spirit, Spirit of Whoredoms,

Unclean Spirit, Destroying Spirit, Evil Spirit, Spirit of Divination, Another Spirit, Spirit of Bondage, Hasty of Spirit, Spirit of Error, Haughty Spirit, Spirit of False Doctrines, Perverse Spirit, Spirit of Jealousy, Seducing Spirits, Sad Spirit, Jealous Spirit, Wounded Spirit, Lying Spirit, Proud in Spirit, Spirit of Burning, Familiar Spirit, Spirit of Egypt, Spirit of Heaviness, Spirit of Unclean Devil, Spirit of the World **and all other families of Ungodly Spirits.**

Godly Spirits

Lord Jesus Christ, we ask that you direct the angels to minister to our needs. We loose warring angels, ministering angels, the Holy Spirit and the Seven-Fold Spirit of God. We loose legions of angels including the following Godly spirits:

Spirit of Wisdom, Poor in Spirit, Spirit of God, Spirit of Your Father, Spirit of the Lord, Strong in Spirit, Right Spirit, Spirit of Truth, Holy Spirit, Spirit of Life, Broken Spirit, Spirit of Adoption, Spirit of Princes, Fervent in Spirit, Faithful Spirit, Spirit of Meekness, Humble Spirit, Spirit of Faith, Excellent Spirit, Spirit of Jesus Christ, Spirit of Man, Eternal Spirit, Patient in Spirit, Meek and Quite Spirit, Spirit of the Ruler, Spirit of Glory, Spirit of Judgment, Spirit of Prophecy, Spirit of Understanding, Spirit of Elijah, Spirit of Counsel/Might, Contrite Spirit, Spirit of Knowledge, Good Spirit, New Spirit, Spirit of Deep Sleep, Spirit of Holy Gods, Spirit of Living Creature, Spirit of Grace and Supplication, Spirit of Holiness, Spirit of Christ, Spirit of Grace, Quickening Spirit, Free Spirit **and all other Godly Spirits.**

Cursed Objects and Demon Infestation

Lord Jesus, I ask that you forgive me for having cursed objects in my home. Show me by the Holy Spirit what to destroy:

1. Books and objects identified with anything related to Satan's Kingdom.
2. Sinful activities of former residents that left curses.
3. Knocking or noisy ghosts and apparitions (poltergeist).
4. Owl and frog images of all types.
5. Witch's mask and fetishes used by witch doctors.
6. Objects and literature that pertain to false religions, cults, the occult and spiritism.
7. Graven images of gods (demons).
8. Objects dedicated to demons (idols and artifacts).
9. Ouija boards or other occult paraphernalia.
10. Prayers and worship to demons bring curses on home.
11. Mexican sun gods; idols, incense; Buddhas; hand carved objects from Africa or the Orient; anything connected with astrology, horoscopes, fortune telling, etc.; books or objects associated with witchcraft, good luck charms or cult religions (Christian Science, Jehovah's Witnesses, metaphysics, etc.); rock and roll records and tapes.
12. Jewelry given to a person by someone in witchcraft, hex signs, ancient geometric and mystical motifs, jewelry designed to bring good luck and act as talisman to chase evil.
13. Egyptian ankh, Polynesian tikkis of gods, broken cross (peace symbol), chais, African jujus, Italian horn, protectors from the evil eye, hand with index and little fingers pointing up, crosses, clovers, stars, wishbones, lucky coins, mystic medals, horseshoes, religious fetishes and statues.
14. Products with cryptic curses (hidden, secret, occult curses).
15. Puppets, cult objects or representations. Dolls used for witchcraft and magic.

SECTION 18 - DELIVERANCE WARFARE PRAYERS

SHORT PRAYER

Lord Jesus Christ, I believe you died on the cross for my sins and rose again from the dead. You redeemed me by your blood and I belong to you, and I want to live for you. I confess all my sins, known and unknown, I'm sorry for them all. I renounce them all. I forgive all others as I want you to forgive me. **(Pause to allow forgiveness of others as The Holy Spirit leads.)** Forgive me now and cleanse me with your blood. I thank you for the blood of Jesus Christ which cleanses me now from all sin. And I come to you now as my deliverer. You know my special needs--the thing that binds, that torments, that defiles; that evil spirit, that unclean spirit--I claim the promise of your word, 'Whosoever that calleth on the name of the Lord shall be delivered.' I call upon you now. In the name of the Lord Jesus Christ, deliver me and set me free. Satan, I renounce you and all your works. I loose myself from you, in the Name of Jesus. I command you to leave me right now in Jesus' Name. Amen!

MEDIUM PRAYER

Thank you, Lord, for dying for my sins, for your glorious resurrection, and for making me a new creature in Christ by faith in your precious blood. Dear Lord, I have a confession to make:

1. I have sought supernatural experience apart from you.
2. I have disobeyed your Word.
3. I want you to help me renounce all these things and cleanse me in body, soul and spirit in Jesus' name.
4. I renounce witchcraft and magic, both black and white.
5. I renounce Ouija boards and all other occult games.
6. I renounce all séances, clairvoyance and mediums; ESP, second sight, and mind reading.
7. I renounce all fortune telling, palm reading, tea-leaf reading, crystal balls, Tarot and other card laying.
8. I renounce all astrology and interest in horoscopes.
9. I renounce the heresy of reincarnation and all healing groups involved in metaphysics.
10. I renounce all hypnosis under any excuse or authority.
11.I break any curse placed on me from any occult source, in Jesus' name.
12. I renounce all curiosity about either future or past, and which is outside Thy Will.
13.I renounce water witching or dowsing, levitation, body lifting, table tipping, psychometry and automatic writing.
14.I renounce astral projection and other demonic skills.
15. I renounce all literature I have ever read in any of these fields and vow that I will destroy such books in my own possession.
16.I now break, in the name of Jesus Christ, all psychic heredity, and any demonic hold upon my family line as a result of the disobedience of any of my ancestors. I also break any bonds of physical or mental illness, in Jesus' name.
17.I also break all demonic subjection to my mother, father, grandparents or any other human being.
18. In the name of Jesus Christ I renounce everything psychic and occult.
19. I renounce every cult that denies the Blood of Christ.
20.I renounce every philosophy that denies the Divinity of Christ.
21.I call upon the Lord to set me free.

22. Lord, I have another confession to make. I have not loved, but have resented certain people. I call upon you, Lord, to help me forgive them. I do now forgive **(Here we pause for several minutes while each person puts the names in the prayer which the Lord brings to mind, either of persons living or dead.)**

23.I do now forgive myself.

24. I renounce every evil spirit that binds or torments me and I call upon the Lord to set me free.

LONG PRAYER

Forgiveness

Lord, I have a confession to make: I have not loved, but have resented certain people and have unforgiveness in my heart, and I call upon you, Lord, to help me forgive them. I do now forgive **(name them, both living and dead)** and ask you to forgive them also, Lord. I do now forgive and accept myself, in the name of Jesus Christ.

General Confession

Lord Jesus Christ, I believe that you are the Son of God, that you are the Messiah come in the flesh to destroy the works of the Devil. You died on the cross for my sins and rose again from the dead. I renounce unbelief and doubt as sin. I confess all of my sins and repent. I ask you to forgive me. I believe that your blood cleanses me from all sin.

Pride, Ego And Vanity

Father, I come to you in the Name of Jesus Christ. **These six things doth the Lord hate: yea, seven are an abomination unto him: a proud look, a lying tongue, hands that shed innocent blood, a heart that deviseth wicked imaginations, feet that be swift in running to mischief, a false witness that speaketh lies, and he that soweth discord among brethren.** Father, I renounce these and turn away from them. I humble myself before you and come to you as a little child.

Come To Jesus, The Deliverer

I come to you, Jesus, as my Deliverer. You know all my problems **(name them)**, all the things that bind, that torment, that defile and harass me. I now loose myself from every dark spirit, from every evil influence, from every satanic bondage and from every spirit in me that is not the Spirit of God. I command all such spirits to leave me now in the Name of Jesus Christ.

Prince's Blood Of Jesus

Through the Blood of the Lord Jesus Christ, I am redeemed out of the hand of the Devil. All my sins are forgiven. I am justified, made righteous, just as if I'd never sinned. I am made holy, set apart to God. My body is a temple for the Holy Spirit, redeemed, cleansed, sanctified. **The Blood of Jesus Christ, God's Son,** cleanses me continually from all sin. Therefore Satan has no part in me, no power over me. I renounce Satan, loose myself from him, command him to leave me, in the Name of the Lord Jesus Christ!

Church's Command

In the name of the Lord Jesus Christ, I command Satan and his demons to loose my mind. I ask you to send angels to break, cut and sever fetters, bands, ties and bonds, whether they be by word or deed. I ask you to loose the Seven-Fold Spirit of God: Spirit of the Lord, Fear of the Lord, Counsel, Might, Wisdom, Knowledge, and Understanding into me and my family.

Restoring The Soul

You can insert the name of the person or persons that you are praying for, rather than your name in the prayer.

Father, I come to you in the name of Jesus Christ. I ask you to send angels to gather and restore my soul to its rightful place in me. I ask for you to send your angels to unearth and break earthen vessels, bonds, bands and bindings that have been put upon my soul, willingly or unawares. I ask you to have them free my soul from bondage by whatever means is required. I agree and say Father, that the Lord Jesus Christ is all powerful and effective to do this.

Father, I ask you to send your angels to gather and restore the pieces of my fragmented mind, will and emotions to their proper place. Bring them into their original positions perfectly as you planned them when you formed Adam and Eve in the Garden of Eden.

I have the power and authority of Jesus Christ that has been delegated to me. In the authority of Jesus Christ, I break, cast out and return to the sender, the power of curses upon my head and soul.

Warfare

Heavenly Father, I bow in worship and praise before you. I cover myself with the Blood of the Lord Jesus Christ as my protection. I surrender myself completely and unreservedly in every area of my life to you. I take a stand against the workings of Satan that would hinder me in my prayer life. I address myself only to the true and living God, and refuse any involvement of Satan in my prayer. Satan, I command you, in the Name of the Lord Jesus Christ, to leave my presence with your demons. I bring the Blood of the Lord Jesus Christ between us. I resist the endeavors of Satan and his wicked spirits to rob me of the will of God. I choose to be transformed by the renewing of my mind. I pull down the strongholds of Satan.

MOODYS' PRAYERS

Sins Of Ancestors, Curses, Soul Ties, Fragmented Soul And Subconscious Mind

I forgive my ancestors **(upwards)**, descendants **(downwards)**, and anyone else **(outwards)** that has sinned against me or hurt me in any way **(those outside of me)**. I ask you to forgive them for their many sins and mistakes. I remit all their sins, sever any demonic ties, and set myself free. **I ask God to bless them with all spiritual blessings, bring them into all truth, and meet all of their needs out of His Riches in Glory through Christ Jesus.** I ask that God will forgive me **(Godwards)** for my many sins, and I forgive myself **(inwards)** for sins against my body.

I now take authority over Satan and all the forces of evil according to the Holy Bible, the complete Word of God, and command that you obey it. **In the Name of Jesus Christ, I command these things to be done.**

I break all curses, charms, spells, jinxes, psychic powers, hexes, vexes and demonic ties that bind. I break all soul ties caused by witchcraft, sorcery, bewitchment or sexual sins. Lord Jesus, restore my fragmented soul: mind, will and emotions; send your angels out to recover anything that Satan has stolen from me. Lord Jesus, stir up the demons in my subconscious mind so that they can be identified and cast out. **All these things I pray in the blessed name of Jesus Christ: My Lord, Master and Savior, and command the forces of evil to obey in the Name of Jesus Christ. Amen.**

Taking Spiritual Authority Over The Meeting

Satan, we come against all powers, principalities, evil forces in this world and spiritual wickedness in high places. We come against all demons inside or outside of anyone present, over this city, state, nation and world, in Hell or out of Hell. The Bible says, **Behold, I give unto you power to tread on serpents and scorpions, and over all the power of the enemy: and nothing shall by any means hurt you.** We intend to exercise that power to set ourselves free. Satan, we come against you by the power and blood of Jesus Christ, by the Word of God, by the name of Jesus, by the authority of the believer, in the unity of our spirits. Satan, we tell you that we sit in heavenly places with our Christ Jesus. We are over you, your fallen angels, your demons and all forces of evil. We command you to line up in rank and file and order, and come out quickly. We bind every power that you have and loose ourselves from you in the name of Jesus.

Lord Jesus Christ, we ask that you would send the gifts of the Holy Spirit as needed to minister to the needs of the people and to accomplish what you want done here today. We are careful to give you all the glory, honor, praise and credit for everything that is said or done. We ask all these things in the blessed name of Jesus Christ, our Lord and Master and Savior. And we take authority over Satan according to the whole Word of God. For it's in Jesus name we pray. Amen!

SECTION 19 - PRAYERS AND LISTS OF DEMONS FOR INDIVIDUAL AND MASS DELIVERANCE

ATTACK - ATTACK - ATTACK

ALMIGHTY GOD, WE ASK FORGIVENESS FOR OUR SINS. WE ASK IN THE NAME OF JESUS CHRIST OUR LORD, MASTER AND SAVIOR. AMEN.

CONTENTS

PREFACE

There are various types of demons. They have structure, ranks, functions and orders. There are **powers, principalities, evil forces in this world and spiritual wickedness in high places**. Some categories are **spirit guides, fallen angels, wizards, ghosts, phantoms, vampires, spooks, genii, monsters, sylphs, aliens, gnomes, imps, demons, devils, nature spirits and evil spirits (male and female)**. **Gnomes** would include **dwarfs, elves and minihunes** which are one of the four divisions of **earth spirits**. **Nature spirits** have to do with **fire, water, wind and earth**. **Evil spirits** work in different areas such as magic.

A great deal of time has been spent by both brilliant Christians and satanic magicians to chart out the names, ranks and structure of the demonic army that Satan commands. One accurate method of ranking demons has 365 ranks of demons, with No. 1 being the highest level of demons. The numbers of top level demons are numbered in the trillions, while the lower level imps are incredibly numerous. **Satan has a vast army of evil spirits to use against humans.**

Early Christians and the occult have often divided up the evil spirits (nature spirits) under fire, water, wind, and earth. The power of Enochian magic comes from the Watchtowers of these four elements. The principalities and powers exercise dominion over spirits. Each of these types of evil spirits has a number of specialists in a family.

Where sin flings wide the gates, the vital thing to remember is that there can be a demon of anything. There is a name of a demon for everything that is contrary to THE WORD OF GOD! The demons prefer to be called spirits; probably because of their pride.

DELIVERANCE WARFARE PRAYERS

Short Prayer

LORD JESUS CHRIST, I believe you died on the cross for my sins and rose again from the dead. You redeemed me by your blood and I belong to you, and I want to live for you. I confess my sins, known and unknown, I'm sorry for them. I renounce them. I forgive others as I want you to forgive me. **(Pause to allow forgiveness of others as THE HOLY SPIRIT leads.)**

Forgive me and cleanse me with your blood. I thank you for THE BLOOD OF JESUS CHRIST which cleanses me from sin. I come to you as my deliverer. You know my special needs: the thing that binds, that torments, that defiles, that evil spirit, that unclean spirit. I claim the promise of your word, **Whosoever that calleth on THE NAME OF THE LORD shall be delivered.** I call upon you; deliver me and set me free. Satan, I renounce you and your works. I loose myself from you.

Medium Prayer

LORD JESUS CHRIST, thank you for dying for my sins, for your glorious resurrection and for making me a new creature in CHRIST by faith in your precious blood. I have sought supernatural experience apart from you and disobeyed your Word.

I want you to help me renounce these things and cleanse me in body, soul and spirit. I renounce witchcraft and magic, both black and white; Ouija boards and occult games; séances, clairvoyance and mediums; ESP, second sight, and mind reading; fortune telling, palm reading, tea-leaf reading, crystal balls, Tarot and card laying; astrology and interest in horoscopes; the heresy of reincarnation and healing groups involved in metaphysics; hypnosis;

curiosity about future or past, and which is outside Thy Will; water witching and dowsing, levitation, body lifting, table tipping, psychometry and automatic writing; astral projection and demonic skills; literature I read in these fields and vow that I will destroy such books in my own possession; psychic and occult; cults that deny THE BLOOD OF CHRIST; philosophies that deny THE DIVINITY OF CHRIST; and evil spirits that bind and torment me.

I break curses placed on me from occult sources; psychic heredity, and demonic holds upon my family line as a result of the disobedience of my ancestors; bonds of physical and mental illness; and demonic subjection to my mother, father, grandparents and human beings. I call upon THE LORD JESUS CHRIST to set me free.

Long Prayer

Forgiveness

ALMIGHTY GOD, I have a confession to make: I have not loved, but have resented certain people and have unforgiveness in my heart, and I call upon you to help me forgive them. I do forgive (**name them, both living and dead**) and ask you to forgive them. I do forgive and accept myself.

General Confession

LORD JESUS CHRIST, I believe that you are THE SON OF GOD, that you are the Messiah come in the flesh to destroy the works of the Devil. You died on the cross for my sins and rose again from the dead. I renounce unbelief and doubt as sin. I confess my sins and repent. I ask you to forgive me. I believe that your blood cleanses me from sin.

Pride, Ego And Vanity

ALMIGHTY GOD, I come to you. **These six things doth THE LORD hate: yea, seven are an abomination unto him: a proud look, a lying tongue, hands that shed innocent blood, a heart that deviseth wicked imaginations, feet that be swift in running to mischief, a false witness that speaketh lies, and he that soweth discord among brethren.** I renounce these and turn away from them. I humble myself before you and come to you as a little child.

Come To Jesus, The Deliverer

ALMIGHTY GOD, I come to you as my Deliverer. You know my problems (**name them**), the things that bind, that torment, that defile and harass me. I loose myself from evil spirits and influences, and satanic bondages.

Prince's Blood Of Jesus

Through the Blood of THE LORD JESUS CHRIST, I am redeemed out of the hand of the Devil. My sins are forgiven. I am justified, made righteous, just as if I'd never sinned. I am made holy, set apart to GOD. My body is a temple for THE HOLY SPIRIT, redeemed, cleansed, sanctified. **THE BLOOD OF JESUS CHRIST** cleanses me from sin. Satan has no part in me, no power over me. I renounce Satan, loose myself from him, command him to leave me, in THE NAME OF THE LORD JESUS CHRIST!

Church's Command

In THE NAME OF THE LORD JESUS CHRIST, I command Satan and his demons to loose my mind. I ask you to send angels to break, cut and sever fetters, bands, ties and bonds, whether they be by word or deed. I ask you to loose the Seven-Fold Spirit of God: Spirit of the Lord, Fear of the Lord, Counsel, Might, Wisdom, Knowledge, and Understanding into me and my family.

Restoring The Soul

You can insert the names of the person / persons that you are praying for, rather than your name in the prayer:

ALMIGHTY GOD, I ask you to send angels to gather and restore my soul to its rightful place in me. I ask for you to send your angels to unearth and break earthen vessels, bonds, bands and bindings that have been put upon my soul, willingly or unawares. I ask you to have them free my soul from bondage by whatever means is required. THE LORD JESUS CHRIST is powerful and effective to do this.

I ask you to send your angels to gather and restore the pieces of my fragmented mind, will and emotions to their proper place. Bring them into their original positions perfectly as you planned them when you formed Adam and Eve in the Garden of Eden.

I have power and authority that has been delegated to me. I break, cast out and return to the sender, the power of curses upon my head and soul.

Warfare

ALMIGHTY GOD, I bow in worship and praise before you. I cover myself with the Blood of THE LORD JESUS CHRIST as my protection. I surrender myself completely and unreservedly in areas of my life to you. I take a stand against the workings of Satan that would hinder me in my prayer life. I address myself only to the true and living GOD, and refuse involvement of Satan in my prayer. Satan, I command you to leave my presence with your demons. I bring the Blood of THE LORD JESUS CHRIST between us. I resist the endeavors of Satan and his wicked spirits to rob me of the will of GOD. I choose to be transformed by the renewing of my mind. I pull down the strongholds of Satan.

MOODYS' PRAYERS

Sins Of Ancestors, Curses, Soul Ties, Fragmented Soul And Subconscious Mind

I forgive my ancestors **(upwards)**, descendants **(downwards)**, and others **(outwards)** that have sinned against GOD and hurt me **(those outside of me)**. I ask you to forgive them for their sins and mistakes. I remit their sins, sever demonic ties, and set myself free. **I ask GOD to bless them with spiritual blessings, bring them into truth, and meet their needs out of His Riches in Glory through CHRIST JESUS.** I ask that GOD forgive me **(Godwards)** for my sins, and I forgive myself **(inwards)** for sins against my body.

I ask You to send the gifts of THE HOLY SPIRIT to minister to the needs of the people and accomplish what you want done. I am careful to give you the glory, honor, praise and credit for what is said and done. **These things I ask in the blessed NAME OF JESUS CHRIST: LORD, MASTER AND SAVIOR.**

I command the forces of evil to obey in THE NAME OF JESUS CHRIST. I take authority over Satan and the forces of evil according to the HOLY BIBLE, the complete WORD OF GOD, and command that you obey it. I break curses, charms, spells, jinxes, psychic powers, hexes, vexes and demonic ties that bind. I break soul ties caused by witchcraft, sorcery, bewitchment and sexual sins. Restore my fragmented soul: mind, will and emotions; send your angels out to recover what Satan has stolen from me. Stir up the demons in my subconscious mind so that they can be identified and cast out.

Taking Spiritual Authority Over The Meeting

Behold, I give unto you power to tread on serpents and scorpions (big and little demons)**, and over all the power of the enemy: and nothing shall by any means hurt you** (Luke 10:19). We come against powers, principalities, evil forces in this world and spiritual wickedness in high places. We come against demons inside or outside of anyone present, over this city, state, nation and world, in Hell or out of Hell. We come against you by THE POWER AND BLOOD OF JESUS CHRIST, by THE WORD OF GOD, by THE NAME OF JESUS, by the authority of the believer, in the unity of our spirits, to set ourselves free. We sit in heavenly places over Satan, fallen angels, demons and forces of evil. We command you to line up in rank, file and order, and come out quickly. We bind the power that you have and loose ourselves from you in THE NAME OF JESUS CHRIST of Nazareth. We take authority over Satan and the kingdom of evil according to THE WHOLE WORD OF GOD. Amen!

DELIVERANCE WARFARE PRAYERS WITH LISTS

Biblical Curses

ALMIGHTY GOD, I forgive my ancestors and others that have cursed me. I ask that GOD forgive me and them. I break curses placed on me and my descendants from uttering a wish of evil against one; to imprecate evil, to call for mischief and injury to fall upon; to execrate, to bring evil upon and to; to blast, vex, harass and torment with great calamities. I break the curses back to ten generations and even to Adam and Eve on both sides of my family, and destroy legal holds and grounds that demons have to work in my life.

I rebuke, break, loose myself and my children from evil curses, charms, vexes, hexes, spells, jinxes, psychic powers, bewitchment, witchcraft and sorcery that have been put upon me and my family line from persons, occult and psychic sources, and I cancel connected and related spirits and command them to leave me. I thank you, LORD, for setting me free. **But it shall come to pass, if thou wilt not hearken unto the voice of THE LORD THY GOD, to observe to do all His commandments and His statutes which I command thee this day; that all these curses shall come upon thee, and overtake thee.** I break these curses and those that follow in The Name Of THE LORD JESUS CHRIST.

Mistreating God's Chosen People, Willing Deceivers; Adultery, Harlotry and Prostitution; Disobedience to Bible, Idolatry, Keeping Cursed Objects, Refusing To Fight For God, House of Wicked, Not Giving To Poor, Stealing, Swearing Falsely By God, Failing To Give Glory to God, Robbing God of Tithes, Dishonoring Parents, Hearkening to Wives Rather Than God, Making Graven Images, Cheating People Out of Property, Taking Advantage of Blind; Oppressing Strangers, Widows and Orphans; Bestiality, Incest With Sister or Mother, Murder Secretly and For Hire, Pride, Putting Trust In Man, Doing The Work of God Deceitfully, Rewarding Evil For Good, Abortion and Causing Unborn To Die,

Having Bastards, Murdering Indirectly, Striking Parents, Kidnapping, Cursing Parents, Not Preventing Death, Sacrificing to Gods, Witchcraft, Turning Someone Away From God, Following Horoscopes, Rebelling Against Pastors, Losing Virginity Before Marriage, False Prophets, Rape, Not Disciplining Children, Teaching Rebellion Against God, Cursing Rulers, Refusing To Warn Sinners, Defiling The Sabbath, Sacrificing Humans, Seances and Fortune Telling, Intercourse During Menstruation, Homosexuals and Lesbians, Necromancers,

Blaspheming Lord's Name, Being Carnally Minded, Oral and Anal Sex, Children Rebelling, Nonproductivity, Fugitive and Vagabond, Improper Family Structure, Destruction of Family Priesthood, Refusing To Do The Word of God, Family Disorder, Failure and Poverty, Sins Worthy of Death, Touching God's Anointed, Perversion of Gospel, Loving Cursing, Choosing That Which God Delights Not In, Looking To World For Help, Stubbornness and Rebellion, Offending Children Believing CHRIST, Adding To and Taking Away From Bible, **and Biblical Curses not listed Above.**

Soul Ties

ALMIGHTY GOD, I break and renounce evil soul ties with engagements, lodges, adulterers, close friends, husbands, wives, cults and binding agreements between buddies.

Forgive me for developing evil soul ties. I forgive those who would control me. I renounce these evil soul ties, break them and wash them away with the shed blood of THE LORD JESUS CHRIST:

Beasts; Those I Have Had Sex With Outside of Marriage; Divorced Mates; By Incest, Rape, Fornication, Adultery, Homosexuality, Bestiality and Lesbianism; Bloodless Religions and Religious Cults; Blood Brothers and Sisters By Rites; Witchcraft, Occult and Satan Worship; Fortune Tellers and Mediums; Psychiatrists, Social Workers, Psychologists and Mental Institutions. **Finally, I break agreements with those that form evil soul ties.**

Occult And False Religion

ALMIGHTY GOD, I confess seeking from Satan the help that should only come from You. I confess occultism and false religions as sin. I repent and renounce these sins and ask you to forgive me. I renounce Satan and his works: I hate his demons; I count them my enemies. I close the door on occult practices, and I command such spirits to leave me.

I renounce, break and loose myself and my children from psychic powers, bondages, and bonds of physical and mental illness, upon me and my family line, as the results of parents and other ancestors.

I renounce, break and loose myself from demonic subjection to my mother, father, grandparents, and other human beings, living and dead, that have dominated me.

I forgive my ancestors and ask that you would forgive me for participating in occult and false religion. I renounce fortune telling, magic practices and spiritism, cults and false teachings, and Satan worship. I break curses and soul ties brought about by psychic heredity, occult contacts and religious cults. I break demonic holds on my family line due to supernatural experiences apart from GOD including the following forbidden practices:

Enchantments, Wizardry, Necromancy, Witchcraft, Observer of Times, Fortune Telling, Consulting With Familiar Spirits, Occult Practices, Spiritism, Sorcery, Magic Practices, Son or Daughter Passing Through Fire, Divination, Charmers, False Religious Cults **and other Occult and False Religious Practice.**

Ungodly Spirits

ALMIGHTY GOD, I forgive my ancestors and ask that you forgive me for the following families of ungodly spirits and command that they come out as their name is called:

Spirit of Infirmity and Weakness, Spirit of Antichrist, Spirit of Fear, Deaf Spirit, Perverse Spirit, Dumb Spirit, Sorrowful Spirit, Blind Spirit, Spirit of Slumber, Foul Spirit, Spirit of Whoredoms, Unclean Spirit, Destroying Spirit, Evil Spirit, Spirit of Divination, Another Spirit, Spirit of Bondage, Hasty of Spirit, Spirit of Error, Haughty Spirit, Spirit of False Doctrines, Perverse

Spirit, Spirit of Jealousy, Seducing Spirits, Sad Spirit, Jealous Spirit, Wounded Spirit, Lying Spirit, Proud in Spirit, Spirit of Burning, Familiar Spirit, Spirit of Egypt, Spirit of Heaviness, Spirit of Unclean Devil, Spirit of the World **and other families of Ungodly Spirits.**

Godly Spirits

ALMIGHTY GOD, we ask that you direct the angels to minister to our needs. We loose warring angels, ministering angels, THE HOLY SPIRIT and THE SEVEN-FOLD SPIRIT OF GOD. We loose legions of angels including the following Godly spirits:

Spirit of Wisdom, Poor in Spirit, Spirit of God, Spirit of Your Father, Spirit of the Lord, Strong in Spirit, Right Spirit, Spirit of Truth, Holy Spirit, Spirit of Life, Broken Spirit, Spirit of Adoption, Spirit of Princes, Fervent in Spirit, Faithful Spirit, Spirit of Meekness, Humble Spirit, Spirit of Faith, Excellent Spirit, Spirit of Jesus Christ, Spirit of Man, Eternal Spirit, Patient in Spirit, Meek and Quite Spirit, Spirit of the Ruler, Spirit of Glory, Spirit of Judgment, Spirit of Prophecy, Spirit of Understanding, Spirit of Elijah, Spirit of Counsel and Might, Contrite Spirit, Spirit of Knowledge, Good Spirit, New Spirit, Spirit of Deep Sleep, Spirit of Holy Gods, Spirit of Living Creature, Spirit of Grace and Supplication, Spirit of Holiness, Spirit of Christ, Spirit of Grace, Quickening Spirit, Free Spirit **and other Godly Spirits.**

Cursed Objects And Demon Infestation

ALMIGHTY GOD, I ask that you forgive me for having cursed objects in my home. Show me by THE HOLY SPIRIT what to destroy:

1. Books and objects associated with witchcraft and Satan's Kingdom.
2. Sinful activities of former residents left curses.
3. Knocking and noisy ghosts and apparitions (poltergeist phenomenon).
4. Owl and frog images.
5. Witch's masks and fetishes used by witch and fetish doctors.
6. Objects and literature that pertain to false religions, cult religions (Christian Science, Jehovah's Witnesses, metaphysics, etc.), the occult and spiritism.
7. Graven images of gods (represent demons).
8. Idols and artifacts dedicated to demons.
9. Ouija boards and other occult paraphernalia.
10. Prayers to and worship of demons bring curses.
11. Rings, bracelets, necklaces, charms and other jewelry given to a person by someone in witchcraft.
12. Hex signs, and ancient geometric and mystical motifs being incorporated into designs for clothing, jewelry, decorative objects and china.
13. Rings, pendants, pins and various kinds of jewelry originally designed to bring good luck and to act as a talisman to chase evil.
14. Egyptian ankh (cross with a loop at the top which was an ancient fertility symbol); ancient witchcraft sign of the broken cross (called peace symbol); chais (consists of Hebrew characters spelling life); polynesian tikkis carved to represent various gods; African jujus shaped like snakes, hands, figures and other things; wiggley tail which is called Italian horn; protectors from evil eye; hand with the index and little fingers pointing up (satanic witchcraft sign); rock and roll records and tapes; and a great variety of crosses, clovers, stars, wishbones, lucky coins, mystic medals, horseshoes and other items.

15. Religious fetishes and statues may have dangerous resident demon power.
16. Mexican sun gods, idols, incense, Buddhas, and hand carved objects from Africa and the Orient.
17. Astrological symbols, horoscopes and fortune telling.
18. Products with cryptic, hidden, secret, occult curses.
19. Puppets, cult objects and representations. Dolls used for witchcraft and magic.
20. There is no way to list every demonic object. The list seems to go on and on.

SPECIAL
Prayer

ALMIGHTY GOD, please forgive me for practicing mind control over anyone or having anything to do with programming the total mind control slave. I forgive those who have practiced mind control over me in anyway. I command the following spirits to come out of me in THE NAME OF JESUS CHRIST:

General Deliverance

Spirit guides, fallen angels, wizards, ghosts, phantoms, vampires, spooks, genii, monsters, sylphs, aliens, gnomes, dwarfs, elves, minihunes, imps, demons, nature spirits (fire, water, wind and earth), evil spirits, magic, principalities, powers, structures, ranks, functions and orders.

Deliverance And Inner Healing

Empire, Domination, Control, Blocking, Hate, Fear, Envy, Lust, Slander, Narcolepsy, Soporific, Megalomania, Self Exaltation, Black Wraith, Rancor, Suspicion, Criticism, Sexual Violence, Emotional Stifling, Defilement, Abaddon, Infirmity, Unworthiness, Devouring, Floating In Space, Failing Eyesight, Self Condemnation, Hostility, Deafness, Despair, Incubus, Succubus, Astral Lovers, Sexual Perversion, Rape, Molestation, Bitterness, Denial, Oppression, Uncleanness, Shirkism, Shrike.

Deeper Insights Into The Illuminati Formula

Some Common Types Of Evil Spirits: Anti-Christ, Bondage, Divination, Death, Deaf, Error, Familiar, Fear, Haughtiness, Heaviness, Infirmity, Jealousy, Lying, Perverse, Seducing, Whoredoms, Commanders.

Principal Monarch System Demons: Aesculapius, Apollos, Sacred Snake, Absolom, Amon, Apollyon, Fear, Destruction, Apollo, Astar, Star, Ashtareth, Ashtaroth, Astarte, Ishtar, Balilo, Beelzebub, Beliah, Beliel, Bes, Blackwell, Blood, Black Mass, Choronzon, Dameon, Dagon, CTHULHU, Electra, Enigma, Geb, Gerberus, Guardian Angels, Javen, Kali, Kemosh, Leviathon, Dragon, Tiamet, Lilith, Druidism, Dragon, Wyvern, Nwyvre, Winged Lion, Mammon, Meganosis, Metatron, Enoch, Moriah, Moloch, Molech, Mormo, Nanna, Nemo, Octopus, Orion, Ronwe-Squat, Shu, Typhon, Verono, Vultar, Val, Pan, Rege and Bacchus.

Other Important Demons Involved With Mind Control: Abduscius, Abigor, Abyss, Absu, Nar Mattaru, Cutha, Kutu, Archeron, Adramalech, Agaliarept, ISH, Botis, Aguares, Aim, Bonfire Child, Firechild, Alastor, Amduscias, Unicorn, Amon, Andrealphus, Peacock, Andrealphus, Asmodeus, Lust, Martial Discord, Baal, Legion, Freemasonary, Baalberith, Barbatos, Beelzebub, Behemoth, Belphegor, Blackwell, Botis, Captaintto, Astral Projection, Changeling, Crocell, Dantalion, Joker, Decarabia, Pentacles, Flauras, Andras, Foras, Forneus,

Remove, Tongues, Rhetoric, Furcas, Furfur, Guardians, Goblins, Haborym, Haures, Hydra, Lucifer, Oaths, Dragon, Klotilde, Knochers, Leraje, Leraikka, Lucifer, Satan, Devil, Malebranche, Maleficia, Malphas, Mammon, Marax, Astrology, Marbas, Marchosias, Melchom, Mulciber, Murmur, Navky, Murder, Nebiros, Nysrock, Osculum, Paimon, Paymon, Phenex, Philatanus, Sodomy, Pederasty, Procel, Purson, Put Satanachia, Raum, Sabnack, Seera, Seraphim, Shaba Lidoma, Shax, Sitri, Sexual Enchantment, Nudity, Speculum, Succubus, Sytry, Uphir, Volarire, Watchers, Zepar.

Satanism

Spirit: Spirit Guide
Conscience - Intuition - Worship

Soul: Mind - Will - Emotions
Conscious - Subconscious - Unconscious

Body: Physical - Brain - Sexual Organs

Wer Beasts: Vampires - Werewolves - Zombies

Manifestations: Changelings - Incubi/Succubi - Dopple Gangers - Shape Changings

Objects: Familiar Objects - Fetishes - Talismans - Amulets - Marks - Hagstones -Biofeedback

Curses: Spells - Incantations - Hexes - Vexes

Demons: Son of Satan, Mind Control, Death, Occult, Magic, Witchcraft, Drugs, Child Abuse, Fornication, Demonic Healing, Eastern Religions, Demonic Inheritance, Demonic Games, Rock Music, Voodoo, Familiar and Guiding Spirits, Forces and Powers

BASIC DELIVERANCE

Prayer

ALMIGHTY GOD, I forgive those who have rejected me, been bitter against me and have rebelled against me. Please forgive me for rejection, bitterness and rebellion against others.

In THE NAME OF JESUS CHRIST I command the spirits to come out of the Unconscious, Subconscious and Conscious Mind. I command the families of Rejection, Bitterness and Rebellion, and other families to come out of me and bring their works with them as your name is called:

LIST OF DEMONS FOR BASIC DELIVERANCE

Basic Deliverance

Rejection: Fear of Rejection, Self Rejection.
Bitterness: Resentment, Hatred, Unforgiveness, Violence, Temper, Anger, Retaliation, Murder.
Rebellion: Self Will, Stubbornness, Disobedience, Anti-Submissiveness.
Diseases: Cancer, Arthritis and diseases that come in through Bitterness.

Rejection

Feelings of being Rejected, Refused, Repudiated, Declined, Denied, Rebuffed, Repelled, Renounced, Discarded, Thrown Away, Excluded, Eliminated and Jettisoned.

Rejection, Poor in Spirit, Pride - Ego - Vanity, Double Mindedness, **Fear of Rejection, Self Rejection,** Roots of Rejection, Ahab Jezebel Complex, Destruction of Family Priesthood, Dominance, Homosexuality, Lesbianism, Rebellion, Withdrawal, Overpermissive, Too Harsh, Lying, Guilt, Distrust, Inability to Communicate, Witchcraft Control, Ugliness, Schizophrenia, Anger, Rejection from the Womb, Smoking, Drinking, Dementia Praecox, Instability, Agony, Inability to Give or Receive Love, Insecurity, Inferiority, Fantasy, Unreality, Sexual Perversion, Frustration

Passive-Aggressive Behavior, Lack of Confidence, Repression, Co-Dependency, Ignominy, Disappointment & Guilt, Anti-Social Disorder, Vexation, Introversion, Inhibition, Lashing Out, Abuse of Self & Others, Dysfunction, Projection, Addictions, Sex for Love, Depression, Emotional Instability, Anger, Bitterness, Intense Emotional Pain, Shame, Anxiety, Over-Compensation, Negativism, Dejection, Sadness / Crying, Work-A-Holism, Eating Disorder, Over-Sensitivity, Fear, Afraid to be Alone, Hysteria, Mistrust, Humiliation, Grief, Intensive Emotional Pain, Over-Protection, Overweight, Oppression, Eating disorders, Suicide, Isolation, Betrayal, Torment, Emotional Trauma, Feelings of Rejection, Phobia, Loneliness, Emptiness, Neurosis, Grandiosity, Abandonment, Social Isolation, Emotional Victimization, Deception, Psychological Victimization, Denial, Hopelessness, emotional Callousness, Murder, Bashfulness, Disrepute, Disesteem, Discredit, Worthlessness, Insignificance, Disgrace, Emotional / Psychological Rape, Perversions, Need for Approval / Validation, Dishonor, Suspicions, Post-traumatic Stress Disorder, False / Non-Expectations, Discrimination, Segregation, Exile, Eviction, Scorn, Shun, Ignore / Neglect, Insecurities, Disapproval, Repudiation, Comparison, Favoritism, Dysfunctions, Feeling of Not Being Wanted, Nobody Loves Me Syndrome, Justification of Inappropriate Word / Behavior, **Sabotage of Relationships / Organization / Self / Purpose / Destinies**, Low Self-Worth, **Self: Pity, Depreciation, Consciousness, and Fulfilling Prophecy**.

Bitterness

Feelings of being Bitterly Cursed, Rebellious, Sharp, Acrid, Embittered, Poisoned, Violent, Provoked, Vexed, Grieved, Sorrowing, Bitter Herb, Calamity, Bile, Venom, Angry, Chafed, Most Bitter and Provoked.

Bitterness, Resentment, Hatred, Unforgiveness, Violence, Temper, Anger, Retaliation, Murder, Root of Bitterness, Failure To Forgive, Arthritis, Schizophrenia, Mind Binding, Memory Loss, Recall, Broken Relationships.

Rebellion

Feelings of being Disobeyed, Transgressed, Violated, Disregarded, Defied, Infringed, Shirked, Resisted, Mutiny, Rebelled and Revolted.

Rebellion, Greed, **Disobedience,** Lying, **Self-will,** Hate, **Stubbornness,** Evil Plotting and Planning, **Anti-submissiveness,** Evil Control of Others, Destruction, Unrighteous Judgement, Subversion, Rock Music, Resistance, Christian Rock, Interference, Deceit, Friction, Trickery,

Repulse, Betrayal, Defiance, Pride, Aggressiveness, False Love, Scorn, Arrogance, Sorcery, Conniving, Seduction, Confusion, Sullen Masculine Women, Taking Tranquilizers, Effeminate Men, Taking Drugs, Insecurity, Restless, Frustration, Witchcraft, Depression, Unholy Sex, Doubt.

Haughtiness, Independence, Segregation, Wrath, Separatism, Obstinacy, Insubordination, Defensiveness, Vanity, Strife, Conceit, Loftiness, Non-Compliance, Contempt, Recalcitrance, Unruliness, Waywardness, Rejection of Authority, Defiance, Sedition, Disdain, Selfishness, **Self: Centeredness, Importance, Righteousness and Protection.**

Schizophrenia

Inward

INSECURITY, INFERIORITY
LUST: Fantasy Lust, Perverseness (2)
REJECTION: Fear Of Rejection, Self Rejection, Fear Of Judgment (1)
SELF ACCUSATION: Compulsive Confession (3)
JEALOUSY, ENVY **(PARANOIA)**
SELF PITY
FALSE COMPASSION: False Responsibility (4)
DEPRESSION: Despondency, Despair, Discouragement, Hopelessness, SUICIDE
GUILT: Condemnation, Unworthiness, Shame
PERFECTION: Pride, Vanity, Ego, Intolerance, Frustration, Impatience, Anger
UNFAIRNESS
WITHDRAWAL, FANTASY, DAYDREAM, UNREALITY, VIVID IMAGINATION, Pouting
SELF AWARENESS: Timidity, Shyness
LONELINESS
SENSITIVENESS
TALKATIVENESS: Nervousness, Tension
FEARS: People, Insanity, Germs, Other

Outward

CONFRONTATION: Suspicion, Distrust, Persecution, Fears **(PARANOIA)** (5)
ACCUSATION TOWARD OTHERS: Projection (6)
REBELLION: Disobedience, Anti-Submissiveness
SELF WILL, SELFISHNESS, STUBBORNNESS (7)
SELF DELUSION, SELF DECEPTION, SELF SEDUCTION (8)
PRIDE, UNTEACHABLENESS, JUDGMENTAL, CONTROL & POSSESSIVENESS
BITTERNESS: RESENTMENT, UNFORGIVENESS, MEMORY RECALL, ANGER, RETALIATION
HATRED, VIOLENCE, MURDER

General

Schizo, Damnable Seed, a commanding ruler: Double Mindedness; **(Mental Illness)**, **(Rejection)** - Lust, Fantasy Lust, Perverseness, Jealousy, Paranoia, Self-pity, Depression, Suicide, Guilt, Pride, Vanity, Loneliness, Fears, Attention Seeking, Inferiority, Harlotry, Rejection, Unfairness, Withdrawal, Fantasy, Daydreaming, Timidity, Self Awareness, Shyness, Sensitivity, Chattering,

Nervousness, Vivid Imaginations, Fear Of Germs, Frustration, Impatience, Inordinate Affection For Animals, Intolerance, Insanity, Self-Rejection, Self-Accusation, Tension, Fear Of People, Compulsive Confession, Envy, Fear Of Judgment, False Compassion, Fear Of Rejection, False Responsibility, Despondency, Despair, Discouragement, Hopelessness, Condemnation, Unworthiness, Shame, Perfection, Ego. **(Rebellion)** - Fear, Accusation, Rebellion, Selfishness, Pride, Hatred, Resentment, Violence, Murder, Memory Recall Loss, Disobedience, Paranoia, Suspicion, Distrust, Persecution, Confrontation, Self Will, Projection, Stubbornness, Anger, Root Of Bitterness, Judgmental, Self-Deception, Self-Delusion, Self-Destruction, Unteachableness, Control, Possessiveness, Unforgiveness, Retaliation, False Beliefs, Anti-Submissiveness, mental and spiritual spirits.

Comments

1. Keeps one from giving and receiving love - both GOD's and Man's.
2. Weds one to the world for love.
3. Makes one tell all seeking attention, punishment and correction.
4. Includes inordinate affection for animals.
5. With honesty at all costs - seeking evidence for suspicions.
6. Keeps one from looking at self. Projects one's own faults into others.
7. Weds one to selfish desires.
8. Both mental & spiritual. Seductive: to temporally mislead, decoy.
   Delusion: a misleading of the mind, false belief, fixed misconception.
   In psychiatry: a false belief regarding self - common in paranoia.

BASIC DELIVERANCE

Prayer

ALMIGHTY GOD, I forgive those who have rejected me, been bitter against me and have rebelled against me. Please forgive me for rejection, bitterness and rebellion against others.

In THE NAME OF JESUS CHRIST I command the spirits to come out of the Unconscious, Subconscious and Conscious Mind. I command the families of Rejection, Bitterness and Rebellion, and other families to come out of me and bring their works with them as your name is called:

LIST OF DEMONS FOR BASIC DELIVERANCE

Basic Deliverance

Rejection: Fear of Rejection, Self Rejection.
Bitterness: Resentment, Hatred, Unforgiveness, Violence, Temper, Anger, Retaliation, Murder.
Rebellion: Self Will, Stubbornness, Disobedience, Anti-Submissiveness.
Diseases: Cancer, Arthritis and diseases that come in through Bitterness.

Rejection

Feelings of being Rejected, Refused, Repudiated, Declined, Denied, Rebuffed, Repelled, Renounced, Discarded, Thrown Away, Excluded, Eliminated and Jettisoned.

Rejection, Poor in Spirit, Pride - Ego - Vanity, Double Mindedness, **Fear of Rejection, Self Rejection,** Roots of Rejection, Ahab Jezebel Complex, Destruction of Family Priesthood, Dominance, Homosexuality, Lesbianism, Rebellion, Withdrawal, Overpermissive, Too Harsh,

Lying, Guilt, Distrust, Inability to Communicate, Witchcraft Control, Ugliness, Schizophrenia, Anger, Rejection from the Womb, Smoking, Drinking, Dementia Praecox, Instability, Agony, Inability to Give or Receive Love, Insecurity, Inferiority, Fantasy, Unreality, Sexual Perversion, Frustration

Passive-Aggressive Behavior, Lack of Confidence, Repression, Co-Dependency, Ignominy, Disappointment & Guilt, Anti-Social Disorder, Vexation, Introversion, Inhibition, Lashing Out, Abuse of Self & Others, Dysfunction, Projection, Addictions, Sex for Love, Depression, Emotional Instability, Anger, Bitterness, Intense Emotional Pain, Shame, Anxiety, Over-Compensation, Negativism, Dejection, Sadness / Crying, Work-A-Holism, Eating Disorder, Over-Sensitivity, Fear, Afraid to be Alone, Hysteria, Mistrust, Humiliation, Grief, Intensive Emotional Pain, Over-Protection, Overweight, Oppression, Eating disorders, Suicide, Isolation, Betrayal, Torment, Emotional Trauma, Feelings of Rejection, Phobia, Loneliness, Emptiness, Neurosis, Grandiosity, Abandonment, Social Isolation, Emotional Victimization, Deception, Psychological Victimization, Denial, Hopelessness, emotional Callousness, Murder, Bashfulness, Disrepute, Disesteem, Discredit, Worthlessness, Insignificance, Disgrace, Emotional / Psychological Rape, Perversions, Need for Approval / Validation, Dishonor, Suspicions, Post-traumatic Stress Disorder, False / Non-Expectations, Discrimination, Segregation, Exile, Eviction, Scorn, Shun, Ignore / Neglect, Insecurities, Disapproval, Repudiation, Comparison, Favoritism, Dysfunctions, Feeling of Not Being Wanted, Nobody Loves Me Syndrome, Justification of Inappropriate Word / Behavior, **Sabotage of Relationships / Organization / Self / Purpose / Destinies**, Low Self-Worth, **Self: Pity, Depreciation, Consciousness, and Fulfilling Prophecy**.

Bitterness

Feelings of being Bitterly Cursed, Rebellious, Sharp, Acrid, Embittered, Poisoned, Violent, Provoked, Vexed, Grieved, Sorrowing, Bitter Herb, Calamity, Bile, Venom, Angry, Chafed, Most Bitter and Provoked.

Bitterness, Resentment, Hatred, Unforgiveness, Violence, Temper, Anger, Retaliation, Murder, Root of Bitterness, Failure To Forgive, Arthritis, Schizophrenia, Mind Binding, Memory Loss, Recall, Broken Relationships.

Rebellion

Feelings of being Disobeyed, Transgressed, Violated, Disregarded, Defied, Infringed, Shirked, Resisted, Mutiny, Rebelled and Revolted.

Rebellion, Greed, **Disobedience,** Lying, **Self-will,** Hate, **Stubbornness,** Evil Plotting and Planning, **Anti-submissiveness,** Evil Control of Others, Destruction, Unrighteous Judgement, Subversion, Rock Music, Resistance, Christian Rock, Interference, Deceit, Friction, Trickery, Repulse, Betrayal, Defiance, Pride, Aggressiveness, False Love, Scorn, Arrogance, Sorcery, Conniving, Seduction, Confusion, Sullen Masculine Women, Taking Tranquilizers, Effeminate Men, Taking Drugs, Insecurity, Restless, Frustration, Witchcraft, Depression, Unholy Sex, Doubt.

Haughtiness, Independence, Segregation, Wrath, Separatism, Obstinacy, Insubordination, Defensiveness, Vanity, Strife, Conceit, Loftiness, Non-Compliance, Contempt, Recalcitrance,

Unruliness, Waywardness, Rejection of Authority, Defiance, Sedition, Disdain, Selfishness, **Self: Centeredness, Importance, Righteousness and Protection.**

Schizophrenia

Inward

INSECURITY, INFERIORITY
LUST: Fantasy Lust, Perverseness (2)
REJECTION: Fear Of Rejection, Self Rejection, Fear Of Judgment (1)
SELF ACCUSATION: Compulsive Confession (3)
JEALOUSY, ENVY **(PARANOIA)**
SELF PITY
FALSE COMPASSION: False Responsibility (4)
DEPRESSION: Despondency, Despair, Discouragement, Hopelessness, SUICIDE
GUILT: Condemnation, Unworthiness, Shame
PERFECTION: Pride, Vanity, Ego, Intolerance, Frustration, Impatience, Anger
UNFAIRNESS
WITHDRAWAL, FANTASY, DAYDREAM, UNREALITY, VIVID IMAGINATION, Pouting
SELF AWARENESS: Timidity, Shyness
LONELINESS
SENSITIVENESS
TALKATIVENESS: Nervousness, Tension
FEARS: People, Insanity, Germs, Other

Outward

CONFRONTATION: Suspicion, Distrust, Persecution, Fears **(PARANOIA)** (5)
ACCUSATION TOWARD OTHERS: Projection (6)
REBELLION: Disobedience, Anti-Submissiveness
SELF WILL, SELFISHNESS, STUBBORNNESS (7)
SELF DELUSION, SELF DECEPTION, SELF SEDUCTION (8)
PRIDE, UNTEACHABLENESS, JUDGMENTAL, CONTROL & POSSESSIVENESS
BITTERNESS: RESENTMENT, UNFORGIVENESS, MEMORY RECALL, ANGER, RETALIATION
HATRED, VIOLENCE, MURDER

General

Schizo, Damnable Seed, a commanding ruler: Double Mindedness; (**Mental Illness**), (**Rejection**) - Lust, Fantasy Lust, Perverseness, Jealousy, Paranoia, Self-pity, Depression, Suicide, Guilt, Pride, Vanity, Loneliness, Fears, Attention Seeking, Inferiority, Harlotry, Rejection, Unfairness, Withdrawal, Fantasy, Daydreaming, Timidity, Self Awareness, Shyness, Sensitivity, Chattering, Nervousness, Vivid Imaginations, Fear Of Germs, Frustration, Impatience, Inordinate Affection For Animals, Intolerance, Insanity, Self-Rejection, Self-Accusation, Tension, Fear Of People, Compulsive Confession, Envy, Fear Of Judgment, False Compassion, Fear Of Rejection, False Responsibility, Despondency, Despair, Discouragement, Hopelessness, Condemnation, Unworthiness, Shame, Perfection, Ego. (**Rebellion**) - Fear, Accusation, Rebellion, Selfishness, Pride, Hatred, Resentment, Violence, Murder, Memory Recall Loss, Disobedience, Paranoia, Suspicion, Distrust, Persecution, Confrontation, Self Will, Projection, Stubbornness, Anger, Root

Of Bitterness, Judgmental, Self-Deception, Self-Delusion, Self-Destruction, Unteachableness, Control, Possessiveness, Unforgiveness, Retaliation, False Beliefs, Anti-Submissiveness, mental and spiritual spirits.

Comments

1. Keeps one from giving and receiving love - both GOD's and Man's.
2. Weds one to the world for love.
3. Makes one tell all seeking attention, punishment and correction.
4. Includes inordinate affection for animals.
5. With honesty at all costs - seeking evidence for suspicions.
6. Keeps one from looking at self. Projects one's own faults into others.
7. Weds one to selfish desires.
8. Both mental & spiritual. Seductive: to temporally mislead, decoy.
   Delusion: a misleading of the mind, false belief, fixed misconception.
   In psychiatry: a false belief regarding self - common in paranoia.

ABUSED CHILDREN

Call for demon spirits that went in from the abuser (Spirits of Abuse). Call out the Victim Spirit (advertises to be victimized). Come against abuse: mental (mind, will and emotion), physical, spiritual, material and sexual.

BASTARDS AND INCEST

Comments

At least 25 infectious organisms are transmitted through sexual contact. The eight most common include: **Curable (Bacterial) STD's:** Chalamydia, Gonorrhea, Syphilis and Trichomoniasis. **Incurable (Viral) STD's:** Genital Herpes, Human Papilloma Virus (HPV), Hepatitis B and Human Immunodeficiency Virus (HIV) / AIDS. Other diseases are caused by STD's. We curse the bacterial and viral organisms.

Prayer

ALMIGHTY GOD, I forgive my ancestors for creating bastards and committing incest. Please forgive me for the same sins. I break the curses of the bastard and incest on me and my descendents. I command the following spirits of sexual sins and diseases to come out of me in THE NAME OF JESUS CHRIST: (Use the OVERALL LIST OF DEMONS for sex.)

CHARISMATIC WITCHCRAFT

Prayer

ALMIGHTY GOD, please forgive me for practicing charismatic witchcraft. I break the power of the ruler demons over my family and organization. I break demonic ties, bonds and caps. I break soul ties to pastors, religious leaders and any Christian who has been trying to control me. I break curses placed on me by submitting my will to others. I break curses brought by charismatic witchcraft and control. I break the curse of Jezebel and Ahab. I renounce false gifts given by Satan. I drive out demonic works and associated spirits of witchcraft and mind control as follows in THE NAME OF JESUS CHRIST:

Rejection by Christian brothers, sisters, pastors
Rejection of deliverance and Lake Hamilton Bible Camp

Rejection by husband, wife, mother, father, children
Rejection between deliverance workers, pastors
Rejection in womb, of self, of others
Hurts and deep hurts by Christians
Touch me not, inability to give or receive love, conception in lust

False doctrine, hearsay
False preachers, teachers, evangelists, prophets, apostles
False tongues, prophecy, interpretation, demonic gifts
False religions, religious cults, eastern religions
False love, sweetness, sentimentality
False prosperity, love of money, think and grow rich, money by faith
False positive thinking, metaphysical faith, soulish faith
False charismatic movement, false partial gospel
False shaking, quaking, crying, putting on a show
False cooperating, discipleship

Charismatic witchcraft, witches, warlocks
Domination, control, manipulation, dictatorial
Mind control, blanking, blocking, binding, confusion
Witchcraft, occult, antichrist, familiar spirits, divination
Jezebel, Ahab, passivity, destruction of family priesthood, lukewarmness

Commanding angels for riches, imaging, visualization
Greed, covetousness, mammon
Financial poverty of workers, pastors, churches, camps

A different gospel, another Jesus
Apostate religion, almost fooling the very elect
Spirit of error, spirit of the world,, aborted spirit
Ruler demons over workers, pastors, families, churches, camps
Soul ties and curses from control

Despondency, despair, defeat, hopelessness, morbidity
Strife, contention, bickering, quarreling among brethren
Inability to work with other Christians
Denominational spirits, separation, infighting
Spiritual pride, ego, vanity, pre-eminence, haughtiness
Self idolatry, we are gods, worship of man, fear of man

Mormonism, Jehovah Witnessism, bloodless religions
Catholicism, occult, Masonry, religious demons
Evil eye, third eye, Masonic eye, all seeing eye

Christian fantasy, falseness, false love
Playacting, theatrics, affectation, pretension
Hypocrisy, lying, deceit, deception, delusion, compromise

DRUNKENNESS AND GLUTTONY

Prayer

ALMIGHTY GOD, I Forgive those who have rejected me and caused me to seek food and drink for comfort. I ask GOD for forgiveness for drunkenness and gluttony, and any other addictions such as drugs and medicines. I forgive my ancestors who were drunkards and gluttons, and break curses and demonic ties on me. I cast out the following list of demons from myself in THE NAME OF JESUS CHRIST:

Gluttony	Drunkenness
Nervousness	Alcohol
Compulsive Eating	Medications for Drunkenness
Resentment	Desire
Frustration	Addiction to Alcohol
Idleness	Bondage
Self-Pity	Slavery
Self-Reward	Fantasy
Caffeine	Fears
Diet Pills	Flashback
Indulgence	Habit
Surfeiting	Unreality
Addiction to Food	Craving for Alcohol
Craving Particular Foods	Addiction to Any kind of Beverage
I Like To Eat	

PERFECT LOVE

See chapters on **Mind** and **Family** in the **Deliverance Manual**. You will discover demons not on the list. The list is for those commonly found associated with these problems. This could be any spirit that keeps you from loving: Father - Son - Holy Spirit, other people and yourself.

Prayer

ALMIGHTY GOD, I thank You that You loved me so much that You died on the Cross for me. Please forgive me for not loving you, my relatives and others. I forgive my relatives and others for not loving me. I command the following families of inability to give and receive love, and any related spirits to leave me in THE NAME OF JESUS CHRIST:

Lying	Unstable	Fear	Fighting
Fear of loss of love	Unlovable	Pouting	Violent
Fear of being loved	Sly	Cursing	Victim
Manipulation	Cunning	Berating	Alcohol
Drugs	Torment	Suicide	Morbid
Coldhearted	Beating	Lonely	Witchcraft
Unfeeling	Guilt	Inferiority	Uncalled for laughter
Unstable	Destruction	Timid	Silly
Loveless	Jezebel	Shy	Foolishness
Don't Care	Ahab	Suspicious	Pride
Inability To Give And Receive Love			

INGRATITUDE

Prayer

ALMIGHTY GOD, I repent for having ingratitude towards GOD and others. Please forgive me and help me to have an attitude of gratitude irregardless of what happens in my life. Let me have joy in THE LORD and rejoice in THE LORD always. I command these spirits to leave me In THE NAME OF JESUS CHRIST:

Ingratitude to God
Thanklessness
Punishment
Cover-Up Lies
Fear of Failure
Futility
Stupid Speculations
Lack of Knowledge
Sexual Impurity
Incest
Unrighteousness
Covetousness
Envy
Strife
Ill-will
Gossip
Insolence
Inventors of Evil
Without Conscience
Loneliness
Poverty in Soul
Poverty in Purse
Self-centeredness
Proud
Ungrateful
Unholy
Relentless
Troublemakers
Loose Morals
Treacherous
Self-conceited
Anger Towards God
Abusive/Contemptuous
Blasphemous Scoffers
Arrogant & Contemptuous

Dishonor of God
Hatred Towards Gods
Discontent
Cringing Fear
Dishonor of Self
Foolish Reasoning
Senseless Minds
Lack of Wisdom
Homosexuality
(Male or Female)
Iniquity
Grasping Greed
Jealousy
Deceit
Cruel Ways
Slandering
Arrogance
Undutiful To Parents
Faithlessness
Mercilessness
Poverty of Spirit
Want
Insufficiency
Murmuring & Complaining
Boasters
Profane
Unforgiving
False Accusers
Fierce
Betrayers
Hypocrites

Rejection of God & his
dealings with you
Lying To Self
Ineptness
Dishonor of Others
Vain/Godless Imaginations
Foolishness
Idolatry
Indecency
Loathsomeness
Guilt
Malice
Murder
Treachery
Secret Backbiting
Hateful to God
Boasting
Having No Understanding
Heartlessness
Fantasy
Poverty in Body
Lack
Rationalization
Disobedient To Parents
Callous and Inhuman
Lacking Natural Affection
Intemperate
Haters of Good
Rash
Lovers of Sexual Pleasures
and Vain Amusements

SELF

Prayer

ALMIGHTY GOD, please forgive me for thinking more about myself than about You and others that You want me to love. I repent for miserable thoughts about myself. I will rejoice and have joy in You at all times and under all situations. I will love THE LORD MY GOD with all my heart, and with all my soul, and with all my mind. I will love my neighbor as myself. I will love my enemies. I command the family of self demons to come out of me in THE NAME OF JESUS CHRIST:

Rather than calling out each name, you can call out the family of self demons.

Self-abhorring
Self-absorbed
Self-accusation
Self-admiring
Self-affrighted
Self-aggrandizement
Self-applause
Self-approbation
Self-awareness
Self-banished
Self-baptizer
Self-beguiled
Self-betrayal
Self-blinded
Self-concern
Self-condemnation
Self-condemning
Self-conflict
Self-consuming
Self-contempt
Self-criticism
Self-crucifixion
Self-deceiving
Self-degradation
Self-deluded
Self-depraved
Self-depreciation
Self-despair
Self-destroying
Self-devouring
Self-diffidence
Self-diffusive
Self-disparagement
Self-display
Self-loving
Self-made
Self-despraise
Self-deserving
Self-ease
Self-evolution
Self-exaggeration
Self-exalting
Self-exposure
Self-exulting
Self-flattering
Self-forgetfulness
Self-harming
Self-idolized
Self-ignorance
Self-immolating
Self-indignation
Self-indulging
Self-infliction
Self-killed
Self-lauding
Self-loathing
Self-neglecting
Self-oblivion
Self-partiality
Self-pity
Self-pleasing
Self-preference
Self-pride
Self-repression
Self-reproving
Self-repulsive
Self-restriction
Self-reverence
Self-ruined
Self-scorn
Self-interest
Self-righteous
Self-seduction
Self-starved
Self-subjugation
Self-subversive
Self-suppression
Self-suspended
Self-suspicious
Self-tormenting
Self-torturing
Self-unforgiveness
Self-worshiper
Self-abasing
Self-abnegation
Self-absorption
Self-abuse
Self-annihilation
Self-appointed
Self-assumed
Self-begotten
Self-centered
Self-collected
Self-conceited
Self-conscious
Self-contained
Self-contradiction
Self-deception
Self-delusion
Self-destruction
Self-distrust
Self-esteem
Self-hood
Self-hatred
Self-importance
Self-ishness
Self-torture
Self-willed

Self-opinionated
Self-pollution
Self-seeking
Self-wrong

HOW NOT TO DO DELIVERANCE

Prayer

ALMIGHTY GOD, please forgive me for agreeing with the doctrines of demons and not with the truth of THE HOLY SPIRIT, rejecting deliverance and rebelling against THE WORD OF GOD; having fears of deliverance, demons and people; and becoming bitter against GOD and man for me being in bondage. I command the following spirits to come out of me in THE NAME OF JESUS CHRIST:

Fear of Rejection
Fear of Men's Opinions
Fear of Disapproval
Bitterness
Rebellion
Stubbornness
Anti-Submissiveness
Disobedience
Fear of Criticism
Insecurity
Timidity
Inadequacy
Ineptness
Distrust
Fantasy
Compromise
Fear of Failure
Ego
Pretense
Argument
Mockery
Cynicism
Dread
Apprehension
Roving
Restlessness
Unreality
Indifference
Passivity of Mind
Lethargy
Depression
Discouragement
Defeatism
Hopelessness
Heaviness
Burden
Forgetfulness
Rationalization
Deception
Discontent
Fatigue
Selfishness
Hypocrisy
Smug
Shame
Sexual Impurity
Cult Involvement
Embarrassment
Self-Will
Disgust
Worry
Anxiety
Fear of Reproof
Fear of Confrontation
Confusion
Doubt
Unbelief
Indecision
Procrastination
Pride
Play-Acting
Frustration
Hyperactivity
Carelessness
Heedlessness
Complacency

REFERENCES

1. Pigs In The Parlor - Short Prayer.
2. Out In The Name Of Jesus - Medium Prayer.
3. Hegewisch Baptist Church - Long Prayer.
4. Believer's Position of Power & Authority Deliverance Workbook by J.M. Haggard (deceased).
5. Deliverance and Inner Healing by John and Mark Sandford.
6. They Know Not What They Do, **The Illuminati Formula Used To Create An Undetectable Total Mind Controlled Slave**, and **Deeper Insights into the Illuminati Formula** by Fritz Springmeier and Cisco Wheeler, 1630 Stella Rd., Longview, WA 98632.
7. Binding The Strong Man by N. Cindy Trimm.

8. Warfare Prayers; Curses & Soul Ties / Binding & Loosing Spirits; Invading Enemy Territory; Getting Started in Deliverance; The Satanic Cosmos; and **Principles of Deliverance & Mass Deliverance** by Win Worley

9. Deliverance Manual by Gene and Earline Moody.

10. Spiritual Warfare Manual, **How To Do Deliverance Manual**, **Sexual Deliverance Manual**, **Witchcraft Deliverance Manual**, **Curses Deliverance Manual**, **Healing Deliverance Manual**, **Spiritual Warfare Prayer Book** and **Mini Deliverance Manual** by Gene Moody

SECTION 20 - MAINTAINING YOUR DELIVERANCE FROM EVIL SPIRITS

CONTENTS

SCRIPTURE BRINGING ASSURANCE, CONFIDENCE, DELIVERANCE, PROTECTION, & REDEEMING

Psalms 1:1-3 (Meditate)	Matthew 8:17 (Sicknesses)
17:4 (Words)	Mark 11:23 (Saith)
23:4 (Fear of Evil)	Luke 9:23 (Cross)
31:2 (Defend)	John 8:36 (Free)
34:7, 10, 19 (Deliver)	10:10 (Life)
46:1, 5, 10 (Help)	16:13 (Truth)
55:18, 22 (Sustain	Rom. 8:1, 2, 32 & 37 (Free)
68:19 (Benefits)	I Cor. 2:16 (Mind)
71:1 (Trust)	6:17 (One Spirit)
91:5 (Not Afraid)	10:13 (Temptation)
97:10 (Preserve)	12:7-14 (Gifts)
103:3 (Forgiveness)	14:33 (Peace)
107:2, 6 (Redeemed)	II Cor. 2:14 (Triumph)
119:133 (Order Steps)	3:17 (Liberty)
147:3 (Health)	10:5 (Mind)
Prov. 1:33; 3:26 (Safely)	Galations 6:2 (Burdens)
Isaiah 26:3 (Peace)	Eph. 6:16 (Shield)
41:10, 13 (Help)Phil.	4:7-8, 19 (Needs)
50:7 (Help)	I Thes. 5:14 (Praying)
55:7 (Pardon)	II Thes. 3:3 (Keep)
59:19 (Standard)	II Tim. 1:7 (Power & Love)
61:3 (Oil of Joy)	Hebrews 10:17 (Forgiven)
Jeremiah15:21 (Redeem)	I John 2:14 (Overcome)
Ezekiel33:16 (Live)	3:8 (Destroy Devil)
Micah 7:19 (Compassion)	4:4 (Overcome)

50:7 (Help)
55:7 (Pardon)
59:19 (Standard)
61:3 (Oil of Joy)

Rev. 12:11 (Overcome)

SEVEN STEPS FOR RETAINING DELIVERANCE (EXCERPTS)

Put on the whole armour of God as set forth in Eph. 6:10-18. There are seven pieces of armour:

1. Loins girt about with **truth**.
2. The breastplate of **righteousness**.
3. Feet shod with the preparation of the **Gospel of peace**.
4. The shield of **faith**.
5. The helmet of **salvation**.
6. The sword of the Spirit which is the **Word of God**.
7. **Praying in the Spirit.**

Refuse the thoughts that demons give you and replace them with spiritual thoughts (Phil. 4:8).

Positive confession is faith expressed. Negative confessions characterize demonic influence and will open the door to the enemy (Mark 11:23).

Jesus withstood Satan's temptation by using Scripture. The Word is a mirror to the soul (James 1:22-25); it is a lamp unto the feet for guidance (Psalm 119:105); it is a cleansing agent (Eph. 5:25-26); it is a two-edged sword, laying bare the heart (Heb. 4:12); and it is food for the spirit (I Pet. 2:2 ; Matt. 4:4). No person can long maintain deliverance apart from the Word of God as a primary factor in his life (Psalm 1:1-3)!

Take up your cross daily and follow Jesus (Luke 9:23). If fleshly appetites, desires and lusts are not brought to the cross, a way for demons to return will be left open (Gal. 5:19-21, 24).

Develop a life of **continuous praise and prayer** which silences the enemy. Pray in the Spirit (in tongues) and also in the understanding (I Cor. 14:14). **Pray without ceasing** (I Thes. 5:17).

Maintain a life of fellowship and spiritual ministry. It is the sheep that wanders from the flock that is most endangered. Desire spiritual gifts and yield to their operation through you within the body of Christ (I Cor. 12:7-14).

Commit yourself totally to Christ. Determine that every thought, word and action will reflect the very nature of Christ. Faith and trust in God is the greatest weapon against the Devil's lies (Eph. 6:16).

Doing these seven things will insure that your "house" (life) is filled after having been cleansed. Do not settle for anything less (Romans 5:10)!

HOW TO KEEP FREE FROM OPPRESSING SPIRITS (EXCERPTS)

Fill yourself with the Word of God and be obedient to what the Word says. You become God-possessed as you hear and do the Words of the Father. You become demon-possessed as you hear and do the words of the enemy (John 14:23).

Avail yourself of the **Blood of Jesus**. Learn to ask forgiveness when you sin. Learn to stand tall in His love and grace. Satan must respect the blood (Rev. 12:11).

Take your freedom by faith. This is your position, declare it, stand on the Word, get stubborn with the Devil, this is your heritage (Luke 10:19).

Resist the Devil, be sober and vigilant, resist steadfast in the faith, and he will flee from you (I Peter 5:8-10).

1. **A loving spirit is needed.** Refuse to be hateful and mean; confess love (Matt. 5:44).
2. **A forgiving spirit is needed.** An unforgiving spirit lets the enemy on you again (Mark 11:25).
3. **A tender spirit is needed.** Jesus did not bite back. He was tender: you be like Him. Refuse to yield to the retaliation spirit; away with critical spirits. Learn to recognize the striving spirit, it is from the Devil, do not yield to it; it will bring you into bondage again. Learn to yield to the peaceable spirit; be a peacemaker. Learn to exercise mercy and gentleness; these are Christ-like actions. Remember any enemy spirit that you yield to will bring bondage. Yield to Christ's love, meekness and tenderness, and liberation comes (II Tim. 2:24).

You must forsake sin lest a worse thing come upon you (John 5:14).

HOLDING YOUR DELIVERANCE (TESTIMONY OF A WOMAN)

After Pastor Worley cast out spirits of sinus trouble and migraine headaches, I had three glorious weeks of freedom from any pain.

Suddenly one morning I awoke shocked to find I had all the symptoms of sinus and migraine.

When I realized what was happening, I took authority over Satan and his demons and commanded them to leave me in Jesus' name.

Later the same morning this happened, I received a letter from Pastor Worley warning the Devil would use this very tactic but that I must resist him and refuse to accept his attacks.

I believe that, according to Mark 11:23, many times what we say or confess with our lips can be more important than what we believe. The word **believe** occurs only once in the verse while **say** is repeated three times. The last part of the passage is **he shall have whatsoever he saith**.

The submitted, resisting child of God may expect Satan to flee from him (James 4:7). We must learn to hold the deliverance areas against the onslaughts of a determined foe (Joshua 1:7-9; Deut. 28).

WALKING IN FREEDOM AFTER DELIVERANCE (EXCERPTS)

Have you been delivered from unclean spirits? Praise the Lord (Eph. 6:12; Mark 16:17).

Walking in the Spirit after a deliverance is essential in order to keep a person free (Eph. 6:14-17).

It may be that unclean spirits from which you are now free had been with you for a very long time. In such cases, you can expect several weeks up to a year after deliverance during which the Lord will gradually heal your mind and emotions (Rom. 8:37).

In order to avoid the enemy's snares, **it helps to recognize some of his strategy.**

The Scriptures say that **Satan is the father of lies**. Even though they are now outside of you, unclean spirits still talk to you (John 8:36).

One meaning for the word **Satan is accuser**. You may find yourself feeling guilty for having had unclean spirits or for your past sins (Psalm 13:5).
The enemy may **try to intimidate you** with demonstrations of his power. Don't be frightened if things seem to go wrong for you for a while or if some symptoms from before deliverance seem to reappear.
You may find yourself tempted with old habits or behavior that doesn't fit in with Christian life. The Devil has a way of making the old times seem rosy to us just like he tricked the Israelites in the desert into missing the "leeks and onions" that they left behind in Egypt (John 10:10; Psalm 37).

Recognizing the enemy's strategy is helpful but it does not win the battle for us. It is more important that you learn and practice some positive principles that will enable you to gain ground quickly and hold it. The following five points are easy to remember and will help you tremendously:

1. **Focus your attention on Jesus** (Rev. 12:11).
2. **Allow the Holy Spirit to have His way with you** (John 16:13).
3. **Immerse yourself in the Scriptures;** the Bible is the written Word of God (John 8:31).
4. **Tell the Devil and his unclean spirits in Jesus' name to go away and leave you alone.** Make it clear that you intend to follow Jesus no matter what (James 4:7).
5. **Hang onto other Christians.** The Christian walk is not a solo performance (Gal. 6:2).
6. If you practice these five faith principles, your post-deliverance problems will be minimal and your progress steady (Luke 4:17-21).

BY THIS I OVERCOME THE DEVIL (EXCERPTS)

1. Through the blood of Jesus, I am **redeemed** out of the hand of the Devil (Eph. 1:7).
2. Through the blood of Jesus, all my **sins are forgiven** (Psa. 107:2).
3. The blood of Jesus Christ, God's Son, continually **cleanses** me from all sin (I John 1:7).
4. Through the blood of Jesus, I am **justified**, made righteous, just-as-if I'd never sinned (Rom. 5:9).
5. Through the blood of Jesus, I am sanctified, made holy, set apart to God (Heb. 13:12).
6. My body is a **temple of the Holy Spirit**, redeemed, cleansed, by the blood of Jesus (I Cor. 6:19-20).
7. Satan has no place in me, no power over me, through **the Blood of Jesus and the Word of God** (Rev. 12:11).

TAKE HEAVEN BY FORCE

We are not **wrestling** against the Father, Son and Holy Spirit, but against Satan and his forces of evil. God has given us the abundant life but we have to take it by **force** from Satan! This is analogous to Israel; God gave them the promised land and then told them to take it by force (Eph. 6:12).

Two verses clearly illustrate this Bible principle:
Matt. 11:12Kingdom of heaven suffereth **violence** and the violent take it by **force** (abode of God is to be seized and the forces seized it).
Luke 16:16Kingdom of God is preached, and every man **presseth** into it (rule of Supreme Deity is preached and every man **forces** into it).

Some other good **fighting** verses are:
Psalm 57:6They have digged a pit before me.
Isa. 54:17No weapon formed against thee shall prosper.
Matt. 15:26The woman fought for deliverance for her child (15:21-28)!
II Cor. 10:3-6Weapons of our warfare.
Eph. 6:10-18Put on the whole armour of God.
Rev. 12:11And they overcame him.

HOW TO TREAT DEMONS

Matt. 9:33**Cast** - to eject, drive out, pluck (Dumb Demoniac).
Matt. 9:34**Casteth** - thrust out, expel (Dumb Demoniac).
Matt. 17:18**Rebuked** - censure, admonish, tax upon (Epileptic).
Mark 1:34**Suffered** - to send forth (Sick or possessed with demons).
Luke 11:14**Casting** - put out, send away (Demon that was dumb.).
Eph. 4:27**Place** - location, condition (Gave no opportunity to the Devil.).
James 4:7**Resist** - oppose, withstand (Resist the Devil.).
II Pet. 2:11**Railing** - blasphemer, slanderous, profane, wicked (Judgement)
I John 3:8**Destroy** - loosen, break up, put off (Destroy works of Devil.).
Jude 9**Railing** - vilification, evil speaking (Reviling Judgement).

As you can see from the above scripture, we forcefully drive demons out of Christians but we do not rail at demons.

Luke 9:1 says we have **power and authority** (mastery, superhuman force, violence, control) and Luke 10:7 says the demons **are subject** (subordinate, obey) to Christians.

STUDY OF THE BLOOD OF JESUS

The Old Testament told of rites and bloody **sacrifices** of the law to redeem the people from their sins which foretold the shedding of the blood of Jesus Christ.

The New Testament told of **dignity and perfection** of the blood and sacrifice of Jesus Christ.

The following scriptures will give you an **overall** view of what the Bible says about the blood of Jesus **(Bold verses are more important):**

Gen. 4:10; Exodus **12**:7, **13**, 22-23; **24**:6, **8**; 29:12, 16, 20-21; Lev. 4:6-7; 5:9; 7:2; 8:24; **17:11**; Num. 19:4; Joel 3:21; Rom. **3:25**-26; 5:9; Eph. 1:7; Heb. **9**:7-**14**; **10:19**-22; 12:24; 13:20; I Peter **1**:2, **19**-22; I John 1:7; **5**:7-**8**; Rev. **12:11**

CURSING DEMONS AND INFIRMITIES

The Psalms contain imprecations (call down curses and evil) upon enemies and transgressors. For a good study, see "Strong's" or "Young's" Concordance for "curse, cursed, curses, cursest, curseth, **cursing**, accursed and cursedst". The following verses describe the meaning of cursing:

Gen. 9:24-27**Execrate** - to abhor, loathe, detest (Cursed younger son.).
Num. 22:6 & 23:8**Blaspheme** - perforate, bitterly curse (King of Moab asked Balaam, prophet, to curse Israel.).
Deut. 11:26-28; 27:15-26; 28:15-68(Blessing and curse, curses and more curses.)
Judges 5:23**Execrate** - (Curse bitterly its inhabitants.).
II Sam. 16:10-12**Vilification** - revile, slander (Curse David).
II Kings 2:23-25**Despise** - speak evil of (Cursed them in the name of the Lord.).
Job 3:1-10**Contempt** - vile (Cursed the day of his birth.).
Mark 11:21**Doom** - execrate, imprecate (Fig tree which you cursed.).
Gal. 1:8-9**Anathema** - solemn curse, excommunicated (Let him be accursed.).

EARLINE'S TESTIMONIES ABOUT DELIVERANCE

Scriptural basis is Rev. 12:11 for overcomers. Earline Moody has a good testimony about **how the soul (mind, will and emotions) works** in maintaining her deliverance. She was a school teacher.

Maintaining Deliverance

The scriptural basis for giving a testimony is found in Rev. 12:11 where we overcome Satan by three things: **the blood of Jesus, our testimony, and not loving our lives to the death. God told me that if I was unwilling to tell about my deliverance, I would lose it. And furthermore, if I was ashamed of Him and His provisions, He would be ashamed of me in Heaven.**

In James 4:7 we are told how to make the Devil flee. We often quote part of the verse **"resist the devil and he will flee from you"**. This gives us a false sense of security. The truth is you must first submit yourself to God. This is not a careless submission but true submission to God which requires us to read, study and obey the Bible. As we submit this way to God and then resist the Devil, he will indeed flee from us. God does not require us to know all the Biblical requirements before He will help us but we must be making every effort to obey all that we have learned, and be diligent about learning and applying more.

After all deliverances, some decisions must be made and never changed no matter how much pressure is applied to you from whatever source to change or go back to old sins. **Here are some decisions which must be made: 1. Study God's Word and accept His principles as your own. 2. Discipline your life and accept responsibility for your actions and thoughts in the areas where you have been delivered. 3. Enter His presence with thanksgiving for all with which He has blessed you. 4. Joyfully obey God's direction even if you have to force yourself in the beginning.**

The day after I received my main deliverance, I had an empty feeling and did not know what to do. My reaction was to ask God continually for direction.

We cannot do what God directs if we never apply His Word to our life. If we do not apply His Word to our thoughts and actions we are not truly subject to God. Therefore the Devil will not flee from us and we are only fooling ourselves if we think the demons will leave us alone. While we kid ourselves, the Devil and his demons eat our dinner and by the time we face the truth dinner is nearly over.

I learned that I didn't really know God's Word. I didn't know how to use God's Word or how to use my mind. I asked God to take my thoughts. **He told me that He wouldn't touch my thoughts with a ten foot pole; that His thoughts were higher than mine and that I must control my thoughts bring them into submission to Jesus Christ (II Cor. 10:5).**

I started marking everything that God said in the Bible in red. I found there is much said about the mind in Deuteronomy and throughout the Bible. Next I was impressed to underline every verse in the New Testament that told me something that I should do.

I soon realized that I really didn't know what I should think with my mind. It occurred to me that my mind is to be an instrument for my spirit's use and not the other way around. The hands, feet, eyes, ears and body obey, so why not make the mind obey? To make the mind obey, I needed to know what to make it do.

I had to learn how to tell the difference between God's and the Devil's thoughts. **The battleground for the Christian is primarily for his soul, not body or spirit.** The demons want to re-enter through your mind.

See Romans 6:16-18. Do you not know that if you continually surrender yourselves to any one to do his will, you are the slaves of him whom you obey, whether it be to sin, which leads to death, or to obedience which leads to righteousness - right doing and right standing with God. But thank God, though you were once slaves of sin you have become obedient with all your heart to the standard of teaching in which you were instructed and to which you were committed. And having been set free from sin, you have become the servants of righteousness - of conformity to the divine will in thought, purpose and action.

How do we yield ourselves to anyone (God or Devil)? Is it not in the mind? A human always plays with sinful thoughts, then he acts it out. It is not by accident we sin. A lot of people do not want to accept the responsibility for their sinfulness and want to blame it on someone else. The only trouble with this idea is that God will not be fooled by it neither will your enemy, the Devil.

Temptation - **For no temptation - no trial regarded as enticing to sin (no matter how it comes or where it leads) - has overtaken you and lied hold on you that is not common to man - that is no temptation or trial has come to you that is beyond human resistance and that is not adjusted and adapted and belonging to human experience, and such as man can bear. But God is faithful to His Word and to His compassionate nature and He (can be trusted) not to let you be tempted and tried and assayed beyond your ability and strength**

of resistance and power to endure, but with the temptation He will (always) provide a way out - the means to escape to a landing plane - that you may be capable and strong and powerful patiently to bear up under it (1 Cor. 10:13).

This tells me temptation in common to mankind; therefore, it is common for the Devil and the demons to use it. If they tempt us, we have not sinned. We have sinned when we enjoy and continue to invite the temptation, then yield and obey the temptation. It also shows we were not watchful for the escape route and we did not take it.

Situations around you will not necessarily change immediately now that you have changed. Just as you practiced obedience to the demons' words, now practice obedience to God's Word.

This is my first encounter with the Devil after I was delivered. Before I was delivered, I would get very angry and depressed when I cleaned house. At that time, we had wall-to-wall furniture. The living room was really badly cluttered. Each piece of furniture had to be moved to vacuum around it. I was happy and didn't hate this house anymore.

As I was vacuuming the living room, I dropped a table on my toe and was having trouble getting the vacuum nozzle under the sofa. I raised up and let out a loud "I hate this---". **God quickly warned me that "life and death is in the tongue, and they that love it will eat the fruit thereof" (Prov. 18:21). God also told me at this time that He had given it to my family. If I didn't have an attitude of gratitude about the house and furniture, He could easily remove them from me.** I knew that I must not complete the sentence or I would be back where I started from. I repented and repeated until I believed it, "I love this house and I thank God for it".

Another of Satan's tactics is to use gradualism on us. He will give us a sin to look at and consider. He will cover it over with pretty lies (pretty young people smoking, never an old person dying of lung cancer). **Satan will use rejection to trap you.** He will never tell the true ending (where does illegal sex lead?). He knows that the more we see it, hear it and consider it, the more likely we are to give in to it. A good example of the use of gradualism is Humanism. Forty years ago it was very mildly given to people mainly by pastors and teachers. People considered it and accepted it because it was given by people they trusted. Not considering what was the basic theory behind it (worship of self - therefore idolatry), people allowed this theory to so invade them that now we cannot recognize it for what it is. Many of us say we are against it but we live by it instead of the Bible.

We do not recognize God's provisions for us. We think our life should have no problems or privations. We are not grateful to God for all. **Because you did not serve the Lord your God with joyfulness of heart and mind in gratitude for the abundance of all with which He had blessed you, therefore you shall serve your enemies whom the Lord shall send against you, in hunger and thrust, in nakedness, and in want of all things; and He will put a yoke of iron upon you neck, until He hath destroyed you.** (Deut. 28:47-48)

This verse presents some interesting ideas 1. Are you having problems because you are ungrateful to God? 2. Do you know which problems are from God to help you learn to endure to the end or which ones are brought on because of being ungrateful? 3. Which ones have you invited by yielding to temptations of the enemy? If you will know the answer to these questions, you will have to seek God. He has promised to give wisdom to all who ask for it not wavering (James 1:4-8). If you ask God for wisdom and He gives you wisdom, you must not waver following His wisdom. For example: if you have been one to look at dirty magazines, God's wisdom tells you this will lead you to want to do what you see; then you must stop it. You may need deliverance for the demons you have let in plus you must change your habits. No one can change your thought life by casting out your demons. Casting out your demons is one of God's escape routes. **The deliveree must discipline the mind and actions.**

The best attack against habit, and the attempts of demons to trick you and get back in that I found was 1. to tell them to leave in Jesus' name once and 2. immediately take control of your mind. I would do it this way: I would tell them Jesus has given me authority over you (Luke 10:19, Matt. 28:18-20), therefore I command you to leave me now. If I did not sense they were gone, I would say, "Since you are still here, I would like to read to you about what Jesus Christ has done for me." I would open the Bible to **Matt. 26-28, Mark 14-16, Luke 22-24 and John 17-21** and read it aloud to them. Of course they did not want to hear of God's love and provision for me. The pressure they had placed on me and their thoughts were long gone but I would read on and bless myself in God's Word. Some times the pressure from the demons trying to get back in was strong enough that I would have to walk and read very loudly to them. I will still do this if I come under attack; it always works. After a time, you will be able to tell them the facts without reading it to them.

God also told me at this time that He had given it to my family. If I didn't have an attitude of gratitude about the house and furniture, **God could easily remove them from me** (Deut. 27:48).

My next attack was sent through people. **When asked why I looked so much better and was losing weight, I would answer truthfully and say "I was delivered of demons and no, I was not dieting".** If three people were present, you would get three distinct reactions. One would leave pronto, one would regard you as if you were radioactive, and one would grab your arm and want to know more.

Then you'd hear whispers - she had demons! They only talk about demons; do they worship them? They are fanatical; they believe there is a demon under every bush!

Next I was tempted to go back to some of my old habits of retaliation, etc. I must crucify the flesh - **God said that vengeance belongs to Him** (Rom. 12:19). I must not habitually sin or else I become the demon's house in that area again (I John 3:8-9).

Mental suggestions by the Devil must be put down. He will suggest a what if, could be or maybe. If this happens, what will you do (fear and more fear)? Unless you have facts to base your knowledge on, don't let the Devil play you along.

One of his tactics was to attack me about Marie: what if Marie can't adjust to her brother's death? Before deliverance, I would cringe in fear and worry. After deliverance, I learned to tell Satan that Marie can do all things through Christ who strengthens her; I can too!

You don't have to be perfect to give a word of encouragement, share an experience, help someone or even cast out a demon. If God demanded perfection, nothing would ever get done. I'm over fifty years old and **I have yet to meet a perfect person.**

You must have a total commitment to Jesus Christ. Rely totally on Him and His Word. Do these things and you will continue to get free and stay free. Don't be double minded: deciding and undeciding. Remember that a double-minded man is unstable in all his ways. Give very careful study to what you read in THE BIBLE and carefully compare it to the thing you need to make a decision on. When you have judged it by the Biblical instructions, then don't waver.

I found a verse, Heb. 12:4, to put my temptations in prospective. Begin reading at verse one which contains instruction on keeping pure. **Strip off and throw aside every encumbrance and sin which so readily (deftly and cleverly) clings to and entangles us, and let us run with patient endurance and steady and active persistence the appointed course of the race set before us. Looking away (from all that will distract) to Jesus, Who is the Leader and the source of our faith (giving the first incentive for our belief) and is also its Finisher, (bringing it to maturity and perfection). He, for the joy (of obtaining the prize) that was set before Him endured the cross, despising and ignoring the shame, and is now seated at the right hand of the throne of God. Just think of Him who endured from sinners such grievous opposition and bitter hostility against - reckon up and consider it all in comparison with your trials - so that you may not grow weary or exhausted, losing heart and relaxing and fainting in your minds. You have not yet struggled and fought agonizing against sin, nor have you yet resisted and withstood to the point of pouring out your (own) blood.**

If we are able with every temptation to resist to the shedding of our blood maybe, then we might have an acceptable excuse for failing to resist the Devil and him having to flee.

God will not make you over; He will work with you and help you. See Mark 16:20. A miracle is taking place as you go obeying The Word in the areas you have received instruction and deliverance.

A study of Matthew 5 will help anyone see just where they are missing it with their attitudes. It will inspire you to clear your mind of a lot of incorrect ideas and to broaden your understanding of the truth.

Schizophrenia Deliverance

Schizophrenia means split mind (**schizein = to split** and **phren = mind**). I had a lifetime of mental and emotional tension. I was unable to decide what to do and see it through. I had many fears that something bad was going to happen. All of my life I had great fears of bad things happening: fears of failing and fears of people. I was often tense for weeks and I did not know why.

This is the earliest memory I have of going to school. I was so afraid of all the people I could not go into the school but hid behind the well house until my brother, Clyde, came and took me into the first grade. I was disoriented that day; strange feelings and fears tormented me.

I have very few memories from childhood below the age of nine or ten years. Generally speaking I lived in two worlds; home and away from home. I became very good at forgetting everything bad (parents' fights and my own troubles) that happened at home the minute I walked out the door. I felt more freedom and ease away from home.

At high school and college I had trouble with certain subjects like algebra and chemistry. They had things too similar for me to distinguish between them.

Both of these subjects ended in frustration and low grades for me. In my marriage I had some problems of accepting my husband as one who would provide for me, take care of me, and continue to love me. **I was always expecting the marriage to end badly.** After six years of marriage, we had a delightful son and two years later we had a beautiful daughter.

Double mindedness wears the person out, and frustrates and confuses him. Deciding, then undeciding stagnates a person. For example, my mom was here for a while; she couldn't be content for desiring to go home. When at home, she was pressed to stay somewhere else besides her home. When away from home, great fears filled her about the house. She was miserable and made those around her miserable (James 1:5-8).

Deliverance From Indian Curses

What are the effect of curses? I had Cherokee Indian ancestors on both sides of my family. I had a heart condition which was unusual. It never occurred with regularity or under any specific condition.

God gave me a vision of an Indian Shaman Witch Doctor at an elevated funeral pyre which was burning dead bodies. He was chanting and waving, and saying on the descendents and descendents. This was supposed to be a blessing, but in actuality was a curse. Some Indians worship demons and this was an ungodly witch doctor. The curse came down on my family causing heart problems.

While taking a tread mill test, I experienced tremendous pain in the chest, arms and neck. Having been examined by a heart specialist in Minneapolis, who told me that my heart was good but he had written **death by heart attack** on many people's certificates like myself. **These were people who didn't really have anything wrong with their hearts physically but spiritually were cursed.**

A year or so after my dad's death I found my heart acting up again. Sometimes one to five years would elapse between seizures. I began to ask God to show me why my brothers, dad, dad's brothers and his dad all had heart problems.

GOD showed me Exodus 20. He told me to repent for my ancestors and myself for the sin of idol worship in Leviticus 26:40-41. The curse of idol worship follows the blood line. I did these things and have been free for over eleven years. I was only the second generation from previous generations that sinned before God.

NAMES OF DEMONS

Scornful
Destroyer
Fear
Death
Poverty
Afflictions
Trouble
Confusion
Terror
Hate
Diseases
Distress
Domination
Broken Heart
Dismay
Heaviness
Mourning
Infirmities
Sicknesses
Stealing
Murder
Doubt
Condemnation
False Gifts
Imaginations
High Things
Unclean spirits
Resentment
Hatred
Anger
Rejection
Self-Pity
Jealousy
Depression
Worry
Inferiority
Insecurity
Mental Torment
Procrastination
Indecision
Compromise
Rationalization
Loss of Memory
Spiritual Wickedness
False Gospel

Lying
Cursing
Blasphemy
Criticism
Mockery
Railing
Gossip
Fantasy Sex
Masturbation
Lust
Perverseness
Homosexuality
Fornication
Adultery
Incest
Pornography
Harlotry
Nicotine
Alcohol
Drugs
Medicines
Caffeine
Presumptuous
Adultery
Cursing
Philosophies
Mind Sciences
Yoga Exercises
Karate
Mormonism
Self-Willed
Sore Boils
Rosicrucianism
Theosophy
Unity
Corruption
Occult
Spiritism
Seances
Witchcraft
Magic
Ouija Boards
Levitation
Fiery Darts
Sore Boils

Palmistry
Handwriting Analysis
Automatic Handwriting
ESP
Hypnosis
Horoscopes
Astrology
Divination
False Doctrine
Deceiving
Seducing
Asceticism
Vegetarianism
Dishonesty
Proud ness
Madness
Unforgiveness
Yoke of Bondage
Serpents and Scorpions
Blindness
Retaliation
Striving
Sinus Trouble
Migraine Headaches
Negative Confessions
Principalities
Powers
Lust of Flesh
Vanity
Guilt
Temptation
Strongholds
Imaginations
High Things
Evil Thoughts
Disobedience
Evil Weapons
Evil Tongues
Nets and Pits
Wiles
Principalities
Powers
Deceiving
Mockery

Pagan Religions	Affliction
Christian Science	Eastern Religions
Jehovah's Witnesses	Addiction to Food
Lust of Uncleanness	Bloodless Religions
Covetousness	Rulers or Darkness
Provocativeness	Spots and Blemishes
World Rulers of Darkness	
Spiritual Hosts of Wicked	

SECTION 21 - INDIVIDUAL AND MASS DELIVERANCE

ATTACK - ATTACK - ATTACK

CONTENTS

PREFACE

This lesson applies to a group of any size; there is no limit on the number of people that can be ministered to. **Anyone that can hear your voice, can be delivered.** It is organized primarily for mass deliverance of a group.

PERSONAL DELIVERANCE

However, it is also applicable to personal deliverance. You could look at personal deliverance as mass deliverance for a person such as a man, woman or child, or a few persons such as a couple or family. Select the parts of the lesson that are applicable to the people that are being ministered to. For more information on how to minister to a few persons, see **How To Do Deliverance** in the **HOW TO DO DELIVERANCE MANUAL.**

Personal Prayers

The ideal prayer is the one prayed by the individual to cover that person's life. Pray out loud for the most power in the spirit world. **Get the individual to pray about their specific problems and sins. You must personally repent of your sins! No one can repent for you.**

PRAYERS

There are many good deliverance prayers that have been written. Some of these prayers are general and some are for specific subjects. **The next best prayer** is the form prayer which the person or group repeats after the deliverance leader or reads from the printed prayer.

The prayers found in **PRAYERS AND LISTS OF DEMONS FOR INDIVIDUAL AND MASS DELIVERANCE** have been used many times by us and others. They have produced good results. One side benefit is that the people can see what is wrong and evil in their lives by what is contained in the prayers. These prayers can be used for individuals, small groups or large groups equally well.

SUMMARY

If you are working in mass deliverance, lead the group in praying the form prayers. Lead congregation through these scriptures, prayers and commands as fits the situation and as led by THE HOLY SPIRIT. THE BLOOD OF JESUS will cleanse the people, and take away legal rights and grounds that the demons have to remain. Then demons can be cast out.

MASS DELIVERANCE

How To Get Delivered

Relax and cooperate with the deliverance minister and workers. There is nothing to be afraid of. GOD never gives a spirit of fear; all fear is from Satan. We have not lost a deliveree in thirty years of ministry.

Demons are like air. They are usually expelled by the exhaling of breath. This can be by yawning, coughing, deep breathing or gentle exhaling. It is good to take several deep breaths to help get the deliverance started.

Demons can have nests in the body which have substance. They are usually expelled by blowing the nose or coughing up phlegm. Don't feel bad when this happens.

For instance, it is beautiful to see a cancer vomited out of a person during deliverance. I sat at his feet and watched Win Worley deliver a woman from cancer at Lake Hamilton Bible Camp. Paper towels and waste cans may be provided for this reason.

Demons can temporarily take over your body and manifest their characteristics. They can look through your eyes, talk using your voice, cause the body to assume various shapes, temporarily paralyze the body, and throw the body on the floor and cause it to squirm around.

Deliverance is the casting out of demons from your body. Prayer is the infilling of THE HOLY SPIRIT. Leave the passages open so that the spirits can leave.

Do not pray, pray in tongues or chant. Chanting is the repetition of a word or phrase such as saying JESUS repeatedly.

Decide that you want to get rid of the demons within your body. You no longer agree with them and they no longer will be your pets. **Exercise your mind and will to be delivered.** If the demons do not leave, command them, by name, to go. Do this verbally, out loud, for more power.

Do not hold back or be embarrassed. As they come up and out of your chest, let them go even if you have to spit or vomit. It is all right even if they take over some part of your body. If you have too much pride to let the demons manifest to get delivered, you give the demons a right to stay. **GOD hates pride; it is an abomination to Him!**

Deliverance workers should move around quietly. Provide paper towels to those who need them. Lay hands on those who are having trouble, agree with them, and command the demons to come out.

Do not start a conversation with the person during mass deliverance. This interrupts the flow of the deliverance; you then have your own private meeting.

Deliverance is not prayer. You command the demons to go in JESUS' NAME. He will not cast the demons out. He has given us that authority and He expects us to use it.

Babies and children generally get delivered easily. Babies can even get delivered in the womb. Women generally manifest more than men do. Women usually get into and out of spiritual trouble more quickly than men. Men generally get delivered by the simple exhaling of the breath. The more a person is in bondage, the greater the manifestations will be.

Deliverance is dynamic and exciting. It is wonderful to see people getting free from demon bondage. **JESUS CHRIST as glorified when Satan is defeated** by Christians here on earth.

Families should sit together. Husbands are the most effective in casting demons out of their family because they are given spiritual authority over it. This authority is even greater than that of the deliverance minister because it is given by GOD to the husband to be priest and head of the home.

It is not the loudness of a command that moves the demon but the authority of THE NAME AND BLOOD OF THE LORD JESUS CHRIST. You must know your authority or the demons will recognize your weakness. Every Christian has authority to cast out demons in THE NAME OF JESUS CHRIST. By initiating young, interested believers into the battle for deliverance, they soon become seasoned soldiers, learning tactics on the battlefield. Small children who are Christians can cast out demons.

CASTING OUT DEMONS

Basic Deliverance

Start with casting out families of demons that comprise basic deliverance: **Rejection, Bitterness and Rebellion** in that order. People get rejected, become bitter and then rebel.

Advanced Deliverance

After basic deliverance, go on to other demonic families. **The list of names of demons seems to be endless**. There is a name of a demon for everything that is contrary to THE WORD OF GOD. Call the demon out by his characteristic or personality. Demons will answer to their medical names, common names, symptoms or names they are given in the spiritual world.

Lists of Demons

Refer to the **DELIVERANCE MANUAL, Mass Deliverance Manual**, page 271 for a Table of Contents of the Lists of Demons. Use these lists with the lessons or as needed.

MASS DELIVERANCE SUPPLEMENT

Preface

The only way for deliverance to spread around the world is for many Christians to begin to practice deliverance. I encourage you to take this guide, begin to practice deliverance and help others as you grow stronger.

Mass deliverance is simply deliverance for everyone that can hear your voice. You can use this lesson for your family, prayer meeting or church. Normally we only work on one area of a person's life at a time in mass deliverance. We do not try to cover all areas. If you are thirty years old, I would say that you have spent thirty years and nine months collecting demons.

There is nothing mysterious about deliverance; any Christian can cast out demons. As a teacher, I am worthless if I can not show you how to practice what I teach. **The Bible is also worthless unless you put it into practice.**

AIDS TO CASTING OUT DEMONS

General

Practice systematic deliverance: basic to advanced to mass. Work on one area of a person's life at a time in mass deliverance. You can not cast out all of the demons at one time! **The deeper the pit that the person and their ancestors have dug, the longer it takes to climb up out of the pit.**

Pray deliverance prayers - break Biblical curses and soul ties - renounce occult and false religions - loose Godly Spirits - destroy or exorcise cursed objects - make positive confessions in CHRIST - read deliverance Scripture - do anything else that THE HOLY SPIRIT tells you to do.

If The Demons Do Not Leave

No demon can resist THE NAME OF JESUS or disobey THE WORD OF GOD when they are being used properly in deliverance. If this happens, then they have a **legal right before GOD to remain.**

You must **search out this legal right and remove it.** The person being ministered to must do their part! Generally, the right to remain has to do with what other people have done to that person or what that person has done to their self. The most common ground is **unforgiveness.** Other common grounds are **sins of ancestors or anyone who had authority over that person,** or the **personal sins of that person.**

If the demons do not leave, find out what their legal right is and remove it. Ask GOD what it is, force the demon to tell you and/or ask the person what sin they or their ancestors committed to get them in that trouble.

Scripture

Read deliverance Scripture out loud to the spiritual world. I have marked my Bible with deliverance scriptures that I read when resistance by the demons is encountered. There are many Scriptures that can be used in the Old and New Testaments. Two scriptures follow as examples:

The weapons of our warfare are not carnal but mighty thru GOD to the pulling down of strongholds, casting down imaginations and every high thing that exalts itself against GOD (II Cor. 10:4).

No weapon formed against thee will prosper; and every tongue that shall rise against thee in judgment thou shall condemn. This is the heritage of the servants of the LORD, and their righteousness is of me, saith the LORD (Isa. 54:17).

COMMENTS

1. People may bind demons but they do not cast them out. If you only bind the demons, they stay within the person. Binding only lasts for a short period, say 24 hours. The bottom line of deliverance is the casting out of demons.
2. You need to identify or expose the primary problem and deal with it in prayer before trying to cast out. Otherwise this results in partial or superficial deliverance, if any at all.
3. You have to go through the proper steps to achieve success such as the Six Steps To Deliverance Of An Individual.
4. Soul ties need to be broken. It is good to ask GOD to restore a persons soul where it has been fragmented by soul ties to others.
5. When the demons come out, they go into the dry places. There is some possibilities of sending them to the Abyss or Tartarus.
6. Demons have names. It is more powerful to call out a demon by its name or at least some characteristic of its actions.
7. There is a name of a demon for everything that is contrary to THE WORD OF GOD. This is the easy way of identifying a demon.
8. It is good to have the person take several deep breaths at different times to expel the demons. This gets the person involved with their deliverance.
9. Demons come out different ways but generally by the exhaling of breath when they have no legal right to be within a person.
10. If demons have a legal right to stay, they may become violent or not come out.

SPIRITUAL WARFARE DIRECTIONS

Work this lesson with PRAYERS AND LIST OF DEMONS FOR INDIVIDUAL AND MASS DELIVERANCE.

1. Teach one lesson or several lessons.
2. Customize the deliverance around what was taught.
3. **Deliverance Warfare Prayers** - These can be used in various ways as indicated by the subtitles.
4. **Moodys' Prayers** - These are good combination prayers.
5. **Deliverance Prayers With Lists** - These can be used in various ways as indicated by the subtitles.
6. **Tactics To Win The War Against Satan** - These can be used to drive out demons.
7. **Tormenting Demons** - These are used to torment the demons with their impending doom by using statements based on Scripture and using scriptural quotations as a weapon to drive out demons.
8. **Prayers and Lists of Demons for Mass Deliverance** - These are lists to be used for mass deliverance in various ways as indicated by the subtitles. Other lists are found in the **Mass Deliverance Manual** of the **DELIVERANCE MANUAL.**

9. Customize the deliverance to the situation that is presented. There are many factors to be considered such as time allowed, sequence of events and spiritual climate.

10. **Sequence of Events**

1. **Teach** - Teach one or more lessons.

2. **Pray** - Have the people stand up and repeat after you the following prayers that you have selected.

3. **Cast Out** - Cast out the demons in mass deliverance from selected lists of demons. It is good to start with **Basic Deliverance** of the families of **Rejection**, **Bitterness** and **Rebellion**, and then go on to other families. A good list to use always is **Fifty-Three Common Demon Families**.

4. **Deliverance Manual** - There are many lists of demons in the manual. The lists can be selected by topic being taught to the people or with the lesson in the **Deliverance Manual.**

5. **Audios and Videos** - An excellent tape is **Mass Deliverance** by Win Worley. There are audio and video tapes that have mass deliverance on them after teaching about various topics.

REFERENCE

Deliverance Manual by Gene and Earline Moody

Pigs In The Parlor by Frank and Ida Mae Hammond

SECTION 22 - MASS DELIVERANCE

HOW TO GET DELIVERED

Relax and cooperate with the deliverance minister and workers. There is nothing to be afraid of. We have not lost a deliveree in about twenty-five years of ministry. God never gives a spirit of fear; all fear is from Satan.

Demons are like air. They are usually expelled by the exhaling of breath. This can be by yawning, coughing, deep breathing or gentle exhaling of breath. Demons can have nests in the body which have substance. They are usually expelled by blowing the nose, coughing up phlegm or vomiting. Don't feel bad when this happens. For instance, it is beautiful to see a cancer vomited out of a person during deliverance. Paper towels and waste cans are provided for this reason.

Demons can temporarily take over your body and manifest their characteristics. They can look through your eyes, cause the body to assume grotesque shapes, temporarily paralyze the body, throw the body on the floor and cause it to squirm around, and talk using your voice.

Deliverance is the casting out of demons from your body. Prayer is the infilling of the Holy Spirit. Leave the passages open so that the spirits can leave. Do not pray, pray in tongues or chant. Chanting is the repetition of a word or phrase such as saying Jesus repeatedly.

Decide that you want to get rid of the demons within your body. You no longer agree with them and they no longer will be your pets. **Exercise your mind and will to be delivered.** If the demons do not leave, command them, by name, to go; do this verbally, out loud, for more power.

Do not hold back or be embarrassed. As they come up and out of your chest, let them go even if you have to spit or whatever. It is all right even if they take over some part of your body. If you have too much pride to let the demons manifest to get delivered, you give the demons a right to stay. **God hates pride; it is an abomination to Him!**

Deliverance workers should move around quietly. Provide paper towels to those who need them. Lay hands on those who are having trouble, agree with them, and command the demons to come out. Do not start a conversation with the person during mass deliverance. This interrupts the flow of the deliverance and you then have your own private meeting.

Deliverance is not prayer. You command the demons to go in Jesus' Name. He will not cast the demons out. He has given us that authority and He expects us to use it.

Babies and children generally get delivered easily. Babies can even get delivered in the womb. Women generally manifest more than men do. Women usually get into and out of spiritual trouble more quickly than men. Men generally get delivered by the simple exhaling of the breath. The more a person is in bondage, the greater the manifestations will be.

Deliverance is dynamic and exciting. It is wonderful to see people getting set free from demon bondage. Jesus Christ is glorified when Satan is defeated by Christians here on earth.

Families should sit together. Husbands are the most effective in casting demons out of their family because they are given spiritual authority over it. We believe this authority is even greater than that of the deliverance minister.

It is not the loudness of a command that moves the demon but the authority of the name and blood of the Lord Jesus Christ. You must know your authority or the demons will recognize your weakness. By initiating young, interested believers into the battle for deliverance, they soon become seasoned soldiers, learning tactics on the battlefield.

DELIVERANCE PRAYERS

General - There are **many good deliverance prayers** that have been written and printed in books and in loose-leaf form. Some of these prayers are general and some have been written for specific purposes.

The ideal prayer is the one prayed by the individual to cover the specific area of that person's life that is being ministered to at that time. The next best prayer is the form prayer which the person repeats after the deliverance leader.

The following prayers have been used many times by us and **have produced good results**. One side benefit is that the people can see what is wrong and evil in their lives by what is contained in the prayers.

These prayers can be used for individuals, small groups or large groups equally well.

Short Prayer - "Lord Jesus Christ, I believe you died on the cross for my sins and rose again from the dead. You redeemed me by your blood and I belong to you, and I want to live for you. I confess all my sins--known and unknown--I'm sorry for them all. I renounce them all. **I forgive all others as I want you to forgive me**. (Pause) Forgive me now and cleanse me with your blood. I thank you for the blood of Jesus Christ which cleanses me now from all sin. **And I come to you now as my deliverer.** You know my special needs--the thing that binds, that torments, that defiles; that evil spirit, that unclean spirit--I claim the promise of your word, 'Whosoever that calleth on the name of the Lord shall be delivered.' I call upon you now. In the name of the Lord Jesus Christ, deliver me and set me free. Satan, I renounce you and all your works. I loose myself from you, in the name of Jesus, and I command you to leave me right now in Jesus' name. Amen!"

This is my favorite prayer because it is short and effective. The first part is **salvation** and the last part is **deliverance**. You can pause after the sentence highlighted about **forgiveness** and let the people forgive others as the Holy Spirit leads them. This prayer was written by Derek Prince.

Moody's Prayers - The first thing we do is get the people **to pray about their specific problems and sins**, so that the blood of Jesus can cleanse the people and take away legal rights that the demons have to remain, and God can begin to act. You must personally repent of your sins!

Then we get the people to repeat the **Short Prayer** out loud with sincerity after me.

Finally, we lead the people in a prayer out loud that covers **Sins of Ancestors, Curses, Soul Ties, Fragmented Soul, and Subconscious Mind** as follows:

"Lord Jesus Christ, I forgive my ancestors and descendants, and I ask you to forgive and bless them. Forgive me for my many sins and I forgive myself for sins against my body. I break all curses, charms, spells, jinxes, psychic powers, hexes, vexes and demonic ties that bind. I break all soul ties caused by witchcraft, sorcery, bewitchment or sexual sins. Lord Jesus, restore my fragmented soul: mind, will and emotions; send your angels out to recover anything that was stolen from me. Lord Jesus, stir up the demons in my subconscious mind so that they can be identified and cast out. All these things I ask in the blessed name of my Lord Jesus Christ: My Lord, Master and Savior. I now take authority over Satan and all the forces of evil according to the whole Word of God and command that you obey it. In the Name of Jesus Christ, I ask these things. Amen."

After the people have prayed and been led in prayer, then **I take spiritual authority over the meeting** as follows:

"Satan, we come against all powers, principalities, evil forces in this world and spiritual wickedness in high places. We come against all demons inside or outside of anyone present, over this city, state, nation and world, in Hell or out of Hell. The Bible says, **Behold, I give unto you power to tread on serpents and scorpions, and over all the power of the enemy: and nothing shall by any means hurt you.** We intend to exercise that power to set ourselves free. Satan, we come against you by the power and blood of Jesus Christ, by the Word of God, by the name of Jesus, by the authority of the believer, in the unity of our spirits. Satan, we tell you that we sit in heavenly places with our Christ Jesus. We are over you, your fallen angels, your demons and all forces of evil. We command you to line up in rank and file and order, and come out quickly. We bind every power that you have and loose ourselves from you in the name of Jesus.

Lord Jesus Christ, we ask that you would send the gifts of the Holy Spirit as needed to minister to the needs of the people and to accomplish what you want done here today. We are careful to give you all the glory, honor, praise and credit for everything that is said or done. We ask all these things in the blessed name of Jesus Christ, our Lord and Master and Savior. And we take authority over Satan according to the whole Word of God. For it's in Jesus name we pray. Amen!"

BIBLICAL CURSES

"I forgive my ancestors and anyone else that has cursed me. I ask that God forgive me and them. I break any curses placed on me or my descendants from uttering a wish of evil against one; to imprecate evil, to call for mischief or injury to fall upon; to execrate, to bring evil upon or to; to blast, vex, harass or torment with great calamities. I break these curses in Jesus' name. I break the curses back to ten generations or even to Adam and Eve on both sides of my family, and destroy every legal hold and every legal ground that demons have to work in my life. I break curses that follow in the name of the Lord Jesus Christ."

Mistreating God's Chosen People, Willing Deceivers, Adultery, Harlotry and Prostitution, Disobedience to Bible, Idolatry, Keeping Cursed Objects, Refusing To Fight For God, House of

Wicked, Not Giving To Poor, Stealing, Swearing Falsely By God, Failing To Give Glory to God, Robbing God of Tithes, Dishonoring Parents, Hearkening to Wives Rather Than God, Making Graven Images, Cheating People Out of Property, Taking Advantage of Blind, Oppressing Strangers, Widows, Orphans, Bestiality, Incest With Sister or Mother, Murder Secretly or For Hire, Pride, Putting Trust In Man, Doing The Work of God Deceitfully, Rewarding Evil For Good, Abortion or Causing Unborn To Die, Having Bastards, Murdering Indirectly, Striking Parents, Kidnapping, Cursing Parents, Not Preventing Death, Sacrificing to Gods, Witchcraft, Turning Someone Away From God, Following Horoscopes, Rebelling Against Pastors, Losing Virginity Before Marriage, False Prophets, Rape, Not Disciplining Children, Teaching Rebellion Against God, Cursing Rulers, Refusing To Warn Sinners, Defiling The Sabbath, Sacrificing Humans, Seances and Fortune Telling, Intercourse During Menstruation, Homosexuals and Lesbians, Necromancers, Blaspheming Lord's Name, Being Carnally Minded, Oral and Anal Sex, Children Rebelling, Nonproductivity, Fugitive and Vagabond, Improper Family Structure, Destruction of Family Priesthood, Refusing To Do The Word of God, Family Disorder, Failure and Poverty, Any Sin Worthy of Death, Touching God's Anointed, Perversion of Gospel, Loving Cursing, Choosing That Which God Delights Not In, Looking To World For Help, Stubbornness and Rebellion, Offending Children Believing Christ, Adding To or Taking Away From Bible, Any Biblical Curse not listed Above

But it shall come to pass, if thou wilt not hearken unto the voice of the Lord thy God, to observe to do all His commandments and His statutes which I command thee this day; that all these curses shall come upon thee, and overtake thee (Deut. 28:15). I believe that there is a curse for every verse that you disobey and a blessing for every verse that you obey. If you obey half the Bible, you are half blessed and half cursed.

SOUL TIES

"Forgive me for developing soul ties with anyone. I forgive those who would control me. I renounce these evil soul ties, break them and wash them away with the shed blood of the Lord Jesus Christ. I break all evil soul ties with the following:"

Beasts
Anyone I Have Had Sex With Outside of Marriage
Divorced Mates
By Incest, Rape, Fornication, Adultery, Homosexuality, Bestiality, Lesbianism
Bloodless Religions, Religious Cults
Blood Brothers/Sisters By Rites
Witchcraft, Occult, Satan Worship
Fortune Tellers, Mediums
Psychiatrists, Social Workers, Psychologists, Mental Institutions
Finally, I break any agreement with anyone that forms an evil soul tie.

OCCULT AND FALSE RELIGIONS

"I forgive my ancestors and ask that you would forgive me for participating in occult and false religions. I renounce all fortune telling, magic practices and spiritism, cults and false teachings, and Satan worship. I break every curse and soul tie brought about by psychic heredity, occult contacts and religious cults. I now break any demonic hold on my family line due to supernatural experiences apart from God including the following forbidden practices and all that they entail."

Enchantments, Wizardry, Necromancy, Witchcraft, Observer of Times, Fortune Telling, Consulting With Familiar Spirits, Occult Practices, Spiritism, Sorcery, Magic Practices, Son or Daughter Passing Through Fire, Divination, Charmers, False Religious Cults

LOOSING GODLY SPIRITS

We can bind and loose spirits (Matt. 18:18-20). We can loose ministering spirits from the Lord. We **bind** the spirits (demons) of Satan and **loose** the spirits (angels) of God. We cast demons out of people and ask God to direct the angels to minister to our needs.

Godly spirits commonly mentioned are spirit, Spirit of God, Spirit of the Lord, Holy Spirit (human spirit, angels and Holy Spirit). Ungodly spirits commonly mentioned are evil spirits, demons and devils. There is actually only one Devil, Satan; demons are the correct terminology. There are millions of fallen angels and billions of demons.

"Lord Jesus Christ, we ask that you direct the angels to minister to our needs. We loose warring angels, ministering angels, the Holy Spirit and the Seven-Fold Spirit of God. We loose legions of angels including the following godly spirits."

Spirit of Wisdom, Poor in Spirit, Spirit of God, Spirit of Your Father, Spirit of the Lord, Strong in Spirit, Right Spirit, Spirit of Truth, Holy Spirit, Spirit of Life, Broken Spirit, Spirit of Adoption, Spirit of Princes, Fervent in Spirit, Faithful Spirit, Spirit of Meekness, Humble Spirit, Spirit of Faith, Excellent Spirit, Spirit of Jesus Christ, Spirit of Man, Eternal Spirit, Patient in Spirit, Meek and Quite Spirit, Spirit of the Ruler, Spirit of Glory, Spirit of Judgment, Spirit of Prophecy, Spirit of Understanding, Spirit of Elijah, Spirit of Counsel/Might, Contrite Spirit, Spirit of Knowledge, Good Spirit, New Spirit, Spirit of Deep Sleep, Spirit of Holy Gods, Spirit of Living Creature, Spirit of Grace and Supplication, Spirit of Holiness, Spirit of Christ, Spirit of Grace, Quickening Spirit, Free Spirit

CURSED OBJECTS AND DEMON INFESTATION

If you have a cursed object, you become cursed by God! Remove all cursed objects from your being and from your home; destroy by breaking, burning or at least throw them in the trash can. Do not keep the cursed silver or gold of the object. If the cursed object belongs to someone else and you can not throw it away, then anoint with oil and cast the demons out of it. Anoint your house with oil and cast out evil spirits from your house and possessions.

"Lord Jesus, I ask that you forgive me for having cursed objects in my home. Show me by the Holy Spirit what to destroy. Amen".

1. Books and objects identified with anything related to Satan's Kingdom.
2. Sinful activities of former residents left <u>curses</u>.
3. Knocking or noisy ghosts (poltergeist) and apparitions.
4. Owl and frog images of all types.
5. Witch's mask and fetishes used by witch doctors.
6. Objects and literature that pertain to false religions, cults, the occult and spiritism.

7. Graven images of gods (demons).
8. Objects dedicated to demons (idols and artifacts).
9. Ouija boards or other occult paraphernalia.
10. Prayers and worship to demons bring curses on home.
11. Mexican sun gods; idols, incense; Buddhas; hand carved objects from Africa or the Orient; anything connected with astrology, horoscopes, fortune telling, etc.; books or objects associated with witchcraft, good luck charms or cult religions (metaphysics, Christian Science, Jehovah's Witnesses, etc.); rock and roll records and tapes.
12. Jewelry given to a person by someone in witchcraft, hex signs, ancient geometric and mystical motifs, jewelry designed to bring good luck and act as talisman to chase evil.
13. Egyptian ankh, broken cross (peace symbol), chais, Polynesian tikkis of gods, African jujus, Italian horn, protectors from the evil eye, hand with index and little fingers pointing up, crosses, clovers, stars, wishbones, luck coins, mystic medals, horseshoes, religious fetishes and statues.
14. Products with cryptic curses (hidden secret, occult curses).
15. Dolls used for witchcraft and magic; puppets, cult objects or representations.

CASTING OUT DEMONS

Basic Deliverance - Start with casting out families of demons that comprise basic deliverance: Rejection, Bitterness and Rebellion in that order.

Rejection	**Bitterness**	**Rebellion**
Fear of Rejection	Resentment	Self-Will
Self-Rejection	Hatred	Stubbornness
	Unforgiveness	Disobedience
	Violence	Anti-Submissiveness
	Temper	
	Anger	
	Retaliation	
	Murder	

Advanced Deliverance - After basic deliverance, go on to other demonic families. **The list of names of demons seems to be endless**. There is a name of a demon for everything that is contrary to the Word of God. Call the demon out by his characteristic or personality. Demons will answer to their medical names, common names, symptoms or names they are given in the spiritual world.

LISTS OF DEMONS

Abused Children (Deliverance for the Subconscious Mind)
Ahab and Jezebel (The Curse of Ahab and Jezebel)
Bad Habits of Thinking and Reacting
Baldness - Beards - Hair
Bastards (The Curse of the Bastard)
Biblical Curses
Catholic Spirits
Charismatic Witchcraft
Children Drug Addicts

Children's Deliverance
Christian Fantasy - Lies not Truth
Christmas - Pagan or Christian Holiday?
Classical Mythology (How to Identify Godly and Ungodly Spirits)
Common Demon Groupings (How to Minister Basic Deliverance)
Cursed Objects (Cleaning Your House)
Cursing Others and Being Cursed
Drugs and Medicines
Drunkenness and Gluttony
Effeminacy - Sins of Sodom
Fears Of (How to Identify Godly and Ungodly Spirits)
Good Homemakers
Grief and Bitterness (Deliverance from Grief and Bitterness)
Hate, Vengeance, Envy and Strife
Holidays
Humanism
Idols Worshipped by Countries (How to Identify Godly and Ungodly Spirits)
Indians (Indian Curses)
Infirmity, Weakness, Sickness, Disease (Body - Cured and Healed by Deliverance)
Ingratitude (An Attitude of Gratitude)
Lies, Deceit and Flattery
Maintaining Your Deliverance from Evil Spirits
Mass Deliverance Supplement
Mind (The Mind: Freeing - Restoring - Protecting)
Occult (Forbidden Practices of the Occult)
Passive Mind
Perfecting Love
Psychoneurosis (The Neurotic Personalities)
Psychoneurotic (The Delinquent Personalities)
Psychopsychosis (The Pathologic Personalities)
Rebellion
Rape
Religious Error (Spirits of Religious Error)
Respect, Fear and Nervousness
Satan, Fallen Angels and Demons (Learn About the Real Enemy - Satan/Followers)
Schizophrenia and Paranoia (Schizophrenia)
Schizophrenia and Related Diseases (How to Identify Godly and Ungodly Spirits)
Scripture (Deliverance Scripture)
Selected Topic Studies
Self (How to be Miserable)
Sexual Harassment - Abuse - Assault - Violence
Sexual Sin and Diseases (Sexual Diseases, Impurities and Demons)
Toys and Games (Children's Deliverance)
Ungodly Spirits (How to Identify Godly and Ungodly Spirits)
Valentine's Day (What's Wrong with Valentine's Day?)
When Demonization of Christians is Denied (Can a Christian Have a Demon?)
Witchcraft (Winning over Witchcraft)

Women's Inheritance (Our Inheritance from Woman's Viewpoint)
Women's Weaknesses (From Eve to Jezebel - Women's Weaknesses)

SECTION 23 - MASS DELIVERANCE SUPPLEMENT

PREFACE

The only way for deliverance to spread around the world is for many people to begin to practice deliverance. I encourage you to take this guide, begin to practice deliverance and help others as you grow stronger. God told us to help train an army to minister deliverance.

Mass deliverance is simply deliverance for everyone that can hear your voice. You can use this lesson for your family or church. Normally we only work on one area of a person's life at a time and do not try to cover all areas at the same time in mass deliverance.

There is nothing mysterious about deliverance; any Christian can cast out demons. As a teacher, I am worthless if I can not show you how to practice what I teach. **The Bible is also worthless unless you put it into practice.**

SIX STEPS TO DELIVERANCE OF AN INDIVIDUAL

1. Find out what the individual's problems are.
2. Forgive, pray and get yourself right with God.
3. Break the curses and soul ties on you and your descendents.
4. Cast out the demons.
5. Pray for healing of soul and body.
6. Discipline your life by changing your way of thinking and acting.

It is easy to cast out demons but hard to discipline your life!

AIDS TO CASTING OUT DEMONS

General - Practice systematic deliverance: basic then advanced - mass and individual. Work on one area of a person's life at a time in mass deliverance. You can not cast out all of the demons at one time!

Pray deliverance prayers - break Biblical curses and soul ties - renounce occult and false religions - loose Godly Spirits - destroy or exorcise cursed objects - make positive confessions in Christ - read deliverance Scripture.

Scripture - Read deliverance Scripture out loud to the spiritual world. There are many Scriptures that can be used in the Old and New Testaments. Several Scriptures follow:

The weapons of our warfare are not carnal but mighty thru God to the pulling down of strongholds, casting down imaginations and every high thing that exalts itself against God.

No weapon formed against us will prosper.

Statements - Make positive confessions to God and to each other about living our life for Christ. Some of these types of statements follow:

We forgive everyone that has hurt or sinned against us, and we pray for our enemies.

We exercise honesty - humility - repentance - renunciation - forgiveness - prayer - warfare.

We seize the Kingdom of Heaven and take it by force from Satan.

We overcome Satan by the Blood of the Lamb, by our testimony for Jesus Christ, and **we love not our lives unto death.**

We send back every fiery dart and demon attack that has been sent against us. We give no opportunity to the Devil.

We cast out the demons and their works. We eject, drive out, pluck out, thrust out, expel, rebuke, censure, admonish, send away, put out, loosen holds, break up nests, and put off works of demons.

We have power, authority, mastery, superhuman force and control over all the works of the enemy; you must obey and subordinate yourselves to our commands.

We resist, despise, have contempt for, speak doom to, abhor, loathe, detest and hate everything that God hates, all sin and evil, Satan, fallen angels and demons.

We break the power of cursed objects, hex signs, demonic toys and games, and objects infested by demons.

We put on the Whole Armor of God and cover ourselves with the Blood of Jesus Christ. **We accept Jesus Christ is our Lord, Master and Savior!**

We close all doorways for Satan in the occult, addictions, sexual impurities, demonic healing, demonic religions, rock music, inheritances and any others known or unknown.

Casting Out - I now command all controlling spirits to come out of the human being as follows:

Soul: Mind - Will - Emotions
    Conscious - Subconscious - Unconscious
Body: Physical - Brain - Sexual Organs

I now command all special demons to manifest and come out or leave as your name is called:

Wer Beasts: Vampires - Werewolves - Zombies
Manifestations: Changelings - Incubi/Succubi - Dopple Gangers
Objects: Familiar Objects - Fetish, Talisman and Amulets - Marks - Hagstones - Biofeedback
Curses: Spells - Incantations - Hexes - Vexes

I now command all demons associated with the above practices to come out as well as the following demonic families:

Demons: Son of Satan - Mind Control - Death - Occult - Magic - Witchcraft - Drugs - Child Abuse - Fornication - Demonic Healing - Eastern Religions - Demonic Inheritance - Demonic Games - Rock Music - Voodoo - Familiar and Guiding Spirits - Forces and Powers

SECTION 24 - EARLINE'S TESTIMONY ABOUT MAINTAINING DELIVERANCE

CONTENTS

PURPOSE OF DELIVERANCE

The purpose of salvation and deliverance is to bring honor to God among the heathen. In the Old Testament, God became very upset about the shame Israel brought upon His name through their disobedience and sins.

For Israel's uncleanness, shedding innocent blood and worshipping idols, God scattered them among the heathen and dispersed them into many nations. For they had profaned His holy name (Ezk. 36:17-21). When we do these things, we also profane His name. See also Rom. 1:16-24.

As Christians, we must be very careful not to profane God's name. For profaning His name, we will be punished. Demons have a right to enter you if you persist in disobedience.

Our desire and duty is to honor God's name. Read I Tim. 6 and Titus 2 for directions on how to honor God.

Maintaining your deliverance is important to other Christians. It brings honor to God and encouragement to others. **We overcome Satan first by God's provision, the Blood of the Lamb; secondly by our testimony, not just our words but our lives; and thirdly by not loving our lives to the death** (Rev. 12:11; Sing this verse.)

This is why it is so important for you and me to keep getting and maintaining our deliverance until it is complete, and we are established and settled.

BACKGROUND

I have an Indian-English-German-French background. There are curses on each of these people. Indians worshipped devils. Some English and Europeans were Druids who worshipped Satan.

In innocence, my father participated in some occult practices - wart removal and water witching. From my father came curses of Masons and Indians. Physical problems came as a result of curses on Indian worship: inactive thyroid, female disorders and heart disease.

My mother was a paranoid schizophrenic with an Indian-English background. Her emotional illness caused me to need a lot of deliverance from emotional problems.

The following testimony will help you understand how the soul (mind, will and emotions) works. It will also show you how Satan attacks the physical body with demons through curses.

MAIN TESTIMONY ABOUT DELIVERANCE

In July of 1975 I came into deliverance. For most of my life, I was your average daughter, wife, mother and woman. In my mind there was never any real peace, only a sort of make-believe peace. I was not particularly moody, not often angry and not often depressed. **Do you know it is truly possible to have peace in your mind?** (Do you have the peace of God that passes understanding?)

Life for me after I married was a continual move - new places - new people - new houses, all of which I enjoyed. Our homes were among the best and most beautiful around. Decorating them was a lot of joy for me. Taking my children to new places and introducing them to new experiences was exciting. We toured all of the U.S., Canada and Mexico. The greatest fun was watching the children enjoy all the new and unusual things we came across. Life was very exciting.

On May 22, 1973 we were devastated. Our son died from an accident at play. Now all of these lovely homes, beautiful furniture, exciting places, fun people and fun times seemed like trash. At this time we came to know the love of Jesus and the power of God. Never would we be the same again.

After five months passed, we returned south from Minneapolis. In Baton Rouge at the Full Gospel Business Men meetings, we heard about divine healing and the Baptism in the Holy Spirit; I needed both. In time I was healed of my allergies, bad back, etc. and got the Baptism in the Holy Spirit.

Gene and I went to meetings, testified and prayed for people, and saw miracles of healing and Baptisms. For about six months things went fine but as time passed, some attitudes and hurts began to show up and I was very unhappy, moody and depressed.

I spent hours telling Gene how badly he had treated me. I came to believe he had done things that he had not. If you look at my previous statement, you'll see I enjoyed moving. One time when I was ill, I didn't want to move. The rest of the time I enjoyed it. So, I let myself come to believe that he moved just to hurt me and to make life bad for me. I accused him of shutting Marie and me out of his life since Byron died. Gene never knew what to expect when he got home - maybe a frying pan on the noodle (Earline never did). No amount of Bible reading, prayer or fasting helped for more than a week or two at the most.

I was trying to help Marie who was going through all kinds of adjustments to her brother's death but only made matters worse. She also became full of resentment and hurt, and was bitter and angry.

Gene, Marie and I fasted, prayed and talked. I was fasting and praying that God would fix Gene up. I was so blind I was sure that I was perfect - well almost.

After a year or so, I was sitting reading Psalm 91. I had always loved it but suddenly like a bucket of ice water it hit me. The Psalm was not true for me. I had no peace, and was always angry and moody. I (when you are persuaded by the Devil to look on others as the problem) was even beginning to wonder if God was just being bad to me.

I sat on the couch and began to pray: **God if you don't help me tonight I am going out of church, and into the world for good.** I told God that Gene is worse off than me; he's all of my problems.

God just stopped talking so I started praying again the same prayer. **God said again, "Get Gene to pray deliverance for you".** I asked about having our pastors do my deliverance. **God didn't answer; it was like he pulled down a shade or veil.**

Being one of determination I started out again **God I must have help tonight; if I don't get it, I flat quit. He said, "Get Gene to pray deliverance for you". God was not harsh, neither was he condemning. He seemed to be pleased that I had finally asked for help and really meant it.**

I called Gene; he didn't seem particularly impressed. He also suggested the same people and the same excuses. But the best one was **I don't know what deliverance is; I don't know how to do that.**

After some discussion, we decided to go to the bedroom and get in the middle of the bed. We were sitting facing each other, Gene starts praying, and my mind starts wandering. He prayed a while in tongues and started saying strange things such as, **You come out of my wife in the name of Jesus.** One thing I remember well was that at the beginning when each demon was named, I had a thought, **I don't have that.**

As he called out Rejection, its hurts and kindred spirits, I was being shown by the Holy Spirit how these spirits had gained entrance into me, and how they had checked and bound me in all attempts to be myself. Rejection kept me just short of my goals in life. Mostly it kept me from doing what God said to do due to a fear that the other person would disagree or reject me and my idea. I always worked better and succeeded best in those things that I did alone.

Next came Bitterness; I never even considered myself bitter. But as he called out demons under this ruler, I saw hate, violence and anger. I had much trouble with temper. Not that I was always violent, on the contrary I was seldom angry to the observer. When I did get angry or lose my temper, my husband and children usually found some other more suitable place to be.

At the naming of Rebellion, I thought I surely don't have this spirit. As he called it out again, I balled up my fist, drew back to back-hand him, and was consumed with a fit of coughing and mucus.

As this was going on, I was shown how there is only one real rebellion, and it is pointed toward God. Even if we say, **My husband just does not accept God's way so I am going to---.** In the end when it's traced back, it is rebellion to God for God gave directions about how to live with an unsaved mate (I was saved). If it is against circumstances, God says, **In every thing give thanks: for this is the will of God in Christ Jesus concerning you** (I Thes. 5:18). **Let your**

conversation be without covetousness; and be content with such things as ye have: for he hath said, I will never leave thee, nor forsake thee (Heb. 13:5).

One of my rebellions was against circumstances. I had always had such lovely homes with rooms to spare, so that Gene always had an office, and I always had a sewing and craft room. When we came here, Gene bought a three bedroom house with only two baths. His reason was that I couldn't set up Byron's bedroom; I became bitter. I said, "Yes, but you still have your office; I don't have a room. You always get what you want." And I became more rebellious.

When I first moved here I didn't hate this house but little by little it crept up on me. At first it was just the things packed together. Then it grew until I hated the house twenty-four hours a day. Then my ingratitude reached other branches of my life. My wheels were the wheels of a camper truck. I didn't like the truck anymore. Next came Gene, and then living in this bug-infested hot climate with people who can't speak good English. Next the ungrateful person begins to blame others even if he sees it's as much his fault as the other persons. He lies to himself until in his eyes, at least, the other person is entirely at fault.

God showed me my attitude in light of His Attitude letting me know that He could take even this house away; that He had provided it and I was ungrateful for His provision. Oh my, this really was sobering me up. After these three main ruler demons were cast out, I gave up if he called a demon out. I just agreed and became free of it.

I had a habit of getting my work done as fast as I could because I didn't like being in the house alone. So, I roved all over this town looking for plants and cloth to work on the house, but I never worked on it. I did a lot of visiting with other Christian women which is not necessary. Since neither Gene nor I knew anything about this turn of events, I asked God to teach me so I wouldn't go backwards. I rather liked the changes in my mind and attitude.

I found Romans 12 contained my answer. In verse 2, I am told to renew my mind and attitudes with God's instructions. By doing this, I would prove for myself what is the good and acceptable and perfect will of God. In response to your obedience and surrender, God will help you change bad attitudes and habits.

Attitudes submitted to God's word will follow with actions of obedience.

In studying Eph. 5:25-32, I saw how my home was meant to show Christ's relationship with the Church. To my dismay, I saw it reflected my relationship with Christ. It was not a relationship to bring others to Christ.

I also saw how the Church is rebelling against Christ just as in our family members were in rebellion.

The morning after this experience I came down the hall to the kitchen and was greeted pleasantly by my daughter. Now, this was a surprise because she was not so pleasant at that time either. I noticed that she began to change. I asked God about this often and learned that my condition had put such a strain on her that she was being broken under it. I didn't tell her about my deliverance;

I didn't know I should. She became a very obedient and joyful person. I began to enjoy Marie and not worry about her so much.

TESTIMONY ABOUT OVEREATING

(Black Americans have twice the illnesses that White Americans have.) The morning after the first deliverance took place I prepared a nice breakfast for us. Sitting down to read the Bible, I thought about getting something to eat. In fact I said **I think I'll get me something.** This thought alarmed because I was now approaching 180 pounds. I prayed asking God to show me what this is. **To my amazement something inside me said "I said get me something to eat."** I asked who are you? **It said "My name is I LIKE TO EAT."** I said that often. After casting out the demon, **I LIKE TO EAT**, I told God how I had tried dieting and I knew that was hopeless.

I was told obedience is better than sacrifice, and I knew how to eat but was not doing it. Plenty of fresh fruits and vegetables, not much meat and very little sweets is the basis of a proper diet.

Asked if I'd do what I was told, I assured God that I would. **He said that food can be divided into two groups: God's and Devil's. Devil's food includes sweets to excess, junk food, and liquids which are mostly empty calories.**

It's not bad manners not to eat sweets or any other food when you know your body has not used up the last meal. I was intelligent enough to know if I truly needed food.

Here are God's suggestions in summary:

1. **Eat fruit and vegetables; include leafy greens.**
2. **Do not each much meat - three or four servings weekly.**
3. **Don't eat unless you truly need to.**
4. **Don't let others stuff you.**
5. **Seldom eat sweets.**
6. **Almost never eat junk food.**
7. **Remember those whose God is their belly.**
8. **Cook all foods simply.**
9. **Use little fat and cut fat from meat.**

TESTIMONY ABOUT DELIVERANCE FROM INDIAN CURSES

I had a heart condition which was unusual. It never occurred with regularity nor under any specific condition.

While taking a tread mill test, I experienced tremendous pain in the chest, arms and neck. Having been examined by a heart specialist, he told me that my heart was good but he had written **death by heart attack** on many people's certificates like myself. These were people who didn't really have anything wrong with their hearts.

A year or so after my dad's death I found my heart acting up again. Sometimes one to five years would elapse between seizures. I began to ask God to show me why my brothers, dad, dad's brothers and his dad, all had heart problems. He showed me **Exodus 20 and Ezekiel 18**. He told me to repent for my ancestors and myself for the sin of idol worship in **Lev. 26:40-41**. The curse of idol worship follows the blood line. I did these things and have been free for over thirteen years. I was only the second generation from this Indian worship and also had curses from previous generations.

TESTIMONY ABOUT SCHIZOPHRENIA

Schizophrenia means split mind (schizein = to split and phren = mind). I had a lifetime of mental and emotional tension. I was unable to decide what to do and see it through. I had many fears that something bad was going to happen.

All of my life I had great fears of bad things happening: fears of failing and fears of people. I was often tense for weeks and I did not know why.

This is the earliest memory I have of going to school. I was so afraid of all the people I could not go into the school but hid behind the well house until my brother came and took me into the first grade. I was disoriented that day; strange feelings and fears tormented me.

I have very few memories from childhood below the age of nine or ten years. Generally speaking I lived in two worlds: home and away from home. I became very good at forgetting everything bad (parents' fights and my own troubles) that happened at home the minute I walked out the door. I felt more freedom and ease away from home. At high school and college I had trouble with certain subjects like algebra and chemistry. They had things too similar for me to distinguish between them. Both of these subjects ended in frustration and low grades for me.

In my marriage I had some problems accepting my husband as one who would provide for me, take care of me, and continue to love me. I was always expecting the marriage to end badly.

After six years of marriage, we had a delightful son and two years later we had a beautiful daughter.

Double-mindedness wears the person out, and frustrates and confuses him. Deciding, then undeciding stagnates a person. For example, my mom was here for a while; she couldn't be content for desiring to go home. When at home, she was pressed to stay somewhere else besides her home. When away from home, great fears filled her about the house. She was miserable and made those around her miserable (James 1:5-8).

TESTIMONY ABOUT MAINTAINING DELIVERANCE

The scriptural basis for giving a testimony is found in Rev. 12:11 where we overcome Satan by three things: **the blood of Jesus, our testimony, and not loving our lives to the death. God told me that if I was unwilling to tell about my deliverance, I would lose it. And furthermore, if I was ashamed of Him and His provisions, He would be ashamed of me in Heaven.**

In James 4:7 we are told how to make the Devil flee. We often quote part of the verse **resist the devil and he will flee from you**. This gives us a false sense of security. The truth is you must first submit yourself to God. This is not a careless submission but true submission to God which requires us to read, study and obey the Bible. As we submit this way to God and then resist the Devil, he will indeed flee from us. God does not require us to know all the Biblical requirements before He will help us but we must be making every effort to obey all that we have learned, and be diligent about learning and applying more.

After all deliverances, some decisions must be made and never changed no matter how much pressure is applied to you from whatever source to change or go back to old sins.

Here are some decisions which must be made:
1. Study God's Word and accept His principles as your own. 2. Discipline your life and accept responsibility for your actions and thoughts in the areas where you have been delivered.
3. Enter His presence with thanksgiving for all with which He has blessed you.
4. Joyfully obey God's direction even if you have to force yourself in the beginning.

The day after I received my main deliverance, I had an empty feeling and did not know what to do. My reaction was to ask God continually for direction. We cannot do what God directs if we never apply His Word to our life. If we do not apply His Word to our thoughts and actions we are not truly subject to God. Therefore the Devil will not flee from us and we are only fooling ourselves if we think the demons will leave us alone. While we kid ourselves, the Devil and his demons eat our dinner and by the time we face the truth dinner is nearly over.

I learned that I didn't really know God's Word. I didn't know how to use God's Word or how to use my mind. I asked God to take my thoughts. **He told me that He wouldn't touch my thoughts with a ten foot pole; that His thoughts were higher than mine and that I must control my thoughts bring them into submission to Jesus Christ** (II Cor. 10:5).

I started marking everything that God said in the Bible in red. I found there is much said about the mind in Deuteronomy and throughout the Bible. Next I was impressed to underline every verse in the New Testament that told me something that I should do.

I soon realized that I really didn't know what I should think with my mind. It occurred to me that my mind is to be an instrument for my spirit's use and not the other way around. The hands, feet, eyes, ears and body obey, so why not make the mind obey? To make the mind obey, I needed to know what to make it do.

I had to learn how to tell the difference between God's and the Devil's thoughts. The battleground for the Christian is primarily for his soul, not body or spirit. The demons want to re-enter through your mind.

Do you not know that if you continually surrender yourselves to any one to do his will, you are the slaves of him whom you obey, whether it be to sin, which leads to death, or to obedience which leads to righteousness - right doing and right standing with God. But thank God, though you were once slaves of sin you have become obedient with all your heart to the standard of teaching in which you were instructed and to which you were committed. And having been set free from sin, you have become the servants of righteousness - of conformity to the divine will in thought, purpose and action (Romans 6:16-18).

How do we yield ourselves to anyone (God or Devil)? Is it not in the mind? A human always plays with sinful thoughts, then he acts it out. It is not by accident we sin. A lot of people do not want to accept the responsibility for their sinfulness and want to blame it on someone else. The only trouble with this idea is that God will not be fooled by it neither will your enemy, the Devil.

For no temptation - no trial regarded as enticing to sin (no matter how it comes or where it leads) - has overtaken you and lied hold on you that is not common to man - that is no temptation or trial has come to you that is beyond human resistance and that is not adjusted and adapted and belonging to human experience, and such as man can bear. But God is faithful to His Word and to His compassionate nature and He (can be trusted) not to let you be tempted and tried and assayed beyond your ability and strength of resistance and power to endure, but with the temptation He will (always) provide a way out - the means to escape to a landing plane - that you may be capable and strong and powerful patiently to bear up under it. (1 Cor. 10:13).

This tells me temptation is common to mankind, therefore it is common for the Devil and the demons to use it. If they tempt us, we have not sinned. We have sinned when we enjoy and continue to invite the temptation, then yield and obey. the temptation. It also shows we were not watchful for the escape route and we did not take it.

Situations around you will not necessarily change immediately now that you have changed. Just as you practiced obedience to the demons' words, now practice obedience to God's Word.

This is my first encounter with the Devil after I was delivered. Before I was delivered, I would get very angry and depressed when I cleaned house. At that time, we had wall-to-wall furniture. The living room was really badly cluttered. Each piece of furniture had to be moved to vacuum around it. I was happy and didn't hate this house anymore.

As I was vacuuming the living room, I dropped a table on my toe and was having trouble getting the vacuum nozzle under the sofa. I raised up and let out a loud **I hate this---. God quickly warned me that "life and death is in the tongue, and they that love it will eat the fruit thereof"** (Prov. 18:21). **God also told me at this time that He had given it to my family. If I didn't have an attitude of gratitude about the house and furniture, He could easily remove them from me.** I knew that I must not complete the sentence or I would be back where I started from. I repented and repeated until I believed it, **I love this house and I thank God for it.**

Another of Satan's tactics is to use gradualism on us. He will give us a sin to look at and consider. He will cover it over with pretty lies (pretty young people smoking, never an old person dying of lung cancer). He will use rejection to trap you; he will never tell the true ending (where does illegal sex lead?). He knows that the more we see it, hear it and consider it, the more likely we are to give in to it. A good example of the use of gradualism is Humanism. Forty years ago it was very mildly given to people mainly by pastors and teachers. People considered it and accepted it because it was given by people they trusted. Not considering what was the basic theory behind it (worship of self - therefore idolatry), people allowed this theory to so invade them that now we cannot recognize it for what it is. Many of us say we are against it but we live by it instead of the Bible.

We do not recognize God's provisions for us. We think our life should have no problems or privations. We are not grateful to God for all.

Because you did not serve the Lord your God with joyfulness of heart and mind in gratitude for the abundance of all with which He had blessed you, therefore you shall serve your enemies whom the Lord shall send against you, in hunger and thrust, in nakedness, and in want of all things; and He will put a yoke of iron upon you neck, until He hath destroyed you (Deut. 28:47-48).

This verse presents some interesting ideas:
1. Are you having problems because you are ungrateful to God?
2. Do you know which problems are from God to help you learn to endure to the end or which ones are brought on because of being ungrateful?
3. Which ones have you invited by yielding to temptations of the enemy?

If you will know the answer to these questions, you will have to seek God. He has promised to give wisdom to all who ask for it not wavering (James 1:4-8). If you ask God for wisdom and He gives you wisdom, you must not waver following His wisdom. For example: if you have been one to look at dirty magazines, God's wisdom tells you this will lead you to want to do what you see; then you must stop it. You may need deliverance for the demons you have let in plus you must change your habits. No one can change your thought life by casting out your demons. Casting out your demons is one of God's escape routes. To deliverance must be added by the deliveree, discipline of mind and action.

The best attack against habit, and the attempts of demons to trick you and get back in that I found was 1. to tell them to leave in Jesus' name once and 2. immediately take control of your mind. I would do it this way: I would tell them Jesus has given me authority over you (Luke 10:19, Matt. 28:18-20), therefore I command you to leave me now. If I did not sense they were gone, I would say, **Since you are still here, I would like to read to you about what Jesus Christ has done for me.** I would open the Bible to Matt. 26-28, Mark 14-16, Luke 22-24 and John 17-21 and read it aloud to them. Of course they did not want to hear of God's love and provision for me. The pressure they had placed on me and their thoughts were long gone but I would read on and bless myself in God's Word. Some times the pressure from the demons trying to get back in was strong enough that I would have to walk and read very loudly to them. I will still do this if I come under attack; it always works. After a time, you will be able to tell them the facts without reading it to them.

My next attack was sent through people. When asked why I looked so much better and was losing weight, I would answer truthfully and say **I was delivered of demons and no, I was not dieting.** If three people were present, you would get three distinct reactions. One would leave pronto, one would regard you as if you were radioactive, and one would grab your arm and want to know more.

Then you'd hear whispers - she had demons! They only talk about demons; do they worship them? They are fanatical; they believe there is a demon under every bush!

Next I was tempted to go back to some of my old habits of retaliation, etc. I must crucify the flesh - God said that vengeance belongs to Him (Rom. 12:19). I must not habitually sin or else I become the demon's house in that area again (I John 3:8-9).

Mental suggestions by the Devil must be put down. He will suggest a what if, could be or maybe. If this happens, what will you do (fear and more fear)? Unless you have facts to base your knowledge on, don't let the Devil play you along.

One of his tactics was to attack me about Marie: what if Marie can't adjust to her brother's death? Before deliverance, I would cringe in fear and worry.

After deliverance, I learned to tell Satan that Marie can do all things through Christ who strengthens her; I can too!

You don't have to be perfect to give a word of encouragement, share an experience, help someone or even cast out a demon. If God demanded perfection, nothing would ever get done. I'm over fifty years old and I have yet to meet a perfect person.

You must have a total commitment to Jesus Christ. Rely totally on Him and His Word. Do these things and you will continue to get free and stay free. Don't be double minded: deciding and undeciding.

I found verses to put my temptations in prospective (Heb. 12:1-4). Begin reading at verse one which contains instruction on keeping pure. It suggests we are to:

Strip off and throw aside every encumbrance and sin which so readily (deftly and cleverly) clings to and entangles us, and let us run with patient endurance and steady and active persistence the appointed course of the race set before us. Looking away (from all that will distract) to Jesus, Who is the Leader and the source of our faith (giving the first incentive for our belief) and is also its Finisher, (bringing it to maturity and perfection). He, for the joy (of obtaining the prize) that was set before Him endured the cross, despising and ignoring the shame, and is now seated at the right hand of the throne of God. Just think of Him who endured from sinners such grievous opposition and bitter hostility against - reckon up and consider it all in comparison with your trials - so that you may not grow weary or exhausted, losing heart and relaxing and fainting in your minds. You have not yet struggled and fought agonizing against sin, nor have you yet resisted and withstood to the point of pouring out your (own) blood. (Heb. 12:1-4).

If we are able with every temptation to resist to the shedding of our blood maybe, then we might have an acceptable excuse for failing to resist the Devil and him having to flee.

God will not make you over; He will work with you and help you. See Mark 16:20. A miracle is taking place as you go obeying The Word in the areas you have received instruction and deliverance.

A study of Matt. Chapter 5 will help anyone see just where they are missing it with their attitudes. It will inspire you to clear your mind of a lot of incorrect ideas and to broaden your understanding of the truth.

Scripture for Preparing Ourselves for Warfare

Josh. 1:7-9 Only be thou strong and very courageous, that thou mayest observe to do according to all the law, which Moses my servant commanded thee: turn not from it to the right hand or to the left, that thou mayest prosper whithersoever thou goest.

Neh. 1:4-7 And it came to pass, when I heard these words, that I sat down and wept, and mourned certain days, and fasted, and prayed before the God of Heaven. And said, I beseech thee, O Lord God of Heaven, the great and terrible God, that keepeth covenant and mercy for them that love him, and observe his commandments: Let thine ear now be attentive, and thine eyes open, that thou mayest hear the prayer of thy servant, which I pray before thee now, day and night, for the children of Israel thy servants, **and confess the sins of the children of Israel, which we have sinned against thee: both I and my father's house have sinned**. We have dealt very corruptly against thee, and have not kept the commandments, nor the statutes, nor the judgments, which thou commandest thy servant Moses.

Prov. 28:13 He that coverith his sins shall not prosper: but whoso confesseth and forsaketh them shall have mercy.

Dan. 9:3-6 And I set my face unto the Lord God, to seek by prayer and supplications, with fasting, and sackcloth, and ashes: And I prayed unto the Lord my God, and made my confession, and said, O Lord, the great and dreadful God, keeping the covenant and mercy to them that love him, and to them that keep his commandments; **We have sinned, and have committed iniquity, and have done wickedly, and have rebelled, even by departing from thy precepts and from thy judgments**: Neither have we hearkened unto thy servants the prophets, which spake in thy name to our kings, our princes, and our fathers, and to all the people of the land.

Matt. 16:23 But he turned, and said unto Peter, Get thee behind me, Satan: thou art an offence unto me: for thou savourest not the things that be of God, but those that be of men.

Matt. 17:18-21 And Jesus rebuked the devil and he departed out of him: and the child was cured from that very hour. Then came the disciples to Jesus apart, and said, Why could not we cast him out? And Jesus said unto them, Because of your unbelief: for verily I say unto you, If ye have faith as a grain of mustard seed, ye shall say unto this mountain, Remove hence to yonder place: and it shall remove: and nothing shall be impossible unto you. **Howbeit this kind goeth not out but by prayer and fasting.**

Matt. 18:32-35 Then his lord, after that he had called him, said unto him, O thou wicked servant, I forgave thee all that debt, because thou desirest me: Shouldest not thou also have had compassion on thy fellow servant, even as I had pity on thee? And his lord was wroth, and delivered him to the tormentors, till he should pay all that was due unto him. **So likewise shall my heavenly Father do also unto you, if ye from your hearts forgive not every one his brother their trespasses.**

Luke 13:11-17 And, behold, there was a woman which had a spirit of infirmity eighteen years, and was bowed together, and could in no wise lift up herself. And when Jesus saw her, he called her to him, and said unto her, Woman, thou are loosed from thine infirmity. And he laid his hands on her: and immediately she was made straight, and glorified God. And the ruler of the synagogue answered with indignation, because that Jesus had healed on the Sabbath day, and said unto the people, There are six days in which men ought to work: in them therefore come and be healed, and not on the Sabbath day. The Lord then answered him, and said, Thou hypocrite, doth not each one of you on the Sabbath loose his ox or his ass from the stall, and lead him away to watering? And ought not this woman, being a daughter of Abraham, **whom Satan hath**

bound, lo, these eighteen years, be loosed from this bond on the Sabbath day? And when he had said these things, all his adversaries were ashamed: and all the people rejoiced for all the glorious things that were done by him.

I Cor. 3:16-17 Know ye not that ye are the temple of God, and that the Spirit of God dwelleth in you? **If any man defile the temple of God, him shall God destroy**; for the temple of God is holy, which temple ye are.

I Cor. 12:8-10 For to one is given by the Spirit the **word of wisdom**; to another the **word of knowledge** by the same Spirit; To another **faith** by the same Spirit; to another the **gifts of healing** by the same Spirit; To another the **working of miracles**; to another **prophecy**; to another **discerning of spirits**; to another **divers kinds of tongues**; to another the **interpretation of tongues.**

I Pet. 5:8-9 Be sober, be vigilant; because your adversary the Devil, as a roaring lion walketh about, seeking whom he may devour: Whom resist steadfast in the faith knowing that the same afflictions are accomplished in your brethren that are in the world.

I John 2:13-16 I write unto you, fathers, because ye have known him that is from the beginning. I write unto you, young men, because ye have overcome the wicked one. I write unto you, little children, because ye have known the Father. I have written unto you, fathers, because ye have known him that is from the beginning. I have written unto you, young men, because ye are strong, and the Word of God abideth in you, and ye have overcome the wicked one. Love not the world, neither the things that are in the world. If any man love the world, the love of the Father in not in him. **For all that is in the world, the lust of the flesh, and the lust of the eyes, and the pride of life, is not of the Father, but is of the world.**

Rev. 20:1-3 And I saw an angel come down from heaven, having the key of the bottomless pit and a great chain in his hand. And he laid hold on the Dragon, that old serpent, which is the Devil, and Satan, and bound him a thousand years, **And cast him into the bottomless pit, and shut him up, and set a seal upon him, that he should deceive the nations no more, till the thousand years should be fulfilled**: and after that he must be loosed a little season.

OVERALL FOR PREPARING OURSELVES FOR WARFARE

1. Be led by the Holy Spirit after you have prepared yourself.

2. Summary:

1. Leader: Teach - Minister - Counsel
2. Congregation: Self Discipline - Continue in Deliverance

3. Six Basic Steps To Your Deliverance

1. Identify your problems.
2. Forgive, pray and get yourself right with God.
3. Break the curses and soul ties on you and your descendents.
4. Cast out your demons.
5. Pray for healing of your soul and body.
6. Discipline your life by changing your way of thinking and acting.

4. Basis for Deliverance

1. Pray deliverance prayers.
2. Break away from ungodly people, religions, and organizations.
3. Break curses, soul ties, and demonic holds.

5. Ministry

1. Cast out demons.
2. Loose Godly spirits.

3. Read deliverance scripture.
6. Make positive confessions to God with His help.
7. Pray for healing of soul and body.
8. Five Steps To Cleaning Your House

1. Five-way prayer of forgiveness: you forgive your ancestors **(upwards)**, descendants **(downwards)** and other people **(outwards)**; ask God to forgive and bless them. Ask God to forgive you **(godwards)** and you forgive yourself **(inwards)** for sins against your body.

2. Break curses and soul ties from ancestors and others (inwards), and to descendants and others (outwards). Break curses of psychic or false religion prayers from others to you, and from you to others.

3. Clean out house of those objects or exorcise objects that you don't own. Exorcism is the anointing with oil, praying about the object, and casting out the demons.

4. Anoint house with oil, and cast evil spirits out of house.

5. Cast demons out of people that came in thru curses. For mass deliverance, see **Cursed Objects and Demon Infestation** in the **Deliverance Manual**.

9. Clean your house and possessions of cursed objects.
10. Discipline your soul and body.
11. Continue study and practice of deliverance.
12. Continue to gain freedom and strength.

SCRIPTURE FOR WARFARE IN THE HEAVENLIES

Matt. 10:1 And when he had called unto him his twelve disciples, he gave them power against unclean spirits, to cast them out, and to heal all manner of sickness and all manner of disease.

Matt. 12:24-29 But when the Pharisees heard it, they said, This fellow doth not cast out devils, but by Beelzebub the prince of the devils. And Jesus knew their thoughts, and said unto them, Every kingdom divided against itself is brought to desolation; and every city or house divided against itself shall not stand: And if Satan cast out Satan, he is divided against himself; how shall then his kingdom stand? And if I by Beelzebub cast out devils, by whom do your children cast them out? therefore they shall be your judges. But if I cast out devils by the Spirit of God, then the Kingdom of God is come unto you. **Or else how can one enter into a strong man's house, and spoil his goods except he first bind the strong man? and then he will spoil his house.**

Matt. 16:18-19 And I say also unto thee, That thou are Peter, and upon this rock I will build my church; and the gates of hell shall not prevail against it. **And I will give unto thee the keys of the Kingdom of Heaven**: and whatsoever thou shalt bind on the earth shall be bound in heaven: and whatsoever thou shalt loose on earth shall be loosed in heaven.

Matt. 28:18-20 And Jesus came and spake unto them saying, All power is given unto me in heaven and in earth. Go ye therefore, and teach all nations, baptizing them in the name of the Father, and of the Son, and of the Holy Ghost: Teaching them to observe all things whatsoever I have commanded you: and, lo, I am with you alway even unto the end of the world.

Mark. 11:22-23 And Jesus answering saith unto them, Have faith in God. For verily I say unto you, That whosoever shall say unto this mountain, Be thou removed, and be thou cast into the sea; and shalt not doubt in his heart, **but shall believe that those things which he saith shall come to pass; he shall have whatsoever he saith**.

Mark. 16:15-20 And he said unto them, Go ye into all the world, and preach the gospel to every creature. He that believeth and is baptized shall be saved; but he that believeth not shall be damned. And these signs shall follow them that believe; **In my name shall they cast out devils**;

they shall speak with new tongues; They shall take up serpents; and if they drink any deadly thing, it shall not hurt them; they shall lay hands on the sick, and they shall recover. So then after the Lord had spoken unto them, he was received up into heaven, and sat on the right hand of God. And they went forth, and preached every where, the Lord working with them, and confirming the word with signs following. Amen.

Luke 9:1-2 Then he called his twelve disciples together, **and gave them power and authority over all devils, and to cure diseases**. And he sent them to preach the Kingdom of God, and to heal the sick.

Luke 10:17-20 And the seventy returned again with joy, saying, **Lord, even the devils are subject unto us through thy name**. And he said unto them, I beheld Satan as lightning fall from heaven. **Behold, I give unto you power to tread on serpents and scorpions, and over all the power of the enemy: and nothing shall by any means hurt you.** Notwithstanding in this rejoice not, that the spirits are subject unto you; but rather rejoice, because your names are written in heaven.

Luke 11:21-22 When a strong man armed keepeth his palace, his goods are in peace: **But when a stronger than he shall come upon him, and overcome him, he taketh from him all his armour wherein he trusted, and divideth his spoils.**

II Cor. 2:10-11 To whom ye forgive any thing, I forgive also; for if I forgave any thing, to whom I forgave it, for your sakes forgave I it in the person of Christ: **Lest Satan should get an advantage of us: for we are not ignorant of his devices**.

II Cor. 4:3-4 But if our gospel be hid, it is hid to them that are lost: **In whom the god of this world hath blinded the minds of them which believe not**, lest the light of the glorious Gospel of Christ, who is the image of God, should shine unto them.

II Cor. 10:3-6 For though we walk in the flesh, we do not war after the flesh; For the weapons of our warfare are not carnal, but mighty through God to the pulling down of strong holds; Casting down imaginations, and every high thing that exalteth itself against the knowledge of God, and bringing into captivity every thought to the obedience of Christ: And having a readiness to revenge all disobedience, when you obedience is fulfilled.

Eph. 1:19-23 And what is the exceeding greatness of his power to us-ward who believe, according to the working of his mighty power, Which he wrought in Christ, when he raised him from the dead, and set him at his own right hand in the heavenly places, **Far above all principality, and power, and might, and dominion and every name that is named**, not only in this world, but also in that which is to come: and hath put all things under his feet, and gave him to be the head over all things to the church, Which is his body, the fullness of him that filleth all in all.

Eph. 2:6 And hath raised us up together **and made us sit together in heavenly places in Christ Jesus**.

Eph. 6:10-18 Finally, my brethren, be strong in the Lord, and in the power of his might, Put on the whole armour of God, that ye may be able to stand against the wiles of the Devil. **For we wrestle not against flesh and blood, but against principalities, against powers, against the rulers of the darkness of this world, against spiritual wickedness in high places**. Wherefore take unto you the whole armour of God, that ye may be able to withstand in the evil day, and heaving done all, to stand. Stand therefore, having you loins girt about with truth, and having on the breastplate of righteousness: And your feet shod with the preparation of the gospel of peace: Above all, taking the shield of faith, wherewith ye shall be able to quench all the fiery darts of the wicked. And take the helmet of salvation, and the sword of the Spirit, which is the word of

God: Praying always with all prayer and supplication in the Spirit, and watching thereunto with all perseverance and supplication for all saints.

Col. 2:15 And having spoiled principalities and powers, he made a shew of them openly, triumphing over them in it.

Heb. 1:13-14 But to which of the angels said he at any time, Sit on my right hand, until I make thine enemies thy footstool? **Are they not all ministering spirits, sent forth to minister for them who shall be heirs of salvation**?

I John. 3:8 He that committeth sin is of the Devil: for the Devil sinneth from the beginning. **For this purpose the Son of God was manifested, that he might destroy the works of the Devil**.

I John. 5:18-19 We know that whosoever is born of God sinneth not; but he that is begotten of God keepeth himself, and that wicked one toucheth him not. **And we know that we are of God, and the whole world lieth in wickedness**.

OVERALL FOR WARFARE IN THE HEAVENLIES

1. We wrestle against spiritual forces, not against flesh and blood.
2. This is an organized kingdom with delegated authorities, world rulers and wicked spirits.
3. We must sound the trumpet, clothe ourselves for battle, take up our spiritual weapons, know our enemy and attack.
4. Satan has limitations, methods of attack and schemes. He temps us, accuses us and deceives us.
5. Methods for disarming the strong man include researching the past, repenting of all sins, forgiving all others, recognizing God's purpose, ministering with compassion, praying with all prayer and speaking to the mountain.
6. The boot camp of spiritual warfare is in our local churches, working with the sheep and ministering deliverance to them one by one.
7. **Ground level warfare is casting demons out of people. Strategic level warfare is coming against territorial spirits.**
8. God sets the battle plan.
9. We have the authority to pull down strongholds. It was given to The Twelve, The Seventy and to The Church.
10. The warfare should be led by those who have spiritual jurisdiction over their territory.
11. We should pull down strongholds. We should bind and loose.
12. Christ's Church, through the exercise of her authority, can change the course of history.
13. You should continue in spiritual warfare until victory comes. Be prepared to wrestle with the enemy. Keep your faith. Remain steadfast in prayer and spiritual warfare.
14. Our strength in the Lord is derived through spiritual exercises: daily prayer and Bible Study, fasting, fellowship with other believers, praise, worship, our testimony and walking in holiness.
15. We are dealing with principalities, powers, rulers of the darkness of this age and spiritual host of wickedness in the heavenlies.
16. Wickedness includes perverseness, greed, witchcraft, occult, cults, false religions, New Age Religion, etc.
17. We must forgive everyone no matter what they did to us.
18. We must sanctify ourselves as individuals and cleanse the Church corporately.
19. After we have cleansed ourselves, we simply speak to the principalities and powers in the authority of Jesus' Name.
20. Put aside jealousy, doctrinal questions, and other factors that separate Christians and churches from each other. Pull down ignorance, fear and prejudice.

21. Help those who are bound by blindness, disease, poverty and fear in the mental, physical, spiritual and material areas.

APPLICATION OF SPIRITUAL WARFARE

1. Personalize commands for your relatives, friends and acquaintances.
2. Personalize commands for Lake Hamilton Bible Camp: those who live there, work there, minister there, and come there to be ministered to.
3. Personalize commands for families; churches and ministries; counties, cities, states and nation; and the world.

REFERENCES

1. **Our Warfare Against Demons and Territorial Spirits** by Frank D. Hammond
2. **The Saints At War - Spiritual Warfare Series Volume I** by Frank D. Hammond

SECTION 26 - SPIRITUAL WARFARE STATEMENTS

CONTENTS

TORMENTING DEMONS

Scripture References

I recommend that you mark these scriptures in your Bible for handy reference in time of battle with the forces of evil. The following scripture verses are to be completely read, out loud, to the demons to drive them out of the people. Probably the most powerful biblical book for warfare is Matthew; start with Matthew and keep reading as long as this weapon is needed. **Demons hate to hear THE WORD OF GOD!**

Matthew 3:7-8; 4:10-11, 23-24; 6:14-15; 7:22-23; 8:2-3, 12, 16-17, 28-33; 9:32-33; 10:1, 7-8; 11:4-6, 11-12; 12:22,24-33, 43-45; 13:41-42, 49-50; 15:19-20, 22-28; 16:18-19, 22-23; 17:14-18; 19:8-9, 18-20, 21-35; 22:13-14; 23:33; 25:30, 41, 46; 28:18-20.
Mark 1:23-27, 32-33, 39-42; 3:10-15, 22-27; 5:1-20; 6:7, 13-14; 7:20-23, 25-30, 34-35; 9:17-29, 38-39, 43-48; 11:15, 21-26; 16:9, 15-20.
Luke 1:71; 4:18-19, 33-35, 38-41; 5:12-14; 6:17-19; 7:21-22; 8:2-3, 26-39; 9:1-2, 37-42, 49-50, 55; 10:17-20; 11:14-22, 24-26; 13:11-17, 31-32; 16:16, 22-24; 22:3.
John 5:14; 6:70; 8:31-32, 44; 10:10; 12:31-32; 13:27; 14:12-14,30; 15:7-8; 16:11.
Acts 1:8; 2:35-36; 5:3-4, 15-16; 8:5-8, 22-24; 10:38; 13:6, 8, 10-11; 15:24; 16:16-18; 19:11-19; 26:18.
Romans 1:21-32; 6:16; 13:12-14; 16:18, 20.
I Corinthians 2:6-8; 3:3; 5:4-8; 10:20-21; 11:3, 10.
II Corinthians 1:10, 24; 2:11; 4:3-4; 7:1; 10:3-6; 11:3-4, 13-15; 12:7.
Galatians 3:1; 4:3; 5:13, 19-24.
Ephesians 1:19-23; 2:1-3, 6-7; 3:10; 4:8-14, 26-27; 5:3-5; 6:10-18.
Philippians 1:28; 2:9-11; 3:19, 21.
Colossians 1:13, 16; 2:9-10, 15,18-19; 3:5-8.

I Thessalonians 2:8, 18.
II Thessalonians 2:7-12.
I Timothy 1:18-20; 4:1-3, 7.
II Timothy 1:7-8; 2:20-22, 24-26; 3:1-5.
Hebrews 1:7, 14; 2:3-5, 7-8, 14-15; 4:12; 12:14-16.
James 1:8; 2:19; 3:14-16; 4:5-8.
I Peter 1:13-14, 223:22; 5:8-9.
II Peter 1:16; 2:4, 14.
I John 2:16; 3:8-9; 4:1-4, 18.
Jude 6, 9.
Revelations 1:18; 12:7-11; 16:13-14; 18:23; 19:20, 20:1-3, 7-10, 14-15.

Tormenting Scripture

Read the scripture reference and scripture out loud:

Matt. 8:12 But the children of the kingdom shall be cast out into outer darkness: there shall be weeping and gnashing of teeth.
Matt. 8:29 --- art thou come hither to torment us before the time?
Matt. 12:43 When the unclean spirit is gone out of a man, he walketh through dry places, seeking rest, and findeth none.
Matt. 13:42 And shall cast them into a furnace of fire: there shall be wailing and gnashing of teeth.
Matt. 18:8-9 --- rather that having two hands or two feet or two eyes to be cast into everlasting fire and hell fire.
Matt. 18:34 And his lord was wroth, and delivered him to the tormentors, till he should pay all that was due unto him.
Matt. 22:13 Then said the king to the servants, Bind him hand and foot, and take him away, and cast him into outer darkness; there shall be weeping and gnashing of teeth.
Matt. 23:33 Ye serpents, ye generation of vipers, how can ye escape the damnation of hell?
Matt. 25:30 And cast ye the unprofitable servant into outer darkness; there shall be weeping and gnashing of teeth.
Matt. 25:41 Then shall he say also unto them on the left hand, Depart from me, ye cursed, into everlasting fire, prepared for the Devil and his angels.
Matt. 25:46 And these shall go away into everlasting punishment: but the righteous into life eternal.
Mark 1:24 --- art thou come to destroy us? I know thee who thou art, the Holy One of God.
Mark 9:43-48 --- into hell, into the fire that never shall be quenched: Where their worm dieth not, and the fire is not quenched.
Luke 8:28 --- I beseech thee, torment me not.
Luke 16:23-24 --- and in hell he lift up his eyes, being in torments, and seeth Abraham afar off, and Lazarus in his bosom. And he cried and said, Father Abraham, have mercy on me, and send Lazarus, that he may dip the tip of his finger in water, and cool my tongue; for I am tormented in this flame.

Tormenting Statements

The following statements are used to be spoken out loud to the demons within a person or group to torment them and to loosen their hold so that the demons can be cast out. Here is just some of what the Bible says about this horrible place:

In Hell people recognize GOD, pray, see a need for repentance and **beg for salvation of others**. They can see Heaven and those who are enjoying Heaven's rewards.

Hell is not the grave, grave is a resting place, no activity in the grave, **Hell was created for the Devil and his angels,** THE BIBLE is full of warnings, **forever is forever,** there is no soul sleep, the dead are conscious, absent from the body is present in Heaven or Hell, body is not recreated, **Hell is enlarged and frightful,** and **the worm does not die.** The wicked are not annihilated. Perish, lost and destroy do not mean annihilate.

Hell is Sheol and Hades. **Gehenna** is where perpetual fires were kept burning. **Tartaroo** is a special place where the angels which sinned are confined.

Place of wrath, sorrow, fire, consciousness, people able to recognize others, conversations, people having knowledge of events and remembrance of past, torment and pain, people seeing the need of soul-winning, eternal punishment, weeping and gnashing of teeth, fire is not quenched and the worm does not die, without end, perpetuity, eternal and the lake with fire with brimstone.

Everlasting burnings, day of the Lord, vengeance, everlasting contempt, wrath of God, resurrection of damnation, accursed, idolatry, second death, wrath, wickedness, cast into Hell, cast into fire, furnace of fire; angels in Hell, greater damnation, damned, turned into Hell, blackness of darkness, and turned away.

Shame and everlasting contempt, unquenchable fire, fire which never shall be quenched, in danger of hell fire, everlasting fire, damnation of Hell, everlasting punishment, in danger of eternal damnation, being in torments, everlasting destruction, of eternal judgment, everlasting chains under darkness, vengeance of eternal fire, tormented with fire and brimstone, smoke of their torment ascendeth up for ever and ever, they have no rest day or night, a lake of fire burning with brimstone, be tormented day and night forever and ever, and the lake of fire.

Lake of fire, bottomless pit, horrible tempest, devouring fire and furnace of fire. Hell is where they will wail, God is cursed, there's no rest, they scream for mercy, they can never repent, they gnaw their tongues, they feel the wrath of God, the fire never goes out and they don't want their loved ones to come. Place of sorrows, weeping, torments, outer darkness, for the Devil and his angels, weeping and gnashing of teeth, fire is not quenched and the lake with fire with brimstone.

Eternal Punishment

Forever is forever, the worm does not die, eternal punishment, without end, perpetuity, everlasting burnings, everlasting contempt, everlasting punishment, eternal damnation, everlasting destruction, eternal judgment, everlasting chains under darkness, smoke of

their torment ascendeth up for ever and ever, be tormented day and night forever and ever, without end, perpetuity and eternal.

SPIRITUAL WARFARE STATEMENT

In THE NAME OF JESUS CHRIST and THE POWER OF HIS BLOOD, THE HOLY SPIRIT, ALMIGHTY GOD and THE HOLY WORD OF GOD we pray and take authority over the kingdom of evil.

WARFARE SCRIPTURE

1. **The LORD is righteous: he hath cut asunder the cords of the wicked** (Ps. 129:4).
2. **And as ye go, preach, saying, The Kingdom Of Heaven is at hand. Heal the sick, cleanse the lepers, raise the dead, <u>cast out devils</u>: freely ye have received, freely give** (Matt. 10:7-8).
3. **And from the days of John the Baptist until now the kingdom of Heaven suffereth violence, and the violent take it by force** (Matt. 11:12).
4. **Whatsoever ye shall bind on earth shall be bound in Heaven: and whatsoever ye shall loose on earth shall be loosed in Heaven** (Matt 18:18).
5. **And these signs shall follow them that believe. In My Name shall they cast out devils** (Mark 16:17).
6. **Behold, I give unto you power to tread on serpents and scorpions, and over all the power of the enemy: and nothing shall by any means hurt you** (Luke 10:19).
7. **CHRIST hath redeemed us from the curse of the law, being made a curse for us: for it is written, Cursed is everyone that hangeth on a tree** (Gal. 3:13). JESUS CHRIST bore our curses on The Cross.
8. **That at THE NAME OF JESUS every knee should bow, of things in Heaven, and things in earth, and things under the earth; and that every tongue should confess that JESUS CHRIST IS LORD, to THE GLORY OF GOD THE FATHER** (Phil. 2:10-11). Bend your knee to JESUS and confess that JESUS CHRIST IS LORD.
9. **And having spoiled principalities and powers, He made a shew of them openly, triumphing over them in it** (Col. 2:15).
10. **For THE WORD OF GOD is quick, and powerful, and sharper than any two-edged sword, piercing even to the dividing asunder of soul and spirit, and of the joint and marrow, and is a discerner of the thoughts and intents of the heart** (Heb. 4:12). We divide the soul and the spirit.
11. **Ye are of GOD, little children, and have overcome them: because greater is he that is in you, than he that is in the world** (1 John 4:4).
12. **And from Jesus Christ, who is the faithful witness, and the first begotten of the dead, and the prince of the kings of the earth. Unto him that loved us, and washed us from our sins in his own blood** (Rev. 1:5).
13. **I am he that liveth, and was dead; and, behold, I am alive for evermore, Amen; and have the keys of hell and of death** (Rev. 1:18).
14. **And to the angel of the church in Philadelphia write; These things saith he that is holy, he that is true, he that hath the key of David, he that openeth, and no man shutteth; and shutteth, and no man openeth** (Rev. 3:7).
15. The entire chapters of Isa. 47, particularly Rev. 18 and 20, and also Rev. 21 and 22.

THE BLOOD OF JESUS CHRIST

1. We ask that GOD send THE BLOOD OF JESUS CHRIST for warfare.

2. We sprinkle THE BLOOD over the gates of body and soul.
3. We apply THE BLOOD.

WE ASK GOD

1. To send coals of fire from THE ALTER OF GOD to be heaped on demons.
2. To send THE SWORD OF THE LORD, reinforcements, arrows, lances and hornets from Heaven to attack.
3. To destroy spiritual idols, sacrifices, altars, temples and counterfeits within and without.

WE

1. Seize the Kingdom of Heaven and take it by force from Satan.
2. Send back every fiery dart and demon attack that has been sent against us. Give no opportunity to the Devil.
3. Cast out the demons and their works. Eject, drive out, pluck out, thrust out, expel, rebuke, censure, admonish, send away, put out, loosen holds, break up nests and put off works of demons.
4. Exercise power, authority, mastery, superhuman force and control over the works of the enemy; command you to obey and subordinate yourselves.
5. Resist, despise, have contempt for, speak doom to, abhor, loathe and detest. Hate sin, evil, Satan, fallen angels, demons and everything that God hates.
6. Break the power of cursed objects, hex signs, demonic toys and games, and objects infested by demons.
7. Close doorways for Satan in the occult, addictions, sexual impurities, demonic healing, demonic religions, rock music, inheritances and other doorways known or unknown.
8. Break down your spiritual walls even as the walls of Jericho came tumbling down (Josh. 6:5).
9. Break curses coming down the family line on the mother's and father's sides, ten generations backwards and forwards.
10. Come against Babylon The Great, the overall satanic spiritual system that encompasses the earth.
11. Bind the spirits that cause spiritual blindness.
12. Break the covenant of death and other covenants that have no legal right.

BINDINGS

1. We put a hook in your nose, a cord around your tongue and we bore a thorn in your jaw (leviathan - Job 41). (This is very effective Scripture when you're up against a serpent, which is quite often.)
2. We bind you with chains from Heaven. We bind the gate keeper.
3. We cut and cast off cords, ties, bonds, bands, ropes and chains within and without.

STRONGMEN

1.We bind the strongmen in the heavens over this people, church, community, county, city, state, nation and world in Hell and out of Hell (person, family, house, building, etc.)
2. We command the strongmen and their nests of spirits to come out.

DROUGHTS

1. We dry up your waters, seas, rivers and springs. We stand on THE WORD OF GOD, and cause a drought over your land. Pass over to Chittim; you shall find no rest. There is no water; there's only THE BLOOD OF JESUS CHRIST. We make your habitation a desolate wilderness.

2. THE LORD will cause a drought to be upon your waters (Jer. 50:38; 51:36). We will dry up your sea and make your springs dry.
3. We dry up your river, even as Jordan was dried up and the people of GOD went into the promised land on dry ground (Josh. 3:16).
4. We dry up your roots even as THE LORD JESUS dried up the fig tree (Matt. 21:19).
5. We ask GOD to send angels and fires from Heaven to dry up the waters of Death.
6. We dry up and turn back the worms of death with fire from Heaven.

GATES AND GATEKEEPERS

1. We bind the gatekeeper. He who has the Key of David: what gate or door he opens, none shall close; what gate He closes, none shall open. By the authority given us, we tear down your two-leaved gates. We knock down and smash your pillars and walls. No stone shall stand upon another (Rev. 3:7; Isa. 22:22; Eze. 21:15-22).
2. We knock down your two-leaved gates and the gates of Death. The gates shall not be shut. We break in pieces your gates of brass and cut in sunder the bars of iron (Isa. 45:1-2).

JEZEBELS

1. Jezebel, we take away your throne and destroy it. We command you to sit in the dust. You are no queen. Bow your knee. Your are no virgin. Neither are you tender and delicate (Isa. 47:1).
2. You are common. Grind meal, uncover your locks, make bare the leg, uncover the thigh, pass over the rivers. You are exposed (Isa. 47:2-3).

POSITIVE CONFESSIONS

We make positive confessions to GOD and each other about living our life for CHRIST:
1. We forgive everyone that has hurt or cursed us, and we pray for our enemies.
2. We exercise honesty - humility - repentance - renunciation - forgiveness - prayer - warfare.
3. We overcome Satan by the BLOOD OF THE LAMB, by our testimony for JESUS CHRIST and **we do not love lives unto death.**
4. We put on the WHOLE ARMOR OF GOD and cover ourselves with the BLOOD OF JESUS CHRIST. **We proclaim JESUS CHRIST as our LORD, MASTER AND SAVIOR!**

WARFARE STATEMENTS

1. You are going to be cast into The Lake Of Fire And Brimstone, where there will be weeping and gnashing of teeth, where the worm will never die and the fire will never be quenched. You will be cast in there with Satan, fallen angels and demons. You will have maggots on your head and worms on your feet. You will be tormented for ages on ages, eons on eons throughout eternity. You lost your right to go to Heaven.
2. Bow your knee to JESUS CHRIST and go where He is telling you to go and do what He is telling you. Satan and demons will bow their knees in Hell and say the JESUS CHRIST IS LORD OF LORDS and KING OF KINGS.
3. We call for spiritual warfare by the angels. We ask the angels to use the sharp two-edged sword to cut the roots of the demons, put a hook in their jaws, bind them up with chains and take them out to dry places or wherever GOD wants them to go.
4. We shine the LIGHT OF THE HOLY SPIRIT on the demons and give them no place to rest and hide. We light a fire under them as hot as Hell. We command that you look down into Hell and see your punishment.

5. We place the demons in separate boxes and cutoff communications from the demons outside to the demons inside.
6. We command that you reveal what legal rights you have to remain. We command that you speak into the mind or out of the mouth. We command that you speak the truth that will stand-up in The Judgement.
7. We command that you manifest, identify and reveal yourselves as unto JESUS, and come out. We command that you bring your families, works, nests, and every evil spirit and family associated with you known and unknown. We bundle the families up and cast them out.
8. If you leave quickly, we will let you go to the dry places and try to find another body to dwell in. If you have no legal right to stay, we ask the angels to take you to The Abyss or Tartarus and lock you up until The Lake Of Fire And Brimstone.
9. How would you like to be cast into Tartarus where the fallen angels who left their first estate are bound up until The Lake Of Fire And Brimstone? They hate you and will torment you until you are cast into Hell. You have a choice, leave quickly or face this punishment.
10. Burn demon burn from the BLOOD OF JESUS CHRIST.
11. We come against you with THE BLOOD OF JESUS CHRIST, THE WORD OF GOD and THE HOLY SPIRIT. We command that you line up in rank and file and order and come out quickly. We bind every power you have and loose ourselves from you. We are violently taking THE KINGDOM OF HEAVEN BY FORCE.
12. We ask GOD to send an angelic army arrayed for battle: warring angels, ministering angels, THE HOLY SPIRIT and THE SEVEN FOLD SPIRIT OF GOD to place a shield of fire around us to protect us and cutoff communications from the demons outside to the demons inside.
13. We ask GOD to send angels out to recover fragments of souls, restore proper order, quicken, bring them back to life and restore the minds.
14. We come against powers, principalities, evil forces in this world and spiritual wickedness in high places. We bind every demon inside or outside of anyone that has anything to do with us. We bind every force of evil and loose every force of good that we have the power and authority to do so.
15. We ask the angels to read Scripture to the demons constantly to torment them with their impending judgement.
16. We ask the angels to destroy, cut away and dispose of the souls of the demons.

REFERENCES

Spiritual Warfare by Richard Ing, Whitaker House
Deliverance Manual by Gene and Earline Moody

SECTION 27 - TORMENTING DEMONS

SCRIPTURE REFERENCES

I recommend that you mark these scriptures in your Bible for handy reference in time of battle with the forces of evil. The following scripture verses are to be completely read out loud to the demons to drive them out of the people. Probably the most powerful chapter for warfare is Matthew; start with Matthew and keep reading as long as this weapon is needed. **Demons hate to hear The Word Of God!**

Matthew 3:7-8; 4:10-11, 23-24; 6:14-15; 7:22-23; 8:2-3, 12, 16-17, 28-33; 9:32-33; 10:1, 7-8; 11:4-6, 11-12; 12:22,24-33, 43-45; 13:41-42, 49-50; 15:19-20, 22-28; 16:18-19, 22-23; 17:14-18; 19:8-9, 18-20, 21-35; 22:13-14; 23:33; 25:30, 41, 46; 28:18-20.
Mark 1:32-33, 39-42; 3:10-15, 22-27; 5:1-20; 6:7, 13-14; 7:20-23, 25-30, 34-35; 9:17-29, 38-39, 43-48; 11:15, 21-26; 16:15-20.
Luke 1:71; 4:18-19, 33-35, 38-41; 5:12-14; 6:17-19; 7:21-22; 8:2-3, 26-39; 9:1-2, 37-42, 49-50, 55; 11:17-20; 11:14-22, 24-26; 13:11-17, 31-32; 16:16, 22-24; 22:3.
John 5:14; 6:70; 8:31-32, 44; 10:10; 12:31-32; 13:27; 14:12-14,30; 15:7-8; 16:11.
Acts 1:8; 2:35-36; 5:3-4, 15-16; 8:5-8, 22-24; 10:38; 13:6, 8, 10-11; 15:24; 16:16-18; 19:11-19; 26:18.
Romans 1:21-32; 6:16; 13:12-14; 16:18, 20.
I Corinthians 2:6-8; 3:3; 5:4-8; 10:20-21; 11:3, 10.
II Corinthians 1:10, 24; 2:11; 4:3-4; 7:1; 10:3-6; 11:3-4, 13-15; 12:7.
Galatians 3:1; 4:3; 5:13, 19-24.
Ephesians 1:19-23; 2:1-3, 6-7; 3:10; 4:8-14, 26-27; 5:3-5; 6:10-18.
Philippians 1:28; 2:9-11; 3:19, 21.
Colossians 1:13, 16; 2:9-10, 15,18-19; 3:5-8.
I Thessalonians 2:8, 18.
II Thessalonians 2:7-12.
I Timothy 1:18-20; 4:1-3, 7.
II Timothy 1:7-8; 2:20-22, 24-26; 3:1-5.
Hebrews 1:7, 14; 2:3-5, 7-8, 14-15; 4:12; 12:14-16.
James 1:8; 2:19; 3:14-16; 4:5-8.
I Peter 1:13-14, 223:22; 5:8-9.
II Peter 1:16; 2:4, 14.
I John 2:16; 3:8-9; 4:1-4, 18.
Jude 6, 9.
Revelations 1:18; 12:7-11; 16:13-14; 18:23; 20:1-3, 7-10, 14-15.

SCRIPTURE

Read the scripture reference and scripture out loud!

Matt. 8:12 But the children of the kingdom shall be cast out into outer darkness: there shall be weeping and gnashing of teeth.
Matt. 8:29 --- art thou come hither to torment us before the time?
Matt. 12:43 When the unclean spirit is gone out of a man, he walketh through dry places, seeking rest, and findeth none.

Matt. 13:42 And shall cast them into a furnace of fire: there shall be wailing and gnashing of teeth.
Matt. 18:8-9 --- rather that having two hands or two feet or two eyes to be cast into everlasting fire and hell fire.
Matt. 18:34 And his lord was wroth, and delivered him to the tormentors, till he should pay all that was due unto him.
Matt. 22:13 Then said the king to the servants, Bind him hand and foot, and take him away, and cast him into outer darkness; there shall be weeping and gnashing of teeth.
Matt. 23:33 Ye serpents, ye generation of vipers, how can ye escape the damnation of hell?
Matt. 25:30 And cast ye the unprofitable servant into outer darkness; there shall be weeping and gnashing of teeth.
Matt. 25:41 Then shall he say also unto them on the left hand, Depart from me, ye cursed, into everlasting fire, prepared for the Devil and his angels.
Matt. 25:46 And these shall go away into everlasting punishment: but the righteous into life eternal.
Mark 1:24 --- art thou come to destroy us? I know thee who thou art, the Holy One of God.
Mark 9:43-48 --- into hell, into the fire that never shall be quenched: Where their worm dieth not, and the fire is not quenched.
Luke 8:28 --- I beeseech thee, torment me not.
Luke 16:23-24 --- and in hell he lift up his eyes, being in torments, and seeth Abraham afar off, and Lazarus in his bosom. And he cried and said, Father Abraham, have mercy on me, and send Lazarus, that he may dip the dip of his finger in water, and cool my tongue; for I am tormented in this flame.

STATEMENTS

The following statements are used to be spoken out loud to the demons within a person or group to torment them and to loosen their hold so that the demons can be cast out.

Here is just some of what the Bible says about this horrible place. Hell is a lake of fire, bottomless pit, horrible tempest, devouring fire and furnace of fire.

Hell is where they will wail, God is cursed, there's no rest, they scream for mercy, they can never repent, they gnaw their tongues, they feel the wrath of God, the fire never goes out and they don't want their loved ones to come.

Hell is a place of sorrows, weeping, torments, outer darkness, everlasting punishment, everlasting destruction, everlasting burnings, and for the Devil and his angels. **TORMENTING DEMONS**

SCRIPTURE REFERENCES

Mark these scriptures in your Bible for handy reference in time of battle with the forces of evil. The following scripture verses are to be completely read out loud to the demons to drive them out of the people. Probably the most powerful chapter for warfare is Matthew; start with Matthew and keep reading scripture as long as this weapon of our warfare is needed. **Demons don't like to hear what we say, but they hate to hear The Word Of God!**

Matthew 3:7-8; 4:10-11, 23-24; 6:14-15; 7:22-23; 8:2-3, 12, 16-17, 28-33; 9:32-33; 10:1, 7-8; 11:4-6, 11-12; 12:22,24-33, 43-45; 13:41-42, 49-50; 15:19-20, 22-28; 16:18-19, 22-23; 17:14-18; 19:8-9, 18-20, 21-35; 22:13-14; 23:33; 25:30, 41, 46; 28:18-20.
Mark 1:32-33, 39-42; 3:10-15, 22-27; 5:1-20; 6:7, 13-14; 7:20-23, 25-30, 34-35; 9:17-29, 38-39, 43-48; 11:15, 21-26; 16:15-20.
Luke 1:71; 4:18-19, 33-35, 38-41; 5:12-14; 6:17-19; 7:21-22; 8:2-3, 26-39; 9:1-2, 37-42, 49-50, 55; 11:17-20; 11:14-22, 24-26; 13:11-17, 31-32; 16:16, 22-24; 22:3.
John 5:14; 6:70; 8:31-32, 44; 10:10; 12:31-32; 13:27; 14:12-14,30; 15:7-8; 16:11.
Acts 1:8; 2:35-36; 5:3-4, 15-16; 8:5-8, 22-24; 10:38; 13:6, 8, 10-11; 15:24; 16:16-18; 19:11-19; 26:18.
Romans 1:21-32; 6:16; 13:12-14; 16:18, 20.
I Corinthians 2:6-8; 3:3; 5:4-8; 10:20-21; 11:3, 10.
II Corinthians 1:10, 24; 2:11; 4:3-4; 7:1; 10:3-6; 11:3-4, 13-15; 12:7.
Galatians 3:1; 4:3; 5:13, 19-24.
Ephesians 1:19-23; 2:1-3, 6-7; 3:10; 4:8-14, 26-27; 5:3-5; 6:10-18.
Philippians 1:28; 2:9-11; 3:19, 21.
Colossians 1:13, 16; 2:9-10,15,18-19; 3:5-8.
I Thessalonians 2:8, 18.
II Thessalonians 2:7-12.
I Timothy 1:18-20; 4:1-3, 7.
II Timothy 1:7-8; 2:20-22, 24-26; 3:1-5.
Hebrews 1:7, 14; 2:3-5, 7-8, 14-15; 4:12; 12:14-16.
James 1:8; 2:19; 3:14-16; 4:5-8.
I Peter 1:13-14, 223:22; 5:8-9.
II Peter 1:16; 2:4, 14.
I John 2:16; 3:8-9; 4:1-4, 18.
Jude 6, 9.
Revelations 1:18; 12:7-11; 16:13-14; 18:23; 20:1-3, 7-10, 14-15.

SCRIPTURE

Demons, we command that you listen to this scripture about what is going to happen to you:

Matt. 8:12 **But the children of the kingdom shall be cast out into outer darkness: there shall be weeping and gnashing of teeth.**
Matt. 8:29 **--- art thou come hither to torment us before the time?**
Matt. 12:43 **When the unclean spirit is gone out of a man, he walketh through dry places, seeking rest, and findeth none.**
Matt. 13:42 **And shall cast them into a furnace of fire: there shall be wailing and gnashing of teeth.**
Matt. 18:8-9 **--- rather that having two hands or two feet or two eyes to be cast into everlasting fire and hell fire.**
Matt. 18:34 **And his lord was wroth, and delivered him to the tormentors, till he should pay all that was due unto him.**
Matt. 22:13 **Then said the king to the servants, Bind him hand and foot, and take him away, and cast him into outer darkness; there shall be weeping and gnashing of teeth.**
Matt. 23:33 **Ye serpents, ye generation of vipers, how can ye escape the damnation of hell?**

Matt. 25:30 **And cast ye the unprofitable servant into outer darkness; there shall be weeping and gnashing of teeth.**
Matt. 25:41 **Then shall he say also unto them on the left hand, Depart from me, ye cursed, into everlasting fire, prepared for the Devil and his angels.**
Matt. 25:46 **And these shall go away into everlasting punishment: but the righteous into life eternal.**
Mark 1:24 **--- art thou come to destroy us? I know thee who thou art, the Holy One of God.**
Mark 9:43-48 **--- into hell, into the fire that never shall be quenched: Where their worm dieth not, and the fire is not quenched.**
Luke 8:28 **--- I beeseech thee, torment me not.**
Luke 16:23-24 **--- and in hell he lift up his eyes, being in torments, and seeth Abraham afar off, and Lazarus in his bosom. And he cried and said, Father Abraham, have mercy on me, and send Lazarus, that he may dip the dip of his finger in water, and cool my tongue; for I am tormented in this flame.**

STATEMENTS

The following statements are used to be spoken out loud to the demons within a person or group to torment them and to loosen their hold so that the demons can be cast out:

Demons listen to the place where you are going to be tormented. Here is just some of what the Bible says about this horrible place:

Hell is a lake of fire, bottomless pit, horrible tempest, devouring fire and furnace of fire.

Hell is where they will wail, God is cursed, there's no rest, they scream for mercy, they can never repent, they gnaw their tongues, they feel the wrath of God, the fire never goes out and they don't want their loved ones to come.

Hell is a place of sorrows, weeping, torments, outer darkness, everlasting punishment, everlasting destruction, everlasting burnings and for the Devil and his angels.

REFERENCES

Spiritual Warfare Manual, Deliverance Ministries Combination I, Are You On The Road To Hell? for more information.

Deliverance Manual by Gene and Earline Moody (unless otherwise noted)

SECTION 28 - BITTERNESS

CONTENTS
1. SCRIPTURE
2. GENERAL
3. ROOTS
4. DEALING WITH BITTERNESS
5. REFERENCES

SCRIPTURE

Deut. 29:18-20 (Root of Gall & Wormwood).
I Sam. 1:10 (Bitterness of Soul)
I Sam. 15:32 (Bitterness of Death)
II Sam. 2:26 (Bitterness in the latter end)
Ps. 10:7 **(Cursing, Deceit, Oppression, Mischief, Iniquity)**
Pr. 14:10 (Bitterness to Heart)
Pr. 17:25 (Bitterness of Mother)
Ezek. 27:31 (Bitter Wailing)
Zec. 12:10 (Bitterness for only son) **(Loss of Byron, our only son)**
Acts 8:22-24 (Gall of Bitterness, Bond of Iniquity)
Rom. 3:13-14 (Cursing and Bitterness)
Eph. 4:31-32 (Bitterness, Wrath, Anger, Clamor)
Col. 3:8-9 (Anger, Wrath, Malice, Slander, Lies)
Heb. 12:14-16 (Root of Bitterness).

GENERAL

Bitterness includes **Resentment, Hatred, Unforgiveness, Violence, Temper, Anger, Retaliation and Murder** in a common demon family.

Generally, after a person becomes rejected, they become bitter and unforgiving. The opposite of bitterness is forgiveness.

Bitterness is defined as bitterly curse, rebellious, sharp, acrid, grief, embitter, poisonous, violently, provoke, vex, grieve, sorrow, bitter herb, calamity, bile, venom, angry, chafed, most bitterly, rebel and provoke.

Have you had these feelings before? Unforgiveness, which is a form of bitterness, is very common among Christians.

Gall is defined as **poison** or **bile**. Bound is defined as **control** and **uniting**. Root is defined as **root** and **thought**. Wormwood is defined as **cursed**.

ROOTS
(Family Deliverance Manual)

Anger, jealousy, irritating behavior, habits, irritability, loathing, mad, madness, malice, murder, offending, idle, pouting, provoking to wrath, pugnacious, quarrelsome, rage, destructive, enraged, rebellion, repugnance, repulsive, resentment, retaliation, revenge, rough, sassy, sassiness, savage, seething, self-abuse, accusation, blame, condemnation, guilt, criticism, destruction, infliction, punishment, torture, sharp tongue, spite, strife, strong will, struggle, suicide wish, suicide, tempter tantrum, tortured, troubled, torn relations, adolescent, vehement, vicious, violence, warring, wild child, unforgiveness, ugliness, unbridled tongue, uncontrollable child, unforgiveness, unruly child and uncooperative adult.

DEALING WITH BITTERNESS (EXCERPTS)

Bitterness is a hurt that will not heal, a wound in the spirit (Prov. 18:14). It comes into a life because of a failure to appropriate God's grace (Heb. 12:15); by refusing to forgive others (Matt. 6:14-15; 7:1-2; 18:21-35); or refusing to thank God for all things (Eph. 5:20; Phil. 4:6). Forgiveness is the most important thing that God has taught us about deliverance!

However, each time we remember the things which happened, we are suddenly flooded with hurt and/or anger again. This indicates unhealed bitterness. This is called a spirit of memory recall.

Vengeance is mine, I will repay, saith the Lord (Heb. 10:30). It is too heavy for us to carry and besides it belongs to God. Earline had a problem with getting even until God delivered her.

Forgive eagerly (Matt. 18:12), remembering that unforgiveness is torture (Matt. 18:34-35).

We must remember that God loves us (Rom. 8:32-34), and not look at what others say, what we think or even at the situation itself.

We must go to the God of all comfort (II Cor. 1:3) for His Holy Spirit is our Comforter (John 14:16) and He earnestly desires to comfort us (Psalm 103:13).

When we go to God, we will find peace that passes understanding which will keep (guard, garrison) our hearts and minds (emotions and thoughts) (Phil. 4:4-9). God's peace guards our mind!

Focus on God and give Him thanks (Eph. 5:20; Rom. 8:28) rejoicing because your name is written in the Lamb's Book of Life (Luke 10:20; Phil. 4:4) and ask for grace, comfort and peace (Matt.7:7-11). **Say, Lord Jesus give me grace, comfort and peace. Amen.**

Focusing on God and letting Him be our judge is absolutely necessary.

Proverbs 29:25 contrasts the **fear of man** with trust in God. Perfect love for God casts out all fear because we trust in Him! **Say, Lord Jesus forgive me for fear of man. Amen.**

To receive comfort and heal the bitterness in your spirit, you must die to works of righteousness (trying to earn God's love and favor) by drowning in the ocean of God's love and grace, rejoicing that He has chosen you.

REFERENCES

Conquering The Hosts Of Hell, Dealing With Bitterness

SECTION 29 - REBELLION

LIST OF SCRIPTURE

I Sam. 15:23 (for **rebellion** is as the sin of witchcraft, **stubbornness** is as iniquity and idolatry) Are you practicing witchcraft or idolatry?
Heb. 2:2 (**disobedience** received a just reward) You will be punished.
Heb. 13:17 (**submit** yourselves) (**Anti-submissiveness**) Pastors should not try to control their flock; the flock should submit to the pastor.
2 Peter 2:10 (Presumptuous are they, **self-willed**)

GENERAL

Synonyms for Rebellion are Treason, Self-Will, Obduracy, Stubbornness, **Disobedience**, Denunciation, and Anti - submissiveness.

Antonyms for Rebellion are Willfulness, **Obedience** and Submissiveness.

Rebellion includes **Self-Will, Stubbornness, Disobedience and Anti-Submissiveness** in this common demon family.

Generally, after a person has become bitter, they rebel.

Disobedience means to disobey, transgress, violate, disregard, defy, infringe, shirk, resist, mutiny, rebel and revolt.

Have you had these feelings before? Rebellion is very common among Christians. **Obedience is the opposite of Rebellion.**

The word **Rebellion** occurs infrequently in the Bible. Therefore, we must use other words as **rebellious** and **to rebel**. The next best word to describe Rebellion is **Disobedience** or the opposite of **Obedience**.

STUDY OF REBELLION

The best way to study rebellion is as **disobedience to God** and from the opposite view of **the need to be obedient to God**. There are many instances of disobedience to God and the corresponding punishment in the Bible for the sin.

Disobedience To God Scripture

Lev. 26:14-46 (A curse to those that break the commandments) There is a curse for each disobedience.
Numbers 14:11-24 (People murmur - God threatens them) **Are you murmuring?**
Numbers 32:8-13 (Moses reproves the Reubenites and Gadites - rebels.)
Deut. 18:19 (God will require it of you the people if you rebel.)
Deut. 28:15-68 (The curse for disobedience)

Helpful Scripture And Bible Stories Of Rebellion

Genesis Ch. 3 The Fall of Man
II Samuel Ch. 13 Absalom Avenges Tamar

II Samuel Ch. 15 Absalom's Conspiracy
I Kings Ch. 16-22 Ahab/Jezebel Rebellion
Isa. 3:12 **Children Oppress, Women Rule (Ahab/Jezebel Complex) A picture of our society: women will not follow and men will not lead!**
Isa. Ch. 14 Satan's Fall
Eze. Ch. 28 Satan's Rebellion
Malachi 4:5-6 Smite the Earth with a Curse
II Thes. 2:9-12 Strong Delusion, Believing Lies
James 3:13-18 Earthly, Unspiritual, Devilish Wisdom

NELSON'S EXPOSITORY DICTIONARY OF THE OLD TESTAMENT

The words **to rebel, rebellion and rebellious** are defined by the following phrases:

Be contentious, make angry, contend with, dispute with, stubborn headed, opposition to someone motivated by pride, stubborn and rebellious, speech and actions are against the Lord, rebellious attitude against God, disobey, act of defying the command of God, rebellious and defiled, listens to no voice, accepts no correction, make bitter, provoke, reject, not recognize, rebellion and stiff neck, double rebellion and rebellious house.

Rebellion can also be defined as revolt, overthrow, mutiny, breakup, destruction, spasm, convulsion, resistance, interference, friction, withstand, repulse and disobedient.

Rebellious can also be defined as revolutionary, defiance, aggressiveness, dare and scorn.

EVE REBELS (THE ORIGINAL REBELLION OF MAN)

We can trace our curses back to Adam and Eve. Adam also rebelled against God. This is the Jezebel / Ahab Complex. There are **many ingredients** in Eve's rebellion:

1. She was **seduced** by conversation and greed for power and knowledge.
2. The **price of seduction** was experiencing a knowledge of good and evil.
3. The **action of rebellion** resulted in shame, attempting to correct the mistake or cover it up, fear, withdrawing from God's presence, loss of esteemed position, pain in childbirth, hard work and toil, and birth of rebellious children.

ABSALOM REBELS

Absalom's sister, Tamar, was **raped** by his half-brother, Amnon (II Sam. 13).

Hate entered Absalom's heart because of his sister being raped. He plotted and planned for two years to murder Amnon.

Absalom again falls prey to resentment and burns Joab's field because he would not go to David for him. By trying to force David to see him, he is acting out rebellion.

He came to repentance but didn't really repent; it was surface repentance only.

After he had his audience with David, he quickly got busy with his **plans for rebellion**.

Absalom got favor with the people by acting as if he loved them and claiming great concern for their welfare. After he had **seduced them**, he declared himself King.

Some demons that probably were in Absalom were **hate, anger, resentment, deceit, trickery, witchcraft, betrayal, pride, pompousness, false love, backstabbing, lying, arrogance, unrighteous judgement and self-serving.**

JEZEBEL REBELS

She killed God's prophets which is **rebellion against God**. She exhibited hate, retaliation and threatenings.

She turns from role of woman and wife to trying to upstage the King, her husband. She belittled him, connived behind his back, and plotted murder and control of people. **Some women/men today use seemingly pure religious motives to control others such as soulish prophecy - telling others what to do.**

Another motive behind her rebellion was that she wanted **worship and admiration**. Jezebel is **true sorcery**. Rebellious Jezebelic males/females will ask questions aimed at causing the other person to doubt his worth, ability, decisions, etc. She ended up being thrown out a window, run over by chariots and eaten by dogs. **Did she go to Hell; what do you think?**

AHAB REBELS

Worshiping Idols Is Worst Rebellion Against God

This is called spiritual adultery. The **major rebellion was against God** in Baal worship. He went after idols. Abortion is worship of the god of sex, Satan, and is similar to Baal worship!

Ahab exhibited characteristics of **complete confusion, disobedience, resentfulness, sullenness, greed, accomplice to Jezebel, believed lying spirit, refused to believe God, and begat rebellious children.**

PERFECT FAMILY

Eph. 5:22 & 25; 6:1 & 4: Families repeat after me:

1. **Husbands love your wives.**
2. **Wives submit to your husbands.**
3. **Children obey your parents.**
4. **Fathers do not provoke your children.**

CLASSIC EXAMPLES OF REBELLION

1. Nation of Israel - rebelled many times. Study the rise and fall of Israel!
2. Satan and Fallen Angels - original rebellion.
3. Queen Jezebel - rebellious woman.
4. King Ahab - rebellious man

JEZEBEL-AHAB REBELLIOUS INFLUENCE IN WORLD TODAY

1. Divorce - one parent families. Men don't want responsibility - just sex!
2. Felinism - pictures bungling father and clever mother. Watch TV brain washing.
3. Sex - no restrictions. There is no free sex; only curses of God in the future.

4. Young people - confused, rebellious.
5. Drugs - Sex - Music.
6. Society with emotional problems.
7. Effeminate, emotional, weak spiritual and weak physical men.
8. Women's false strength - put to test usually fails.
9. Children - fear, insecurity, frustration, difficulty learning, potential corruption, discord, growth in occult and cults, selfishness, doubt, inability to achieve, hypochondriacs and church splits.

YOU AND PEOPLE AROUND YOU

Such qualities as these **have unnatural power to seduce you**, even overwhelm you. It is not charisma but seduction, and it creates bondage. You may have a friend whom you at times have a great desire to be free of, and the next moment feel guilt or condemnation for desiring your freedom. Consider why you are attracted to your friend.

Look out for mothers/dads who try to dominate married children's lives, and men/women who **cannot delegate authority** but try to mind every detail.

Women/men shouldn't try to force mate into a religious experience but win him/her by quiet and joyful submission to the Christian life **fulfilling your role as God established it**.

SUMMARY

A study of the Bible shows clearly that God hates rebellion and that He will punish the people for their sins.

The people are blessed when they obey the Bible and they are **cursed when they disobey the Bible commandments.** There is a curse for every violation of Bible!

All rebellion is against God. For example, when a wife rebels against her husband, she is not just rebelling against him but against God who put the husband in authority over the wife. Finally, **rebellion can be very costly** while **obedience can be very rewarding**. The Bible applies equally to an individual, family, church, community, nation, etc.

LIST OF DEMONS

Rebellion, Greed, Disobedience, Lying, Self-will, Hate, Stubbornness, Evil Plotting and Planning, Anti-submissiveness, Evil Control of Others, Destruction, Unrighteous Judgement, Subversion, Rock Music, Resistance, Christian Rock, Interference, Deceit, Friction, Trickery, Repulse, Betrayal, Defiance, Pride, Aggressiveness, False Love, Scorn, Arrogance, Sorcery, Conniving, Seduction, Confusion, Sullen Masculine Women, Taking Tranquilizers, Effeminate Men, Taking Drugs, Insecurity, Restless, Frustration, Witchcraft, Depression, Unholy Sex, Doubt

SECTION 30 - REJECTION

CONTENTS

SCRIPTURE

Matt. 5:3 (Rejected are "poor in spirit") Do you feel poorly?
Matt. 5:43-44 (Love your enemies) Would solve a lot of your problems!
Rom. 12:3 (Not to think of himself more highly) Would not get rejected!
I Cor. 10:12-13 (Take heed lest he fall) Pride - Ego - Vanity
II Cor. 5:14-15 (Not live unto themselves) Be generous and think of others!
Eph. 6:4 (Fathers do not provoke children) Not the mothers! Phil. 4:8 (Think on these things)
James 1:5-8 (Double-minded man) Will not receive anything from God!
I Peter 4:12 (Fiery trial) We go through many trials!

GENERAL

Comments

Rejection includes **fear of rejection and self-rejection** in this common demon family. **I am going to spend more time on rejection because it is generally the door opener to demon oppression.**

Except for the sins of the ancestors, rejection is generally where the demons first attack someone and because of the parents, this can be in the womb. Rejection is one of the biggest problems of the human race!

Rejection is defined as reject, refuse, repudiate, decline, deny, rebuff, repel, renounce, discard, throw away, exclude, eliminate and jettison.

Have you had these feelings before? Rejection is very common among Christians. **Love is the opposite of Rejection. The Love of God and God loving through us is a very powerful force which we don't fully understand.**

Man's Rejection
(Family Deliverance Manual)

Rejection of God and the truth, over-protection, wrong sex, broken home, guilt complex, treacherous comparison, envy, conditional love, worthlessness, Jezebel influence, depression, internal temper tantrum, controlled by emotions, thinks with feeling, introspection, guilt, lack of responsibility, worries, doubts, fear, unbelief, anxiety, fear of failure prevents attempting, braggart, criticism, obstinacy, loner, perfectionism, compliance, defiance, shyness, **self-deprecating, discipline, condemnation and hatred**.

Man's Symptoms Of Rejection
(Family Deliverance Manual)

Body is tense, high blood pressure, grinding teeth, goes to the refrigerator for relaxation, feels that one does not fit in, not a part, looks for happiness in things, wounded spirit, drive to lead, to have own way rather than serve, clash easily with other people close to you, easily offended, moralist, needs to receive credit, considers self bold and unafraid, intolerant of neurotic people, impatient of slow movers, trouble submitting, argumentative, quick tempered, angry person, suspicious, over-achiever and timidity.

Man's Inter-Personal Effects Of Rejection
(Family Deliverance Manual)

Wishing you were never born, feelings of inferiority, inability to express feelings, depression, emotional insulation, subjectively, perfectionism, lack of self-discipline, irresponsibility, handicaps, conditional love, self-condemnation, inability to express feelings.

EARLINE'S COMMENTS
Rejection Opens Door To A Multitude Of Curses

Looking up rejection in the Bible, I have found that God has not rejected a single person who has not persisted in rejecting God. See I Sam. 8:7; 10:19; 15:23, 26; 16:1; II Kings 17:15, 29; Isa. 53:2; Jer. 6:19; 7:29-30; etc. All of these scriptures reassure us that if we heed God's call to us, He will not reject us.

We have not found a single person who has escaped the problem of rejection. Even if we are not rejected, rejection works very well when demons can convince us that we are rejected. Rejection is one the best ideas the Devil ever had and it works so well he uses it against all people. Even Jesus did not escape rejection. Isa. 53:3, **He was despised and rejected and forsaken by man, ... He was despised, and we did not appreciate His worth or have any esteem for Him.** Jesus was totally rejected of men. The Devil did not stop using rejection on Jesus even when He was on the cross. Jesus' response was, **Father, forgive them for they don't know what they do.**

The Devil used rejection on Eve when he told her she would be like God. Was not that question in response to what Eve was probably thinking? If she had not been thinking this, she would not have taken the bait.

What does rejection do to you? It makes you open to all kinds of seduction because you do not feel complete nor settled. It may be a respectable seduction like food, work, play, prestige, money or non-respectable like street drugs, abnormal sexual activities, murder, abortion, witchcraft, etc. The person is always trying to find something to fix that spot so they will fell all right.

Rejection is behind over working, lying, greed, denying a problem exists or our ability to control it, deception, etc. The work of the Holy Spirit within us is to bring us into proper self-control, peace and joy (Gal. 5:22-26).

Rejection Leading To Sexual Perversions

Sexual perversions represent an extreme attempt to overcome rejection. Sexual experiences, real or imaginary, can never satisfy the need for genuine love. They are the Devil's substitutes for real love and leave a person ridden with frustration and guilt. **Sex is not love!**

The person who has a deep sense of rejection feels insecure and inferior. Since the person has been rejected or fears rejection he is driven to pamper self ... to push self. He is thereby trying to overcome feelings of rejection. One who feels rejected wants to feel important.

Earline's Testimony About Rejection

Rejection is the basic cause of abuse. All types of rejection work to destroy the mental and emotional health of an individual.

I had often wondered about certain problems I had: (1) an inordinate desire to please, (2) inability to say no to things I didn't want to do, (3) always setting goals, working hard to accomplish them and then stopping short of success, (4) always feeling I had to do things better than anyone else, and (5) trying to make everything around me and about me look better than I thought it was. (Do you have some of the problems that Earline had?)

I cut off part of my finger in an accident loading a horse into a trailer. **It was the first time I had need of a hospital in many years.** (Our family lived in divine health for about a dozen years after we learned about divine healing.) I was put to sleep and my finger was sewn into my palm. The next day I was supposed to be quiet and take it easy.

For five years, I had been trying to help my mom get resettled after my dad's death. At times she would tell me what she wanted me to do and I would start to do it. **Right in the middle of my doing it, she would suddenly, without telling me, change her mind and have one of my brothers doing an entirely different thing.**

Two years ago I took her to Maine to see my brother. Back in Chattanooga she accused me of wanting and trying to kill her. This really puzzled me because I thought we got along very well.

After the operation, I was being still on the sofa praying. I asked God **Why can't I help mom? Why does she think I want to kill her?**

I had a vision. (Have you had visions?) I was standing in the room I had as a child. I was high near the ceiling. I was witnessing a terrible thing. A woman was beating, not whipping, a child. I went down to see who this was and to stop it; I saw it was my mom. I went beside the bed, bent down and looked; the child was me. (Earline was a physically and mentally abused child. Have you been physically and mentally abused?)

Thinking I was hallucinating because of the drugs from the operation the day before, I quickly decided to get up and get busy. One-handed work was hard to find, so I swept the carport.

My brother called me or I called him. Since I sounded a little funny, he asked what was wrong. I told him next time they could sew me up awake. Then I related this story to him. He was silent, then he asked me if I remembered that day.

He said he had told my dad that if my mom didn't stop beating me for no reason, he would kill her. The only words said in the scene were by my dad; he said to my mom that he would kill her if he ever heard of this happening again. I was not a small child. I was ten or twelve years old when the beatings stopped.

For some reason, I simply cannot remember this today. He thought her fear that I wanted to kill her came from the guilt for what she did to me.

About eight to nine years before this incident, Gene and I had fasted and prayed for me for two years. When I got the Baptism of the Holy Spirit, there was only initial joy. Immediately, I began to have more fears than before, my emotions were out of control and I couldn't think clearly. God does not give us a spirit of fear but a spirit of power, love, calm, well-balanced mind, discipline and self control.

Neither of us knew about deliverance from demons, so God had to teach us. After a long time of praying one night, Gene began to call out **Rejection, Rebellion, Bitterness, etc.** I was very different after this.

I had to learn how to stay free by studying the Bible. No one in our town believed a Christian could have a demon, so we had to rely on God and His Word.

I was doing very well until the scene passed before my eyes and I learned of my early life. Immediately, I began to have times of panic for no apparent reason. I was hostile. I noticed a panic when those who had authority over me were present. I would become fearful if a policeman came near me, and when the pastor or principal came into my school room. I felt I had to challenge Gene's decisions.

We prayed and felt that I needed more deliverance. Gene was led to call out the same things as before. **We realized at this point that we were working on my subconscious mind.** (When you have very traumatic events that the conscious mind can not handle, they are submerged in your subconscious min.)

THE ROOTS OF REJECTION (EXCERPTS)

As for my people, children are their oppressors, and women rule over them. 0 my people, they which lead thee cause thee to err, and destroy the way of thy paths" (Isaiah 3:12). Children rule the parents and wife rules the husband; this is a matriarchal society!

The curse of destruction of the family priesthood (which is centered in the father and usually is the result of inherited family curses) paves the way for the spirit of Rejection in a child. Father is the priest and head of the home!

Frustrated by his lack of leadership and her inability to respect him as a man, the woman (who herself may have inherited curses of dominance) begins to take over and direct the home by the Jezebel spirit. Men go after wine, women and song - such as adult toys, outdoors, sports, etc. to escape the wife!

The child is caught up in the conflict between the parents and becomes its chief victim. Children are the main victims of divorce!

The spirits in the mother will coerce the male child, forbidding him to assert his masculinity or to engage in activities which would develop him as a man. This pattern develops homosexual men!

The progression of destruction in the life of a female child is much the same as that of the boy, except that she will consciously or unconsciously absorb and manifest the same attitudes and spirits which drive her mother. Watch how your children have your same bad habits!

There is a definite pattern to the entrance of Rejection, which in turn opens the door for Rebellion:

1. Curse of **destruction of the family priesthood** (centered in father).
2. Curses and spirits of **withdrawal** of the father and **dominance** by the mother.
3. Spirit of improper discipline (usually works through the mother (**either overpermissive or too harsh**) may associate with the curse of rebellion against discipline on the child's part.
4. Spirit of **lying** to escape punishment.
5. Curse and spirits of **guilt**.
6. Curse and spirits of **distrust** (resulting from guilt).
7. Curse and spirits involving **lack of communication** between parents and child.
8. Curse and spirits of **rejection** ("My parents don't love me" or "I can't even talk to them etc.").

REJECTION, WITCHCRAFT CONTROL, AND UGLINESS (EXCERPTS)

The hellish "ping pong" game played with hapless victims by the spirits of Rejection and Rebellion has been spelled out by the Hammonds. Everyone should read **Pigs in the Parlor** by Frank Hammond, with particular attention to the chapter on Schizophrenia. The demons of Rejection and Rebellion whipsaw the people back and forth between these opposite emotions!

Rejection is such a common malady that it is found everywhere to some degree or another.

Discovery of an out-of-wedlock pregnancy usually results in anger, upset and dismay in the parents of their child.

The curse of **Rejection from the Womb** has opened the door for many tormenting spirits in scores of people with whom we have dealt. **Did you know that you can be rejected by your parents while you are in the womb?**

Over and over people have reported life-long trouble by seemingly groundless but crippling rejection and various kinds of fears.

In some individuals, such spirits only produce discomfort and uneasiness.

A knowledge of the binding and casting out of evil spirits, and loosing the spirits of God (to counter and cancel the evil ones) is essential (Matt. 18:18; Mark 16:17-18).

There is a demonic entity called **Witchcraft Control** and he is able to bind other spirits in a person, particularly those involving habits such as smoking, drinking and sexual lapses. In order for the victim to be freed completely, all witchcraft curses must be broken from his family (back to ten generations on both sides) or from any other quarter. All legal holds and legal grounds must be taken from the enemy in the name of Jesus.

We have observed that people with heavy rejection spirits (usually including Rejection from the Womb) sometimes are rather homely and plain. A demon called **Ugliness** is found in many persons.

Perhaps you have noticed that people very often look ten to twenty years younger in their casket than when alive. **Many times in deliverance, we see people change before us. They look younger, softer and more relaxed.** Women, would you like to be more beautiful? Then, get your demons cast out.

SCHIZOPHRENIA (EXCERPTS)

Schizophrenia is a very common problem. Some authorities in the field of mental illness estimate there may be as many schizophrenics as one out of eight persons in the United States. Schizophrenics account for half the population in psychiatric hospitals. Of course there are varying degrees of schizophrenia. Some cases are acute while others are quite mild. Many schizophrenics have never been treated professionally. Schizophrenia has remained a very baffling problem to mental health professionals. The cause and cure has remained shrouded in uncertainty.

The disturbance and disintegration of personality known as schizophrenia or dementia praecox is frequently encountered by the deliverance minister. I would estimate that as many as one fourth of those who come to us for deliverance are found to have the schizophrenic pattern. The Lord has graciously given to Frank and Ida Mae Hammond a special revelation on the problem which enables us to deal with such cases more effectively.

The core of the schizophrenic is Rejection and Rebellion.

Schizophrenia always begins with Rejection! It commonly begins in childhood or infancy and sometimes while the child is yet in his mother's womb. There are many causes for rejection. Perhaps the child was not wanted. It may have been the wrong sex desired by one or both parents. The conditions in the home may have been unsettled. There are many "doors" that lead to rejection. **Did you want your children and were they the right sex? How about your parents?**

For example, suppose the schizophrenic nature is in the mother. The demons will pick out one or more of her children to feed down through. The schizophrenic mother feels rejection. She is the one who is primarily responsible for feeding love into the family. The rejection within herself creates problems in her relationships with the child. **The child is opened for rejection by the mother's instability.**

Now, one can have a rejection spirit and not be schizophrenic. In other words, it is all in the matter of forming a personality. You can have a rejection spirit and still manage to form your own personality and be secure in yourself.

Rejection is the control demon in one of the personalities set up within the schizophrenic. Rejection depicts a **withdrawn** type personality. (It is a feeling within - it is **agony within** - it is a **starvation of love** - it is **insecurity** - it is **inferiority** - it is **fantasy** - it is **unreality** - it is all on the inside - "I don't share in this."). **Do you feel loved? Can you love others? Do you try to avoid contact with other people?**

Sexual perversions represent an extreme attempt to overcome rejection. Sexual experiences, real or imaginary, can never satisfy the need for genuine love. They are the Devil's substitutes for real love and leave a person ridden with frustration and guilt. **Sex is not love; did you know that? How many one-night stands have you had in seeking love?**

The person who has a deep sense of rejection feels insecure and inferior. Do you feel inferior?

Since the person has been rejected or fears rejection, he is driven to pamper self...to push self. He is thereby trying to overcome feelings of rejection. **One who feels rejected wants to feel important.**

PRAYER

I forgive my ancestors, descendents and anyone else for rejecting me. I ask God to forgive me and I forgive myself for rejection. In the name of Jesus Christ I pray. Amen.

LIST OF DEMONS

Man's Rejection, **Man's Symptoms Of Rejection**, and **Man's Inter-Personal Effects Of Rejection** can be used as names of demons.

Feelings of being Rejected, Refused, Repudiated, Declined, Denied, Rebuffed, Repelled, Renounced, Discarded, Thrown Away, Excluded, Eliminated and Jettisoned.

Rejection, Poor in Spirit, Pride - Ego - Vanity, Double Mindedness, Fear of Rejection, Self Rejection, Roots of Rejection, Ahab-Jezebel Complex, Destruction of Family Priesthood, Dominance, Homosexuality, Lesbianism, Rebellion, Withdrawal, Overpermissive, Too Harsh, Lying, Guilt, Distrust, Inability to Communicate, Witchcraft Control, Ugliness, Schizophrenia, Anger, Rejection from the Womb, Smoking, Drinking, Dementia Praecox, Instability, Agony, Inability to Give or Receive Love, Insecurity, Inferiority, Fantasy, Unreality, Sexual Perversion, Frustration

REFERENCES

Battling The Hosts Of Hell, The Roots of Rejection
Demolishing The Host Of Hell Rejection, Witchcraft Control and Ugliness
Pigs In The Parlor, Schizophrenia
Roget's Thesaurus, Rejection

SECTION 31 - UNFORGIVENESS

LIST OF SCRIPTURE

Psa. 85:2 (Forgiven iniquity and covered sin - God)
Psa. 86:5 (Ready to forgive and plenteous in mercy - God)
Psa. 103:3 & 12 (Forgiveth all & removed as far as east from west - God)
Isa. 1:18 (Sins shall be as white as snow - God)
Isa. 43:25 (Blotteth out and will not remember - God)
Matt. 5:44 (Forgive your enemies.)
Matt. 6:14-15 (Forgive men or not be forgiven by God - man)
Matt. 18:21-35 (Law of Forgiveness - man)
Mark 11:25-26 (Forgive men or not be forgiven by God - man)
Luke 17:3-4 (Rebuke man and forgive seven times a day - man)
Eph. 4:32 (King, tenderhearted, forgiving as God does - man)
Col. 2:13 (Forgiven you all trespasses - God)
Col. 3:12-13 (Mercies, kindness, humbleness, meekness, long-suffering, forbearing and forgiving one another - man)
Heb. 8:12 (Merciful to unrighteous and remember not sins - God)
Heb. 10:17 (Remember not sins and iniquities - God)
I John 1:9 (Confessing, forgiveness, cleansing from unrighteousness)

ANALYSIS OF MATTHEW 5:44

But I say unto you, Love your enemies, bless them that curse you, do good to them that hate you, and pray for them which despitefully use you, and persecute you. Forgive your enemies; there are no excuses! Whites forgive blacks; blacks forgive whites.

1. **Love your enemies.** We do not have to love Satan! Love in a social or moral sense: beloved. Enemy is an adversary: foe.
2. **Bless them that curse you.** Speak well of: thank or invoke a benediction upon. Curse is to execrate: to doom.
3. **Do good to them that hate you.** Do good honestly: full well. Hate is to detest: especially to persecute.
4. **Pray for them that despitefully use you and persecute you.** Pray earnestly for: supplicate. Despitefully is to insult: slander and falsely accuse. Persecute is to pursue: to suffer.

GENERAL

Generally a person's demons cannot be cast out if he has unforgiveness in his heart. The opposite of unforgiveness is forgiveness.

Matt. 18:21-35 (**Law of Forgiveness** - Key Chapter); God sends demons to torment these with unforgiveness. Forgive your fellowman 70 x 7 = 490 times.

Kingdom of Heaven (is likened to): God (is The King), the Rich Man (is You); and the Poor Man (is anyone you have not forgiven).

1. Talent = 750 oz. of silver; Pence = 1/8 oz. of silver.
2. 10,000 talents x 750 = 7,500,000 oz. = $52,800,000 ($600,000).

3. 100 Pence x 1/8 = 2 1/2 oz. = $44.00 ($1.00).
4. Forgave 600,000 times as much.
5. Tormentors are Satan and his demons.
6. Prison is being in jail with Satan as warden and his demons as guards.

This is the crucifixion of the flesh until you come to your senses, forgive your fellowman and then ask God to forgive you! **The consequence of unforgiveness is the most important lesson that God has taught us about deliverance.**

Cancer and arthritis can come in through the sin of unforgiveness. If you know a Christian with these diseases, see if they have unforgiveness. They cannot be healed if the demons have a right to be there.

Pattern for being delivered and healed: forgive others, ask God for forgiveness, and forgive self. Cast out unforgiveness and bitterness. Cast out cancer and arthritis. Anoint with oil and pray for healing.

FORGIVENESS (EXCERPTS)

Forgiveness is hard to give because it hurts to extend it to undeserving and hard-hearted ones. To release a wrong-doer instead of exacting a just penalty requires that we reach out in love, rejecting the temptation to hold bitterness and resentment. This is contrary to our natural inclinations, thus the old adage, **To err is human, to forgive divine.**

Forgiveness is not forgetting the wrong done; some hurts are so deep that this would be impossible. We can forget the anger and hurt we felt, but the act is branded in our minds. Forgiveness takes place when the victim accepts the loss and/or injury done him and deliberately cancels the debt owed him by the offending person. This is an act of your will and God will honor it.

Anger must be dealt with openly and honestly, not denied or ignored. Either it must be vented in retaliation or the injured party must accept his own anger, bear the burden of it, and confess it in prayer to release himself and to set the other party free. Revenge always hurts the revenger far more than the one at whom it is leveled.

In other words, our pattern must be the grievous and substitutionary death of Christ. He willingly received all the hurt and evil of the entire human race in His own body on the tree (I Peter 2:21-24) to pay the debt for our guilt. He now offers what He has wrought as a free gift to undeserving and guilty persons so they can be free (Rom. 6:23; John 10:28-30).

As nothing else will, forgiveness takes us into the mysteries of grace where God forgives unconditionally on the basis of the substitutionary payment by another (Mark 11:25-26).

One of the fruits of the Holy Spirit's work in a life is the quality of meekness. It is a quality which is nurtured and abetted by practicing forgiveness.

This highly prized quality will cause us to be able to accept God's dealings with us as good, without disputing or resisting them. Meekness will also cause us to be able to **bear one**

another's burden's cheerfully and for Jesus' sake, enabling us to enter into the mystery of Christ's sufferings.

Because unforgiveness, and the resentment and bitterness it generates is so deadly, it is not optional, but necessary that it be dealt with. Cancer and arthritis spirits definitely root into this fertile ground. To be bitter and unforgiving costs far more than it is worth.

Husbands forgive your wives. Wives forgive your husbands. Children forgive your parents. **In Jesus' Name, I forgive my wife or husband and my parents. Amen.**

REFERENCES

Conquering The Hosts Of Hell, Forgiveness

Made in the USA
Monee, IL
27 March 2025

14762979R00155